AUTOBIOGRAPHY OF A PIONEER:

OR,

THE NATIVITY, EXPERIENCE, TRAVELS, AND MINISTERIAL LABORS

OF

REV. SAMUEL PICKARD,

The "Converted Quaker,"

CONTAINING

STIRRING INCIDENTS AND PRACTICAL THOUGHTS; WITH SERMONS BY THE AUTHOR, AND SOME ACCOUNT OF THE LABORS OF

ELDER JACOB KNAPP.

"The love of CHRIST doth me constrain,
To seek the wand'ring souls of men."

EDITED BY O. T. CONGER.

[ILLUSTRATED.]

CHICAGO:
CHURCH & GOODMAN, PUBLISHERS,
51 LA SALLE STREET.
1866.

CHURCH, GOODMAN & DONNELLEY,
Printers,
51 and 53 La Salle Street,
Chicago.

Stereotyped by
A. ZEESE,
84 Dearborn street,
Chicago.

DEDICATION.

TO THE MANY NEW CONVERTS

with whom I have prayed, wept and rejoiced at the mercy seat; and to the many brethren, sisters, and warm friends who have sat under my ministry, and from whom I have received much help and kindness, is this volume respectfully inscribed by their

Grateful Friend and Brother,

S. PICKARD.

PREFACE.

"O THAT MINE ENEMY WOULD WRITE A BOOK!" This, in former times, passed for as sore an evil as a good man could think of wishing to his worst enemy: but as to my enemies — and I hope that, aside from "the rulers of the darkness of this world," they are very few— I do not know that they have wished me so great an evil; yet, strange to say, my best friends have. Book-making is not my *forte;* but I have been urged to attempt it, and here is the result.

I began to preach in Iowa when it was a Territory, and when there were, perhaps, not to exceed a hundred Baptists within its entire bounds, and have made it my principal field of labor ever since. During all this time my labors have consisted chiefly in traveling from place to place, and holding protracted meetings.

My life has been a stirring one; and it is supposed, and probably is true, that I have preached more sermons in Iowa than any other minister now in it. I have aided in the organization of many churches, and held meetings in a great many places; and it is thought by those who have wished me to produce this book, that the many hundreds of converts who have been brought out in those meetings, and also multitudes of brethren, sisters, and friends, who have in different places sat under my ministry, would gladly receive the volume from my hands, and be much profited by it. That I have been persuaded to this must be my only apology.

In justice to myself I should say, that the book has been hastily prepared within the last few months, under the pressure of ministerial labors, so that very little time could be devoted to giving it literary excellence. Even under these circumstances it has been taken altogether from memory; for I have never kept a journal—a fact which I very much regret. Many incidents, therefore, which would have been interesting and useful I have doubtless forgotten.

In what I have recorded I have endeavored to correct abuses, and to impress proper sentiments on the mind of the reader, by an application of the facts set forth. If I succeed in this, my greatest wish in regard to the book will be accomplished.

SAMUEL PICKARD.

CONTENTS.

PAGE.

CHAPTER XXV.

CHAPTER XXVI.

CHAPTER XXVII.

CHAPTER XXVIII.

CHAPTER XXIX.

PAGE.

SERMONS BY S. PICKARD.

Sermon I.

Sermon II.

APPENDIX.

CHAPTER I.

PARENTAGE—CHILDHOOD—QUAKER HABITS.

I WAS born, October 28th, 1820, in Bartholomew county, Indiana. My parents were natives of Tennessee, and were old-fashioned, honest, respectable Quakers. My father was a farmer.

When I was about seven years old my parents moved to Park county, Indiana, and settled on the Wabash river.

Quakers are much inclined to settle in communities of their own kind, and here was a strong one. Their regulations were such, that in many respects they were, as they always are in such communities, a little nation by themselves; and so completely was I surrounded by and under the influence of Quaker society, that I was a full-grown man before I had any definite idea of society outside of the community. All my neighbors and acquaintances were Quakers; all the schools and religious meetings I ever attended, and all the social gatherings I was in until I became a man, were made up of Quakers.

In those days we had in that county little inducement and less facility for travel; hence I "vegetated" quietly in the one neighborhood, and was trained up in the Quakers' peculiar habits of dress and conversation. My communications were "yea," "nay," and "verily;" and, as might be expected, when I was twenty-one years of age, I was a complete Quaker, "dyed in the wool."

No teacher was employed in the community unless he was a Quaker, and none but Quaker pupils were allowed in the school, unless by special permission of the trustees.

All our schools were conducted under the supervision of the Church.

Our common school would have been a novelty to a person unaccustomed to these people; and it may be interesting to the reader to have a description:

The house was about twenty-five by forty feet in size, and was, for a new country, built with much regard to health and convenience, and was a model of order and cleanliness.

From forty to sixty children, plainly and cleanly attired, sat in order around the room, and behind the writing-desk sat the pedagogue. He wore an old, time-honored broad-brimmed hat, tight-fitting pants and stockings, and a smooth, buttonless, shad-bellied coat; had a grave countenance, a sober and wise look, and was regarded by me as decidedly the most knowing man that was to be found anywhere. "Spare the rod and spoil the child," was no part of his creed. He usually had near at hand a good tough hickory or birch rod, with which he often tanned our jackets in unruly cases, and woe to the little Quaker who was found guilty of misdemeanor. Often was I made to dance jigs and hornpipes to the music of the gad. However, we had a good school, and he made as rapid progress in teaching the young ideas how to shoot, as our mischievous inclinations would permit.

The teacher had a very pleasant way of managing the noon-spell dinner. We were commonly seated with military precision in a hollow square behind the writing-desks. Heads of classes were permitted the official honor of getting the dinner baskets, and placing them before their respective owners, who in turn laid out the dinner on the desk before them. The teacher's seat was considered the head of the table. The victuals being spread, at a motion of his hand all would become perfectly quiet for saying grace, which was done in silence, occupying one or two minutes, and which was broken by another signal from the teacher, when all would eat their dinners. In very pleasant weather he would take us to a shady grove, where our dinner was spread upon the grass, and eaten with the same order and decorum as before mentioned.

Here, with my brothers, sisters and playfellows, I spent the gleeful days of my boyhood in many a youthful sport, drinking again and again from the cup of childish bliss, little dreaming of the stern realities which in after-life I was in the providence of God to experience. I cannot pass this bright period of my life without dwelling a moment upon its sweet memories, or feeling a tender sadness, as I view this weather-beaten, failing tabernacle, in the thought that those merry days will never more return. Parents, I often think it should be one of your most willing and pleasant duties, to seek to make your children happy; for in many respects childhood is the happy part of life. It will soon be past. The little feet of the children are "marching along." They will soon leave the joyous morning and flowery spring behind. Make them happy, then, while you may. Crush not their pleasures, give them no needless sorrow, for full soon they must breast life's cold storms alone!

The place of our settlement on the Wabash was in a new country, and heavily timbered; by reason of which we had much hard work to perform in clearing the forests before we had a comfortable habitation; but by thrift and economy, and general good management on the part of my father, prosperity attended him, and in a few years he was in quite easy circumstances.

With him I learned all about hard work, and was well drilled in chopping, logging, lifting, and many of those kinds of labor that require the free use of muscle. This experience developed my bodily strength and powers of endurance, in a degree which I should not otherwise have enjoyed. This has proved to me a great blessing, and served me in many emergencies in after-life; and my unqualified verdict is, that all boys, whether they expect to be presidents, preachers, or farmers, ought to be taught to do manual labor.

The dense, heavy forests of Park county, in the days of my boyhood, abounded in wild game, and hunting was a common sport with me and my fellows, and we often enjoyed it hugely. We went out hunting as often as we could get permission, and sometimes oftener. My father was very strict in the observance of his religious duties, especially that of attending the regular meetings of his church twice a week. On such occasions we frequently watched the venerable sire, and as soon as he was out of sight, my brothers and I would take our dogs and guns, and slope for the woods. We often hunted at night for coons. This was rich sport, and as they were very troublesome in robbing hen-roosts and cornfields, their room was thought to be better than their company, and as their skins would always command a price in market, the prospect of getting pocket change was always an additional stimulant to us in hunting them. Dogs, well trained to the business, will find them and tree them. When this is done, the next thing to be accomplished is to cut down the tree, or send up some one to shake them off. Many are the anecdotes that are told of coon-hunters. A laughable one is related of a clerical friend, as having occurred during his younger days. He was out with a party, one night, coon-hunting, and the dogs having treed an old coon, it was determined by the party that our friend should climb the tree and shake him off, so that the dogs might catch him. Accordingly he ascended, and stealing softly from branch to branch in search of the coon, he finally espied him snugly ensconced on one of the topmost branches, a somewhat interested spectator of the scene which was transacting below. Proceeding cautiously, he reached the limb below that on which was the coon. Raising himself up for the purpose of reaching the limb which he intended to shake, the one on which he stood was heard to crack, and began to give way.

He was now thirty feet from the ground. Aware of his perilous condition, he cried out to his companions below, "I'm falling!" Seeing his danger, and that nothing scarcely less than a miracle could save him from death, they besought him to pray. "Pray!" said he; "I haven't time; I can't pray." "But you must pray. If you fall you will be killed." He then commenced repeating the only prayer he knew: "Now I lay me down to sleep;" but he could proceed no farther, as the cracking of the limb indicated its speedy severance from the trunk, and he cried out at the top of his voice, "Hold the dogs! I'm coming!" and sure enough, down he came with a crash; and the dogs, thinking him to be the coon, were with difficulty restrained from attacking the coon-hunter. Fortune, however, so favored his fall that he was only stunned.

A negro obtained permission of his master to start out coon-hunting one night, and on seeing his master in the morning, who was anxious to know about his success, related the following: "Well, massa, you know I treed the coon, and I climbs up to shake him off de limb. When I got by him, I begins to shake, and presently I hearn something drap, and what do you think it was, massa?" "Why the coon, to be sure." "No, it wasn't, massa; it was dis here nigger." It appears that instead of shaking off the coon, he shook himself off.

THE QUAKER HABITS

Are peculiar. A community of Friends is almost a world within itself. It is as nearly separated from the world without, and is as nearly distinct from it, as any circle of mortals well can be. All dress in the same plainness of style, the rich as well as the poor. All use the same peculiar phraseology, as *yea*, *nay* and *verily*. Portions of time are designated by numbers instead of names; as, for instance, twelve o'clock is called the first hour of the day, and one o'clock the second hour. Sunday is called the first day of the week, and Monday the second day. January is called the first month, and February the second month, etc. Their houses of worship are usually built neat and plain, with a partition of sliding doors across the audience room, so as to form two rooms of equal size, or have but one room, by sliding the doors, as may be desired. Commonly the doors are closed, and the sisters worship in one room while the brethren worship in the other, but on certain occasions the sliding doors are thrown open and all worship together. The men have the uncommon habit of keeping their hats on during divine service. They are opposed to all fashionable forms of politeness and rules of etiquette in speech and conduct, and repudiate all titles of honor, and refuse to take their hats off even in the presence of magistrates and superiors; being taught to "call no man master on earth." They hold devotional meetings twice each week, and have business meetings once each month. Their meetings for worship are held from one to two hours. They all take seats in their chapel, and there remain usually in perfect silence, as if in communion with their own thoughts. They believe that at such a time the Spirit must move upon them, to act or speak, before they can openly perform any religious service which will be acceptable to God. If one feels that the Spirit moves upon him to speak, he will rise and offer religious remarks, but if not, after they have remained in silence one or two hours, some one of the leading brethren shakes hands with the one sitting next to him. This is taken as a signal for dismission, when suddenly there is a general shaking of hands all around the room, and without farther ceremony they disperse, with perhaps not a word or a whisper having been heard during the whole meeting.

They never sing in their meetings, as they believe that "melody in the heart" should be made unto the Lord. They have no regular ministry brought out and sustained, as is common to most religious sects; but there are those in the order who are gifted with speech, and who devote a portion of their time to the interests of the church and occasional speaking. They hold that it is as appropriate for a sister to publicly preach, exhort and instruct as a brother, and a portion of those who supply the place of the ministry are sisters. They affirm that those who labor in the ministry should do it "without money or price," excepting those employed in foreign work, and then only as they are unable to pay their own expenses; hence they do but little for foreign missions.

As might be expected, these public teachers are comparatively scarce, and preaching is still more scarce. In our community in Park county we would seldom have any preaching, except some traveling

Friend would come along providentially, or accidentally, and would preach, which was not often, and we would sometimes have meetings nearly a year without any public instruction from the Scriptures.

As they never hold prayer-meetings, as others do, nor have any religious exercises that are lively and varied, a stranger finds that after attending their meetings once or twice, all their novelty is gone, and they appear very dull, dry and uninteresting.

Yet the Quakers are so rigid in their habits and rules, and so regular in their ways, that, as the saying is, they are always on hand at their meetings, "fodder or no fodder." In this last respect, I wish our brethren of other churches were as faithful.

CHAPTER II.

QUAKER DOCTRINES.

The doctrines of the Friends harmonize with those of all evangelical denominations, so far as pertains to the fundamental principles of Christianity. They believe in the authenticity of the Scriptures of the Old and New Testaments, as a revelation of the divine will, but do not admit that the Bible is, strictly speaking, the only rule of faith and practice, as they believe that each Christian is more or less under the immediate direction and inspiration of the Holy Ghost, and that it is the duty of all such to inquire what is the mind of the Spirit in relation to supposed duties not clearly pointed out in the Word of God, or the Scriptures of Truth. The term "Word of God," as applied to the Scriptures, they reject, supposing it to be applicable only to Jesus Christ.

They reject the outward forms of baptism and the Lord's Supper, believing water baptism to have been superseded by the baptism of the Holy Ghost, which is the only baptism now valid. Instead of holding to literal communion, they believe that the only true communion is spiritual.

Where both the parents are members, their children are considered as belonging to the church by birthright; hence as soon as they are born they are members. Though they move quietly through the world, in respect to infant church membership they are not so slow, but have thus managed to get a *few days* ahead of the Pedo-Baptist brethren generally.

They believe that war, whether offensive or defensive, is forbidden in the New Testament, and is unqualifiedly evil, and that it is their duty to refuse to bear arms in times of peace or war. Notwithstanding this sentiment, they have through the late rebellion been truly loyal, many of them having served through the war. A good story is told of an old Quaker who lived in the South. At the opening of the rebellion he was much abused and distressed by the rebels, and was finally driven out, with the loss of all his earthly goods. In this condition he sought refuge with a brother in Iowa. As he related to that brother his wrongs, his wrath waxed hot against the rebels, and in his anger he made some severe threats as to how he would use them if he could get the chance. His brother rebuked him for showing such a spirit, saying: "Thee ought not to talk so. 'I say unto you that ye resist not evil; but whosoever shall smite thee on thy right cheek, turn to him the other also.' 'Vengeance is mine, I will repay, saith the Lord.'" "Ah! but, brother," said he, "if thee had been robbed, abused and insulted, as I have been, by those dirty Philistines, thee, too, would have felt *very much like fighting!*" And there were many of the Friends so incensed against the proceedings of the rebels, that they did fall into the ranks and fight manfully. They are all abolitionists "up to the hub," and believe slavery to be exceedingly sinful and villainous, and that it is wicked to make any apology for it. Hence their sympathy for the slave and the fugitive from oppression. The Friends' anti-slavery sentiment is most happily represented in Mrs. Stowe's "Uncle Tom's Cabin," in the character of the "Friend" who assisted George and his wife to escape from their tormentors. I never yet knew a Quaker to show any symptoms of disloyalty. During the rebellion a gunboat was being built in Pennsylvania, when, for want of timber, an old Quaker who had excellent timber was asked if he could not sell enough to complete the boat. His reply was: "I can not sell thee any for such purposes; but thee can look through my woods, and see if there is any that suits thee."

Taking them upon the whole, I think that their fighting inclination is about as well represented in the following incident as by any that I can give:

A vessel which was once sailing upon the ocean was attacked by pirates. There happened to be a Quaker on board, who of course did not believe in fighting, but seeing a pirate who had seized a rope and was trying to climb up the ship's side, he caught up an axe, and stepping up to the edge of the vessel he said, "Friend, if thee wishes to get that bit of rope, I will help thee to it." And so saying, he cut it in twain, when the pirate dropped into the sea and was drowned.

As a sect they are, perhaps, the most strict against the use of ardent spirits of any in the world. They will discipline a member for selling corn to a distillery, or for stopping over night at an inn where liquor is habitually sold; or for furnishing barrels or casks to contain liquor, or in any way aiding the commerce of the article.

No member of the church is allowed to marry a person not belonging to the order. All proposals for marriage must come before the church, and the church decides upon the propriety or fitness of the union, and approves or disapproves as its wisdom may direct.

Much more might be said about the peculiarities of the Quakers, but I will pass on. Suffice it to say, that in this class of people I was born, and I grew up to manhood with their ideas and views deeply rooted in my mind. I had been so little in the world outside of Quaker influence, that I knew but little about other doctrines, and cared but very little about them.

The idea of a change of heart, by the agency of the Holy Spirit, being necessary to my soul's salvation, I had never heard of to my recollection. Though I was a member of the Quaker church when I became a man, I never had been converted to God. But being a member of the church, and supposing her doctrines and practices were just right, I felt no trouble about my soul's safety, because I was a member, and felt of course that all was right.

I leaned upon the church for salvation, and trusted to my identity with it, as the ground of my hope; and, alas! it had well-nigh proved my ruin. The Quakers do hold, doctrinally, in their printed declarations, to the necessity of regeneration, but with them it is too much a dead letter. They practically lay little or no stress upon it, and overlook it, in their concern for smaller things. I can not remember that I ever heard it mentioned in any of their exhortations or discourses. If I did, it was with no force of importance.

They are generally an honest and industrious people, and as such I respect them, and would to God there were none worse than they; but I must render my most solemn verdict against the Quaker church as an ark of safety for souls.

Her practice with reference to church birthright and unregenerate membership, is unwarranted by the Bible, and fruitful in the ruin of souls.

With all their sobriety and moral good, the greater part of them know nothing of regenerating, saving grace, and are deceiving their own souls. I desire to raise the voice of warning and sound the trumpet of alarm throughout the length and breadth of the land, for dying mortals to beware! Place no hope of heaven upon the simple fact that you are a church member, or that you have a church birthright, or that you have been christened in infancy. If you lean upon these things you will be lost! "Verily, verily, I say unto thee, except a man be born again he cannot see the kingdom of God."†

† John iii. 3.

CHAPTER III.

MOVE TO IOWA—WOLF STORY—PRAIRIE BREAKING—SICKNESS—PROSPECTS OF MARRIAGE.

In 1840, the western lands called the Black Hawk Purchase, now Iowa, was much talked of, and a number of the Friends concluded to emigrate. My father's family having become large, and needing a larger tract of land, he determined to go also. But upon consultation it was thought best that two of his boys should first go into the wild country and open a farm, and make some improvements before the family went. Accordingly my elder brother and myself, accompanied by a third brother, who went to assist us in driving the stock and immediately return, took our journey for the wild West. After a trip of usual novelty in moving to a new country, in which we frequently met with Indians, who, though friendly, were strange creatures to us, we arrived safely on the Black Hawk Purchase, and made our cabin near where the town of New Salem now stands, in Henry county, Iowa. We here found ourselves in a wild country indeed. In the latter part of our journey we would often travel from five to twenty-five miles without seeing a human habitation. We were on the borders of civilization. One more day's journey west would have taken us beyond the civilized world, where the Indian was the only sign of humanity. The greater part of Iowa was then a wild, trackless waste. We were almost alone in our glory. Wild deer and wild Indians roamed over the prairies by day, and wild wolves kept up their hideous jargon at night. The wolf is one of the most sneaking and thievish animals in the world, and of the least use. They would sneak about in a cowardly manner in the day-time, but at night one would suppose from their noise that they claimed to be monarchs of the realm. One of them would make such a chorus of howls as to make us think there were a dozen; and when there were a dozen, as was often the case, and sometimes more, their howling was terrific. Nothing is better calculated to make one feel a sense of utter loneliness than to listen from his cabin, on a dark, cheerless night, to their dismal howlings. Though they were cowardly, it was dangerous for us to be caught out at night when there were many, especially if they were hungry. At such times they gave us frequent hints that Quaker bacon would answer for a substitute. A settler, a number of miles from our cabin, determined one fall that as these "varmints" were so troublesome he would try a plan to thin them out a little, and have some fine sport into the bargain.

Having taken his wagon-box about a mile out on the prairie, he moistened a rope with a solution of assafœtida, of which wolves are very fond, and taking his gun and his boy, he trailed the rope through the prairie from different points toward the wagon-box.

About sunset he and the boy got under the box, and having provided port-holes to shoot through, they awaited the result. As it grew dark they heard one howl, then another, and another, and in a short time they were heard apparently in almost every direction for miles around. They drew nearer and howled louder, and increased in numbers, as though they were making a general rally for a grand carnival. Thought the man to himself, "I didn't mean to raise such a tremendous fuss as this. I wish I were at home; this is more than I spoke for, but it's too late now. On they come, like as if all creation was let loose. This old wagon-box looks rather shackling; I wish it were stouter, but it can't be helped now." He was not long in making reflections, for the wolves were soon about him, yelling most terrifically, and he was occupied with shooting them. He killed a number, but they were so greedy for the precious perfume, that they prowled about him in great numbers, and kept him besieged all night. He had no appetite for such an experiment again.

One of the first things that now occupied our attention was breaking up the wild prairie, and we prepared ourselves with a full outfit for our new business. This outfit consisted of five yoke of cattle, with yokes and chains, a large prairie plow, with an extra share; a file and a hammer, and a long buckskin whip. It was arranged that I should carry the whip, drive the oxen, and thus be master of ceremonies. We were at first very awkward Quakers at this new business, but we soon learned the various mysteries of our calling, and thought we were among its master spirits. Oxen are the pioneer laborers of civilization, and as such are the founders of our nation's greatness. No brute slave is more gentle or docile. None are more faithful, and yet none are so much abused. They serve the pioneer the best, because they can live without barns or stalls, almost without provision or expense, and almost without care; hence they must give all their hard toil to the master for little or no remuneration. Shame on the man that will beat and abuse them! When night came we unyoked the oxen from the plow, and hanging a bell upon "Old Tom," who was captain of the company, we would set them at liberty for the night, when they sought the cooling streams and delicious pasturage of nature's wilds, that grew in rich profusion upon every hand. In the morning their sleek coats and full sides showed their preparation for another day's toil. My chief objection to my position was, that on warm days especially, the oxen seemed to be deaf, or hard of hearing, which taxed my lungs to the utmost, and required many loud snaps of the whip to make the team "move up." They were deaf enough, to be sure; but I have since then been calling upon a certain class of creatures to repent, that are more deaf than they.

Our family, for various reasons, did not come as soon as expected; and finding no occupation more respectable or lucrative than prairie breaking, we adopted that as our regular business, and for two years we broke prairie for the new settlers who kept coming in. During this time we broke several hundred acres. There is now a goodly number of fine farms in Iowa, upon which my brother and I were the first to break the sod.

In 1842, my brother having grown tired of the prairies, sold out his western possessions, and returned to Indiana. This misstep he some years after repented and corrected.

I was now left in the new country alone, with no relatives within several hundred miles, and began to feel somewhat lonely. In a short time I took the typhoid fever, and became a great sufferer. I was bed-fast for many long weeks, and for some time lingered between life and death, and I felt that truly dark days were come upon me. Through a merciful Providence, however, I found, in this time of my affliction, a couple of the kindest friends in the persons of William and Nellie Mathews.

Had it not been for them, I verily believe I should have died. But they took me to their cabin and to their hearts, and gave me the best of care. For this I shall ever hold them in kind remembrance, and trust that at the judgment they will hear the Saviour say, "I was a stranger and ye took me in."

After being under lengthy but skillful treatment from Doctor A., I gradually regained my health and strength. The attack, however, so affected my nervous system, that from that time to this, although I have been uniformly robust, my nerves have been so beyond my control that it is with difficulty I write a letter, and sometimes my hands and arms are so tremulous that I can scarcely hold a cup of tea. During this illness I felt, somehow, conscious that I was unfit to die; but my chief feeling was alarm through fear of death. My seriousness was not such as led me to repent and seek the forgiving mercy of God, as I should have done, but I looked to the doctor as my *only* hope. Hence, on my recovery I was indifferent to the subject of vital religion, and as ignorant of it, as ever.

Previous to this illness I had expected marriage with a young Quaker woman of good character and connections; but before my recovery the affair turned out most strangely, and, I suppose the reader will think, with little credit to myself. Feeling, no doubt, solicitous for me, she came a number of miles on horseback to see me, which was certainly very kind.

But while lying on my sick bed I overheard the woman of the house say, as I suppose she saw her in the distance, "Sam's sweetheart is coming!" When I heard it my feelings toward her suddenly changed, in a strange manner, from a state of tender regard to one of uncontrollable repulsiveness; nor could I control this strange impulse sufficiently to speak to her when she came in. The result was that she soon went away, and never spoke to me afterwards. She served me right.

Whether this feeling was caused by my enfeebled condition of body and mind from my long suffering, or had more particularly to do with the far-reaching providence of God, I cannot determine. She was an amiable girl, and, so far as I knew, was all that I could have desired.

CHAPTER IV.

TEACHES SCHOOL—TAKES THE AGUE—CAUSES OF AGUE AND ITS EFFECTS—TEACHES SCHOOL AMONG THE MORMONS—APPEARANCE OF THE SCHOOL HOUSE—CHARACTER OF THE SCHOOL—"TRYING THE MASTER'S PLUCK"—CONQUERING A PEACE.

WHEN I concluded that I could breast the storms of the outer world once more, I found myself out of business, and began to cast about as to what I should do. At this crisis I was urged to teach school, or, as they would say, to "keep school," in a settlement near by. "This," thought I, "is a new business—a step in advance, with new prospects; but am I adapted to it? Can I succeed?"

I hesitated in making such a sudden change, from an ox-driver to a school-teacher, but being urged, I ventured. Enough settlers had gathered in to build a rude log school-house, and rally a good lot of children, and in this house I opened school. It was a rough beginning for a young college, but the world had to move some how, and we managed the best we could. Soon after the term commenced I was attacked with the ague, and generally shook every two days, as long as I remained in the school. However, it so happened that I managed to fully

2*

satisfy my employers and finish the term, and was pronounced "a buncombe school-keeper."

In those days the ague was our chief torment. As the prairie sod which was broken up by the new settlers would rot, its exhalations, together with those of the vast quantities of wild vegetation which decayed every year, loaded the air with such effluvia as to breed ague in abundance.

Scarcely a family could escape it, and it was not a very uncommon thing to see families of which every member, from the oldest to the youngest, had it at the same time. Though it is not a fatal disease, it is exceedingly afflictive. The patient, or perhaps I should say the impatient, after a few shakes becomes weak, poor, and peevish, irregular in appetite and gloomy in feeling. He is not sick enough to keep his bed, except during the shake and fever, nor is he well enough to work; and in this intermediate, helpless condition he sometimes lingers for months, while he sees his business going to ruin. He may escape the chills for one or two weeks, and feel so much better that he will fancy he is almost well, and conclude to work a little; but after a few hours' exertion, alas! he is as sick as ever. The poor creature will vainly try numerous remedies, for nearly every one he meets knows a "sure cure," and perhaps he sullenly resolves at last that he will "wear it out." The disease was so common in those early days of the West, that it was often said that even the dogs and cats were subject to it, and would sometimes shake with chills on a warm day. A certain adventurer, on one occasion, writing a description of the West to his friends East, said, among other things, about as follows: "You wished to know, in your last letter, if we had much ague here, if it is very severe, etc. I reply that it is here in vast abundance—everybody has it. As to its severity, why, bless you! you can have no idea—I can't describe it. A quarrelsome wife is no comparison to it. It shakes all creation out here. It will shake a man out of bed and out of doors, and then shake the bedstead at him."

Many of the first settlers who were much afflicted with ague and fevers, thinking that such diseases would always prevail, became discouraged and returned East with evil reports of the goodly land. This checked the tide of immigration very much for a number of years; but as the fact became known that these troubles arose chiefly from transient causes, the cry was again, "Westward ho!"

Having become known as a teacher, some time after the close of my first term, an offer was sent me to take another school about twenty miles farther south. The condition and character of this school and its community were "hard." It was where the town of Charlestown is now located, and not far from the once notorious city of Nauvoo. The inhabitants were made up chiefly of Mormons, many of whom were as hateful scamps as ever went unhung, and their children were just such progeny as one might expect from a settlement of that kind. They had a wretched house, but a large school. I soon found that I was going to have my hands full. They had usually employed female teachers, who being unable to master the school, would generally be driven out in a short time. Finally they had hired an old gentleman by the name of Meek. He was a decent man, but could not control the pupils. There was among them a number of large boys, or young men, from sixteen to twenty years of age, and knowing that the old man was afraid of them, they treated him with a good deal of impudence, and did about as they pleased; and whenever they took the notion, they would put the teacher out of doors, and raise Cain generally. As the pupils were too numerous for one teacher, it was arranged that I should be at the head of the school, and that the old man should be retained as an assistant. These matters being settled, I went to school one morning and took a survey of my new theatre of action.

The house was built of rough logs, which were put up in such a bungling style that one would suppose that some person had done the carpenter work himself. Where the logs crossed each other at the corners they were from six inches to two feet too long. The crevices between the logs had been chinked with clay, which was still remaining, except such portions as had been knocked out by the boys. The concern was roofed over with clap-boards, but had no ceiling. The floor was made of puncheons which had been smoothed but very little, and the desks and seats were made of the same material, supported by wooden legs polished with an axe and put in with an auger. The door swung on large wood hinges secured by pins. There were two windows in the house, each one being two panes in depth; room had been made for them by cutting out a log on each side. The architectural beauty of the building was finally completed by the fire-place. This was a huge pile built of timber and rocks, and would accommodate a back log six feet in length, with a large quantity of finer wood.

But the school itself beggars description, and I will not attempt it. I verily never had seen such a pack of saucy, shabby, hopeless disciples, and I never have since. Thought I, "Surely I'm in for it." But the success of my first trial in teaching gave me self-confidence, and I resolved to go forward and risk the chances. As I expected, they began to experiment with me the first day, and that for the avowed purpose of "trying the master's pluck."

Modern school teachers and doating parents talk very handsomely about new systems and mild measures, and I am glad of the improvements in our schools, and the growing success of mild measures; yet I think this success is more the result of an improved state of society than anything else. Now, I don't mean to philosophize and forget my story; yet I cannot but wonder how the new order of things would work with such a gnarly lot of imps as those with whom I had to deal.

I let them have rather loose rein the first day. I saw that nothing but strong doses, promptly administered, could cure them. As soon as I dismissed for the night, I prepared, with the concurrence of the old man, a number of strict rules for the school, writing them down in order. I then went to the trustees, showed them the rules, and told them that if I taught the school I should carry out these rules to the letter, and should demand them to sustain me in it, urging that otherwise the attempt for reform would be hopeless. To all this they agreed.

The next morning I cut some heavy whips, toughened them in the hot embers, and again opened school. The next thing I did was to read the rules. I then told the school that the first one who violated them might expect to get very rough handling. I put on a stern look, and assumed a demeanor altogether different from that of the day before, and went forward with the duties.

They were not, however, to be awed into obedience by rules or threats; and it was not long before one overgrown young fellow perched himself upon a seat, and mocked me with all the impudence of a jackanapes. I bade him attend to his book, but he treated my order with contempt. I then went up to him coolly, and before he anticipated my movements, I suddenly caught him by the scalp-lock, jerked him across the writing-desk, keel downwards, and gave his back and hips such a sudden and severe vegetable application that he bawled out lustily for help and mercy.

The ball was now opened in earnest. General disorder prevailed. Cries of "Help! help!" "Pull the master off!" "Knock him down!" came from various quarters. A young man from the back end of the room rushed toward me with a knife drawn; but to my good fortune my old colleague, acting as a reserve corps, met him with the big wooden fire-shovel and split it on his head. The tap proved to be a lucky one for us, for it laid him sprawling on the floor. By this time several of the large boys were coming to the help of their companions; but having tamed the first one, I turned upon them with all the ferocity I could command. At this they hesitated; appearances were against them; blood was flowing pretty freely already, especially from the one lying on the floor. They began to retreat. I then followed them up, and soon had the ground. Many of the smaller ones became frightened, and were for running home; but I forbade them, and told them all to sit down and be orderly, and if they did not I would murder every mother's son of them! They soon became quiet. The old man and I had conquered a peace, won the field, and showed them our "pluck."

They were ever after as afraid of me as death. I had comparatively little trouble with them, and succeeded in carrying out my rules to the letter.

In the opinion of the more influential of the citizens, my reputation as a good "school-keeper" was thoroughly established. I taught this school a long time. During my stay there, however, various changes took place. The Mormons were driven out of the country and a better class of people began to settle in it, so that in a short time the social element of the community became tolerably decent.

CHAPTER V.

RISE OF MORMONS—THEIR STRANGE DOCTRINES—WORKING MIRACLES—JOKE ON A MORMON ELDER—BAPTIZING FOR THE DEAD—MORMON PRAYER-MEETING—FATE OF THE "GENTILES"—MORMON DIALOGUE—THE AUTHOR IS EXPECTED TO JOIN—THE "DANITES"—CORRUPTION OF THE "SAINTS"—SPIRITUAL WIFE SYSTEM—PREACHING OF ONE OF THE APOSTLES—TESTIMONY OF SIXTEEN WOMEN—ARREST OF THE PROPHET—THE MORMONS DRIVEN OUT.

THE history of Mormonism presents one of the most shocking examples, illustrative of human credulity, that the enlightened world ever saw. The success of Joseph Smith, in rising from obscurity and ignorance and building up a sect of followers, gathered from different parts of the world, to the number of two hundred thousand or more, in so short a time, surely entitles him to the name of the "American Mohammed." In an early part of the history of the Upper Mississippi Valley, the Mormons and their enterprise created much public interest, and much was said about them, true and untrue.

Since then, amid other exciting matters of national interest, they have been almost forgotten; yet it will doubtless be instructing and interesting to the reader to hear something about them, from one who was a near neighbor to them, and is personally acquainted with many facts and incidents concerning them. Like all other advocates of heresy, they preach some good doctrines; and under certain circumstances you might listen to a Mormon elder, and hear nothing contrary to sound orthodoxy. But such a discourse would seldom occur. In fact, during my stay among them they labored ten times as much to establish error as to enforce useful truth; and hence not only the religious interests, but the moral well-being of the people was unfavorably affected. Many of their ideas are very strange. For example: They teach that the kingdom of Christ was destroyed at the crucifixion, and has had no existence since until it was reëstablished by Joseph Smith, who is the true prophet of God. They believe that now, since Joseph has done so much, true believers (that is, Latter-Day Saints) can heal the sick, cure the lame, restore the blind, and do all those miraculous things which were done, through faith, by the early Apostles of Christ. To bring in converts, their preachers went into various parts of the country and preached. They often told a miracle performed by the saints. It was a common thing to hear of obstinate diseases and dreadful afflictions suddenly cured by the miraculous power of the true believers; and these reports were speedily circulated among them. But though I lived several years just across the river opposite the Mormon city, and only a few miles from it, in a Mormon community, I never could get to see any such case; nor could I get any other evidence of the truth of such reports than their simple statements.

On one occasion a "Saint" went out from Nauvoo to make converts among the "Gentiles," as all are called who are not Mormons, and took a lame brother along as a traveling companion.

By his request an old preacher of the Christian connection permitted him to hold a meeting in his dwelling. After due notice the neighbors gathered in, and he earnestly preached that the true saints had the power of healing. He told them of a number of examples where he had cured and witnessed the cures of those who had been given up by physicians, and finally urged that all present ought to accept a religion so abundantly approved of God by signs and wonders. When his discourse was ended, he said: "Now, if any one desires to speak, or ask any questions, he may."

The old preacher now arose, and, first addressing the lame brother, said: "Brother J****, do you believe what brother H**** has just preached?"

"Certainly I do," said J****.

Then turning to the Mormon preacher, he said: "Brother H****, do you really believe what you have preached?"

"Most surely I do, with all my heart," said H****.

"Then," said the old preacher, "just turn about now and heal your lame companion, and we'll all believe!"

This was a stumper he could not manage, and there was no chance of relief but for him and his companion to leave the crowd and the community, which they did amid hearty laughter from the company.

They have a singular custom of baptizing the living for their dead friends. I once saw a man baptized seven times for as many dead friends, before he came up out of the water.

They sometimes had prayer meetings in the community where I resided, but not often. On such occasions, where there were seldom any but Mormons, it was shocking to hear them talk and pray. In those days I did not care what people believed; I thought it of little concern to me whether they were saints or sinners; and as I lived among the Mormons and was their school-teacher, I thought best for prudential reasons to have as little dispute with them as possible, and make myself as agreeable to them as I could. From this they became very hopeful for my conversion, and thought I was "not far from the kingdom." In my presence they seemed to feel no restraint in expressing their sentiments; and I had abundant opportunity to thoroughly understand them.

They declared that the day would soon come when God would so help them against their enemies, and visit such judgments on the "Gentiles," that they would flee to the "Saints" (that is, the Mormons) to plead for mercy and beg for bread; and that all that prevented them from doing it then was the forbearance of God. I went once to what they called a night prayer-meeting, in my school-house, to see how they conducted it. I there saw and heard what in substance was about as follows: Mr. Mowry, an elder, and a near neighbor, first arose in the meeting and said: "Brethren, we believe that Joseph

Smith is the true Prophet of God, and we must feel it our bounden duty to comply with any request or order which he may make."

Here one of the brethren inquired, "Suppose he should order us to lay hands on the Gentiles, would not their laws punish us?"

"We do not consider their law as binding upon the true church of the Saints, and this *is* the *order* of Joseph, that if we lay hands on Gentile property and they arrest us, it is our duty to swear each other clear."

Another asked, "Suppose Joseph should order us to go to Missouri and kill those who drove us out, would you go?"

"Certainly I would go; and if we were arrested and tried according to the laws of the d——d Gentiles, I would help in swearing each other clear."

After other questions and remarks more or less of this character, the elder kneeled down and prayed. In that prayer he said, among other things: "O Lord, God of thy Saints, hasten on the day when the true church shall have it in its power to tramp the d——d Gentiles under their feet, until their blood shall rise to the bits of the horses' bridles!"

There was a regular organization within the church, called the "Danite Band." No person could become a member of that band without first joining the church. One young man who belonged to this class, and who expected I would soon become a member of the church, urged that I ought to become a Mormon as soon as possible, and that when I did

I ought to join the "Danites." Partly from curiosity and partly from mischief, I encouraged the fellow until I stole his confidence, when he revealed to me that their business was to gather the Lord's property into the church—that everything belonged to the Lord, and that they gathered it up, wherever and whenever they most conveniently could, among the accursed Gentiles. He said they made their reports to the church every three months, and that it allowed them a certain percentage on all they gathered. They had to be pretty sharp and cautious, but some of them had made a good sum by it. If one of them did get arrested, his comrades were bound to swear him clear, if possible.

I, of course, had heard all this before, though with some doubt as to the details; but in view of the source from which it now came, and the circumstances which called it forth, I was satisfied that a pack of more consummate scoundrels did not live in the West.

The old settlers in the counties adjoining Nauvoo, can well remember how much they were annoyed by this gang of rascals. They skulked about the country so much as to keep people in a constant state of uneasiness, and in consequence of them many quiet citizens moved away. It is true, as has been said, the thieves, gamblers and counterfeiters who infested that region, were not all Mormons. There were more or less of those scamps who haunted the vicinity of the Lower Rapids, who were of a more transient character. But granting this, the fact of their being around there so much shows that Nauvoo was a congenial place for them, and illustrates the saying, that,

> "Birds of a feather
> Will flock together."

The Mormons never publicly advocated the Spiritual Wife System until a short time before they left Nauvoo. I heard Elder Page, one of the twelve Apostles, preach on the subject one evening in a private house, near my school. He tried to argue: First, from the Bible—describing in a very cunning manner the concubinage of Abraham, David, Solomon, and others, and claimed from these precedents the divine sanction of his doctrine. Secondly, from supposed benefits to be derived in the development of the human species. Said he, "Now we wisely follow the more excellent way in our efforts to improve the brute species, and by obeying the law of selection great improvements are made; but of all the animals, man, who was originally the glory of creation, has become the most degenerate." Finally, said he, "I appeal to the good sense of the women. Look at this wretched world, see how it is filled up with poor, miserable, degenerated specimens of humanity. The greater part of them are not men; they are but mere apes of the human kind. Now, had not six or seven of you in company, rather all have one good man—a large, handsome, intelligent, noble, genteel man for a husband, than for each one of you to tie to a poor, scrubby, scabby, ugly, hair-brained, snotty-nosed baboon? To be sure, any sensible woman would."

This doctrine, however, was scarcely introduced, when it resulted in their confusion and dispersion. A Dr. Foster, who had been excommunicated from the church, and a man named Law, commenced the publication in Nauvoo itself, of a newspaper, called the *Expositor*. In the first number they printed the affidavits of sixteen women, to the effect that Smith, Rigdon, and others, had tried to seduce them under the plea of having special permission from Heaven. Soon after this the Mormons destroyed the office of the *Expositor*, and all its contents; and the editors fled for their lives, and took refuge in Carthage. Here they applied for a warrant against Joseph and Hiram Smith, and sixteen others, known to have aided and abetted in putting down the *Expositor* office. The warrant was granted, and served upon Joseph Smith, but he refused to acknowledge its validity, and the constable who served it was marched out of Nauvoo by the city marshal. The authorities of the county could not suffer this affront to the law, and the militia were ordered out to support the county officer in the arrest of the two Smiths and their sixteen confederates. The Mormons in Nauvoo fortified the city, and determined to fight to the last extremity in support of the "Prophet." The "saints," from all parts of the country, hastened to give assistance. Illinois, like Missouri, divided itself into two great camps, the Mormons and the Anti-Mormons, and the circumstances were so menacing that Gov. Ford took the field in person. In a proclamation to the people of Illinois he stated that he had discovered that nothing but the utter destruction of the city of Nauvoo would satisfy the militia and troops under his command, and that if they marched into the city, pretexts would not be wanting for the commencement of slaughter.

Anxious to spare the effusion of blood, he called on the two Smiths to surrender, promising that they should be defended and strictly dealt with according to law. They finally submitted, and were lodged in Carthage jail to await their trial. But the citizens of the adjoining country were so exasperated, that a short time after this, on the evening of the 27th of June, 1844, the guard at the jail was overpowered by a band of nearly two hundred men, with blackened faces, and the prisoners were killed.

After this the Mormons relaxed for a time; Brigham Young was appointed successor to Smith, and they renewed their work on the city and temple. But this state of affairs did not last long. New complaints arose from the citizens of the adjoining counties. Disputes and quarrels became more frequent, until, finally, in September, 1846, the city was besieged, and after three days' bombardment the Mormons were driven off.

Before closing this chapter it is just to say, that there are also many Mormons who are well-disposed and sincere in their belief. This is more especially true of those who have never lived at headquarters, and consequently know nothing of the realities of Mormonism except by report. By its visionary ideas hundreds who have deserved a better fate have been deceived, and I cannot but pity them.

CHAPTER VI.

AWAKENING AND CONVERSION.

DURING the time occupied in events of the two preceding chapters, my father and his family had moved to Henry county, Iowa, and settled on the farm opened by my brother and myself. Many other Quakers had settled there also, and a Quaker village had been built containing three or four hundred inhabitants, called New Salem. They had erected a meeting house, school house, comfortable dwellings, and had around them most of the improvements of a regular "community."

Though the Quakers are strict in the moral training of their children, some of them, of course, are hard to train, and I suppose that I belonged to that class. I was not a law-breaker or a malicious person, yet I must say that I was as full of mischief and frolic as an egg is of meat, and far from God by wicked works. I was about that age when young men are said to "sow their wild oats," and the social influences which had surrounded me in the new country were unfavorable to a sober life.

On renewing acquaintance among the young Quakers at New Salem, I found a number of them who were as fond of sport as I, and they were ever ready for a frolic when they could slip from under the watchful eyes of the old folks.

A Methodist class was organized in the vicinity of New Salem, and we young Quakers were present. It being a new thing to us we thought it a capital show. The praying, preaching, and especially the singing, seemed to us very novel. After attending one of these meetings, we concluded that as they were so interesting we must have one of our own. Accordingly, on the following Sabbath, fifteen or twenty of us went into the woods, arranged some old logs for seats, and held a mock class-meeting. Though we made much awkward work, especially with the singing, we felt that we enjoyed it hugely. We thought there was so much sport in it that we would have another, and we agreed that it should occur in two weeks from that time.

It was arranged that our next meeting should be more systematic. I was to preach, W. W. P. was to do the praying, and the rest were to do the singing and attend to the amens, shouting, rubbing of hands, groaning, etc. In the meantime a preacher's stand was to be erected, and all were to prepare to act well their part. With this understanding we adjourned to our homes.

I privately determined that during that two weeks I would carefully think up a good sermon and have it in readiness, that when the meeting occurred I would astonish them all at my preaching ability.

One would naturally suppose that I must have felt some uneasiness of conscience while, during those two weeks, I was preparing to act out before my young companions such a heaven-daring mockery, and to venture with impudent hardihood upon such ground as angels fear to tread; but no—so hard was my heart and so great was my moral distance from God! I knew it was folly and thought it was a strange experiment, and had some feeling of its awkwardness and inconsistency; but I knew nothing of the doctrine of new birth by the Spirit, and the necessity of a deep repentance of sin at the foot of the cross. I had no knowlege of that faith in Christ which is necessary to salvation. My religious instruction had not been such as to open these doctrines before me, and I went forward in preparations for this mock solemnity without a just conception of its exceeding sinfulness. May God in his mercy blot it from the book of his remembrance!

On the day appointed a good number of us gath ered on the ground, with fine prospects for a jolly time. W. W. P—— made the opening prayer, and did well, considering. A hymn was lined, and singing attempted, but none of us had ever heard singing enough to know how to carry a tune, and the music was a poor apology. This ended, I arose in the stand and announced my text in these words:

"Who is Christ?"

But I could not say another word. By some cause, I knew not what, I suddenly became confused, speechless, and terrified. My companions afterward said that my hair stood erect, and I was as pale as a corpse. I immediately left the ground, with the rest after me, all in great fright. This at once, and forever, put an end to our mock meetings.

It since appears that God, in his mercy, instead of cutting me down in my iniquity, meant to teach me in the severe school of his providence, and by the wonders of his grace, how to preach in earnest, and how to teach doctrines which to me were then unknown, and how to preach a gospel to which I was a stranger.

As soon as I got away from the place of meeting and its vicinity, my fright left me, and my feelings were quiet. I never could tell the real cause of my fear, and cannot yet account for it, otherwise than to regard it as a sudden and special visitation from God. My feelings were frightful, yet they were vague and indefinable; and one thing that still appears strange to me is, that the effect so soon left me.

Some time after this, at the close of a school I had been teaching in another part of the country, I went one night with some young companions to a ball. The fiddle came in due season, and I danced until four o'clock in the morning. At the close of the dance I went to a settlement two miles from M****, and hired to teach another school. I immediately engaged boarding in a tavern, and began to fix myself for a winter's stay. On the first evening, supper being over, while the boarders were seated around the bar-room fire, the conversation turned upon a religious meeting that was to be held at the schoolhouse by a Mr. M****, who was to preach there that evening, and after some talk as to the prospects of an interesting meeting, the majority concluded to go, and I went along. The house was much crowded with people before we arrived, but, though with some difficulty, I found room to stand near the door. The place of worship was built of rough logs, and covered with clap-boards. It had two or three small windows, a large rude fire-place in the back end, and in every way corresponded with the times. As I entered, the people were singing. With this I was delighted, for I had seldom heard it in a religious assembly. The preacher arose to pray. I thought he was certainly a dull, stupid, ignorant man. His hair hung in strings and mats about his neck and shoulders, and half concealed his forehead. In short, his head bore a striking resemblance to a brush-heap. His clothes were worn and tattered, and his figure was lean and crooked. He began his prayer in a very bungling manner. I thought I was "sold" in coming to the meeting, and was more than half decided to go back; for, thought I, I don't care about hearing that man attempt to preach. Yet I did not start. The preacher tried to read a hymn, which he did with much difficulty, being obliged to stop occasionally to spell out the hard words. I thought again I would leave, but waited to hear the singing, which finally went off to my satisfaction. I then thought I would remain a little while and hear what the old man would make out, to satisfy my curiosity. The text was in Matthew, and his subject was the Judgment. He began in a very dull, awkward manner, but after a while he seemed more animated and interesting. His animation increased as he advanced in the discourse, until his intellect seemed to be fully aroused and his soul fixed with inspiration.

His feelings ran up to the highest pitch of sympathy for the sinner, and his exhortations became eloquent and powerful. My mind at length became so riveted upon the speaker that I forgot the crowd of people who were crammed around me, and every thing besides but the preaching and myself. I felt a strange sense of guilt come over me. The sermon, as with a bright lamp, searched by inmost soul. My sins were exposed to view in such a way as I never before imagined. I felt that I was one of the vilest sinners God had ever permitted to live. Yet the preacher went on, and spared me not. He so presented my guilt in the light of the judgment, that I thought he was preaching expressly to me, and my awakened conscience said, "Thou art the man!" I thought that by some means, perhaps supernatural, the preacher knew all about me, and was now exposing me. I trembled with solemn awe.

When meeting was dismissed I went home with my landlord, feeling the keenest remorse, and a most distressing anxiety about my soul's well-being. I soon began to be sorry I had gone to the meeting, and tried to shake off my feelings. I tried to reason with myself, and in this I suppose Satan helped me as follows: "I am a member of the Quaker church, and always have been, and so are my parents. I have no reason to fear; these fears are foolish. Before I went to that meeting I felt well enough, and I stand on the same footing now. I have always enjoyed life; I have had mirth to my full, and if I had kept away from that meeting, I would be happy now; but I have been so silly as to go there, and now I am miserable. I am provoked at myself beyond endurance for having gone there. What a fool I was! The preaching has done me more harm than good; it makes me worse, and unhappy in the bargain; I'll have no more to do with it. These praying and preaching people try to scare folks on purpose; they are nothing but a set of hypocrites; they had better mind their own business. I'll shun their company, that's what I'll do; and I want them to steer clear of me." Thus, with my mind full of rebellious thoughts, I hastened to bed, not wishing to speak to any one; but with all these flimsy arguments I could not banish my troubles; an awful sense of guilt pressed upon me. I commenced my duties in school, yet was often but half conscious of what I was doing; my mind remained gloomy and my feelings morose and sullen. I heard that in two weeks from the previous meeting another was to occur, eight miles distant, and it provoked me to hear of it. I felt determined that I should not go near such a place again. But as the days passed by, in spite of all I could do, my distress of soul continued. I tried various expedients, but to no purpose; and when the time of the meeting arrived, I felt somehow that I *must* go, and I traveled the eight miles through the snow on foot, hoping that some change might be made in my feelings, I thought that possibly they would leave me; I listened attentively to the preaching, and carefully watched all the exercises of the meeting; but, alas! it only revived my sense of guilt, and arrayed my sins anew before me, causing me to feel, if possible, worse than before, and to hate existence. On my journey home I wished I were anybody or anything but Samuel Pickard. In my distress I saw a hog by the road-side, and envied his lot. I heartily wished I was a hog, because, thought I, "I could then quietly eat, drink, and die, without such tormenting, tantalizing fears on account of sin and the great judgment to come. I returned to my school and continued to discharge my duties the best I could; but no permanent change occurred in my feelings, and I feared I should never have another happy day, in time or eternity. A few days after the meeting I heard that a dance was to take place in the neighborhood, and I received it as most welcome news; for, thought I, "I have found delight in such places," and, like Solomon, I said to my heart, "Go to, now, I will prove thee with mirth." I went, but in our first attempt to dance, the fiddle-strings broke, and could not be repaired; thus our prospects were suddenly blasted. We tried to turn the dance into a play, but somehow we could not make it go, and the whole affair turned out a failure and a disappointment. I here met with the young lady who afterwards became my wife, and engaged to escort her home, according to customary civilities; but in this I was doomed to the most mortifying failure of all: we had not gone far on our journey when such a consciousness of my dreadful situation as a sinner came over me, and so affected me, that in spite of all I could do, my knees gave way with weakness, and I sank helpless to the ground. There were very few professors of religion in the country, and I had felt ashamed to reveal my state of mind, for I knew I should be laughed at, and I kept it a dead secret. When my lady saw me sprawled upon the ground, she felt, no doubt, that she had taken up with a poor apology for a beau, and was very much embarrassed; she would walk around me, or stand and look, as though she did not know what on earth to do. I felt sorry for her, and pitied myself, but could not help any. She attempted to raise me up and help me along, but it was no use, my legs would not go; they seemed like strings. Finally, some people from the party came up, on their way home, and carried me back to the house whence we started. I remained in this helpless condition several days, and was urged to try remedies, but refused all medical aid. My friends said, "You ought to quit school; it is killing you, you look so poorly." As soon as I was able to walk I resumed my duties as teacher, but the troubles of my mind now began to tell most seriously upon my health. I lost my appetite, became pale and emaciated, and feared that I should die. Oh, the agony I endured through those long, dreary, weeks of conviction! Well did it teach me how to sympathize with and counsel those who are crushed under the strokes of God's insulted law! Had I sought the company of some warm Christian, I might have been instructed, and led to light and comfort; but no, my proud heart spurned the idea of becoming one of those solemn, praying creatures, whom I had seen conducting meeting; it was contrary to my notions, tastes, and appetites, and repulsive in every respect.

An appointment for an evening prayer meeting to be held five miles distant came round. I did not want to go, yet I felt that I must. At that meeting I saw several go to the anxious seat for prayers; among them my future wife. I wanted to bow there, too, but believed that I was too vile to have any right at such a place. I supposed that those who went to the anxious seat did not think themselves so wicked as I thought myself to be, or they would not have gone there, and I left the meeting with my grief still secret in my soul, to be troubled with gloomy thoughts by day and fearful dreams by night.

Finally, some weeks after this I attended another prayer meeting, and while the people prayed and exhorted I communed with my heart, and felt that I should soon die if I continued in such distressing anxiety. I knew that I had tried every mortal expedient that I could devise for my relief, and all was vain. I thought I should surely not only die in this world, but spend an awful eternity in the world to come, "where the worm dieth not, and the fire is not quenched." I saw that I was brought to a complete extremity, and that God alone could save me through the mercy of Christ. I felt that I had but precious little time left in which to decide the controversy. My feelings at that time are fitly described by a poet:—

"Lo, on a narrow neck of land,
'Twixt two unbounded seas I stand;
A point of time, a moment's space,
Removes me to that heavenly place,
Or shuts me up in hell!"

I felt that I was sinking under the weight of God's wrath, and that I would surely be in hell in a little time if I received not help from him, and from the depths of my heart I pleaded for mercy. My stubbornness was gone. I humbled myself under his mighty hand, and looked with earnest pleadings to Christ. I knew that if I were damned it was just, if saved it was mercy. So intent was I in begging for divine mercy, that I lost sense of what was passing around me.

At last, while the brethren were singing the words—

"Jesus, my all, to heaven is gone,"

the hand of God appeared to be gently placed beneath me, and my soul seemed to rise from its low estate as upon the wings of eagles. The dark night of bitterness and sorrow receded from my soul. The day of hope dawned, and the Sun of Righteousness arose with healing in his wings. I rejoiced with joy unspeakable, and was filled with that peace which passeth all understanding!

"Oh! the rapturous height
Of that holy delight,
Which I felt in his life-giving blood."

Methinks an angel's tongue could not tell half the joy of my first love with Christ. The gift of a crown and scepter I would have prized as insignificant, compared with the gift of immortal hope which I then received through our Lord Jesus Christ. My desire to keep my feelings secret at once vanished, and the brethren rejoiced with me that the dead was alive and the lost was found. It was a moonlight night, and on my way home it seemed to me that the appearance of the world had changed, and that nature had arrayed herself as for some grand festivity to rejoice with me. I thought the whole dome of heaven seemed as one vast amphitheater of glory, and that the stars shone with unearthly luster. The landscape that lay around me, though half concealed in the shadows of the night, seemed of the rarest beauty and sublimity.

Though long years of toil, with their varied scenes of light and shade, have passed since then, I can yet sing—

"Oh happy day that fixed my choice
On thee, my Saviour and my God;
Well may this glowing heart rejoice,
And tell its wonders all abroad."

CHAPTER VII.

CHOOSING A CHURCH.

Up to the time of my conversion I had heard very little said about churches and sects, nor was I disposed to give much attention to the subject. Having been raised a Quaker, I knew something of that church, and supposing it was all right, I thought that was sufficient; but as to creeds outside of that, I was perhaps as ignorant as any convert ever was at my age.

As soon, however, as I received joy in believing, the Bible seemed to me as an unsealed book. I delighted to study it, and it became my daily counselor and companion.

The New Testament showed very clearly, I thought, that churches existed in the days of the Apostles, for it speaks of a church at Jerusalem,* "the church at Smyrna,"† "the church in Pergamos,"‡ and in the same way does it speak in many other places.§ I could see that God had established churches, and that it was the duty and high privilege of a Christian to be in one. I supposed, of course, that the various churches alluded to in the New Testament were of one faith and order, but as I looked around me I

* Acts xv : 2. † Rev. ii : 8. ‡ Rev. ii : 12. § See 1 Cor. i : 2; Col. iv : 16; 1 Thes. i : 1; Rev. ii : 1, 8; iii : 1; iii : 7, etc.

saw that there were a great many different kinds of churches, called by different names, and all more or less at variance with each other in faith and order. It was pleasant for me to know, however, that these churches claimed to love and worship the same God and Saviour, and strive for the same heaven. I felt a strong attachment for the Quakers, but aside from this I had a glowing heart and loved all the praying people with whom I met, and thought it a great pity that there were divisions in sentiment and feeling among Christians. With this unbiased state of mind I resolved to join some church; but when I began to ask counsel as to the best one, some said, "Lo, here!" others said, "Lo, there!" and yet others said, "Lo, yonder!" The consequence was that I became very much confused and knew not what to do.

I finally concluded that they could not all be right in theology and have so many opposites—that God would surely not establish a number of churches, and then give to the world so many different sets of doctrines to suit those churches and accommodate the numerous tastes of men. On reflection, it seemed clear to me that God was a being of one mind.

The question would then arise, "Which is the true Church?" I felt that I must find an answer to the question, if possible, that would satisfy my mind. "For," thought I, "this is a matter of solemn import which concerns my usefulness and happiness for life, and perhaps for eternity."

While reading the Testament, my attention was directed to such passages as the following:

"Search the Scriptures; for in them ye think ye have eternal life; and they are they which testify of me." *

"All Scripture is given by inspiration of God, and is profitable for doctrine, for reproof, for instruction in righteousness; that the man of God may be perfect, thoroughly furnished unto all good works." †

"Ye do err, not knowing the Scriptures." ‡

With passages of this character before me, I resolved to take my time, and study God's Word carefully and diligently, for "doctrine" and "instruction in righteousness."

I believed that God had established a church as a home for his people, and that in his Word its model could be found. I felt satisfied that in taking this course I should get my information from the best authority. I was cautioned in due time by the Book of God, which says that "Some wrest the Scriptures unto their own destruction;" § and I read with a praying heart that I might learn the will of God and be led into the truth.

I soon saw that it was my first duty, as a disciple of Christ, to be baptized. This was clear from the great commission of the Apostles. The Saviour said to them, "Go ye therefore and teach all nations; baptizing them in the name of the Father, and of the Son, and of the Holy Ghost." ‖ "He that believ-

* John v : 39. † 2d Tim. iii : 16, 7. ‡ Matt. xxii : 29.
§ 2d Pet. iii : 16. ‖ Matt. xxviii : 19.

eth and is baptized shall be saved; but he that believeth not shall be damned." *

These, and other passages, showed me that it was not only my right to be baptized, but it was a duty I should not dare to omit.

My practice was, as often as I found a passage relating to any prominent doctrine, to mark down the chapter and verse under its appropriate head, on paper; and thus I would collect in one body all the passages relating to that subject. I then read and meditated upon them with reference to the doctrines they contained, and my duty respecting them; nor did I lay by a particular subject until my mind was at ease concerning it. I of course sought such other helps as could be found; but Iowa at that time was not a land of books or scholars, and the Bible was my dependence.

The mode of baptism next occupied my attention. I noticed upon this subject the fact that John and the Apostles habitually baptized in rivers and places of much water. This was seen in such passages as the following: "And John also was baptizing in Ænon, near to Salim, because there was much water there."† Here it was easy to see that a reason was given why John baptized in Ænon; and this is the reason: "because there was much water there." From this it seemed evident that much water was required in baptizing, or this would not have been given as the only reason. I thought that no other mode of baptism but immersion would require "much water."

* Mark xvi : 16. † John iii : 23.

If the mode had been by sprinkling—which, as is commonly the case, requires only enough water to wet the tips of the administrator's two fore-fingers, which he touches against the forehead—one gallon of water would have baptized thousands, and "much water" would not have been required.

"Then went out to him Jerusalem, and all Judea, and all the region round about *Jordan*, and were baptized of him in *Jordan* confessing their sins." *

"Then cometh Jesus from Galilee to *Jordan* unto John, to be baptized of him." †

"And as they went on their way they came unto *a certain water*, and the eunuch said, See, here is water; what doth hinder me to be baptized?" ‡

"And on the Sabbath we went out of the city by a *river side*.... And a certain woman named Lydia.... heard us .... and when she was baptized and her household," etc.

"John did baptize in the wilderness, and preach the baptism of repentance for the remission of sins, and there went out unto him all the land of Judea and they of Jerusalem, and were all baptized of him in the *river of Jordan*, confessing their sins." §

Again, I noticed that the actions frequently associated with baptism were those of going down *into* the water, and coming up *out of* the water.

For example: "And Jesus, when he was baptized, went up straightway *out of the water*." ‖

"And straightway *coming up out of the water*, he saw the heavens opened."¶

* Matt. iii : 5, 6. † Matt. iii: 13. ‡ Acts viii : 36.
§ Mark i : 4. ‖ Matt. iii : 16 ¶ Mark i: 10.

"And he commanded the chariot to stand still, and they went down *both into the water, both Philip and the eunuch;* and he baptized him. And when they were *come up out of the water*, the Spirit of the Lord caught away Philip, and the eunuch saw him no more." *

I thought, and very naturally, I believe, that such Scriptures pointed to immersion as the true mode of baptism.

Again, I observed that the New Testament represented Christian baptism as a burial. For example:

"Know ye not that so many of us as were baptized into Jesus Christ were baptized into his death? Therefore we are *buried* with him by baptism into death." "For if we have been *planted* together in the likeness of his death, we shall be also in the likeness of his resurrection." †

"*Buried* with him in baptism, wherein also ye are risen with him." ‡

I thought that surely immersion was the only mode of baptism which could be represented by the figure of a burial. By this plan of inquiry I became satisfied as to the mode, and have believed in immersion, as the true apostolic practice, ever since.

Had I not taken to the Bible as my only reliable counselor, I should, perhaps, have never been baptized by any method. The Quakers believe that water baptism has been done away, and superseded by the baptism of the Holy Ghost. Hence, without any prejudice to favor it, I was made an immersionist by the Bible.

* Acts viii : 38, 39. † Rom. vi : 3–5. ‡ Cols. 2 : 12.

Allow me, with due deference, to recommend all my Quaker friends and relatives who may read this narrative, to place less dependence upon their books of discipline and their inculcated opinions, and give more importance to the study of the Bible. Though it be true that your discipline and your instructors, in the main, are good, and teach you many good things, remember that they are not inspired, and the Bible is. They may be wrong, but the Bible cannot be.

While reading the Scriptures, it seemed to me to show that one characteristic feature of the New Testament church was, its being made up of baptized believers. With this impression I searched out the passages which I thought had a bearing upon that point. Some of them I will here quote:

"Then they that gladly received the Word were baptized; and the same day there were added unto them about three thousand souls. And they continued steadfastly in the Apostles' doctrine and fellowship, and in breaking of bread, and in prayers." *

The divine order of things here appears very plain. First, they "gladly received the Word, that is, they believed; secondly, they "were baptized;" thirdly, they were added unto them: from which it is plain that they *all believed and were all baptized before they became members of the church.*

"Paul,....unto the church of God which is at Corinth.....Is Christ divided? Was Paul crucified for you? or were ye baptized in the name of Paul?" †

* Acts ii: 41, 42.

† 1 Cor. i: 1–13.

Here he alludes to the fact of their *having been baptized* into Christ, as a reason why the Corinthian brethren ought to regard him as their supreme head, and not give undue importance to any one of the Apostles.

To the Romans, Paul says: "Therefore we ARE buried with him by baptism."* By this I understood the apostle as recognizing the fact, that the Roman brethren, as well as himself, *had been baptized.* "We ARE baptized." But I cannot dwell, to refer to all the Scriptures which I studied as relating to this point.

I was fully convinced at an early period of my studies, that the New Testament showed that a person must be a believer, before he was a fit subject for baptism. I could find no place where it recognized any other as a suitable candidate. Among the many proofs I found, here are a few: "He that *believeth* and is baptized shall be saved."† "They that gladly *received* the Word were baptized."‡ Of the Samaritans it is said, "But when they *believed* Philip, preaching the things concerning the kingdom of God and the name of Jesus Christ, they were baptized, both men and women."§ The eunuch said before he was baptized, "I *believe* that Jesus Christ is the Son of God." "Philip said, If thou *believest with all thine heart* thou mayest."‖ Which I thought equivalent to saying, "If you do not believe with all your heart you may not be baptized." "Many of the Corinthians hearing, *believed* and were baptized."¶

* Rom. vi : 4. † Mark. xvi : 16. ‡ Acts iii : 41. § Acts viii : 12. ‖ Acts viii : 37. ¶ Acts xviii : 8.

So it was in the case of Lydia,* the Philippian jailor,† Saul of Tarsus,‡ and others.

Having heard that it was the practice of many churches to sprinkle infants, I supposed the doctrine could be found in the Bible, and in my reading I looked carefully for it. Not finding it as readily as I expected, I thought at first that I must have overlooked it; but finally, after diligent search, I was unable to find a single passage of Scripture that gave any authority or encouragement for the practice, nor have I been able to find one to this day. I learned afterward, however, that the leading advocates of the doctrine said, "We do not claim to find any express command in the Bible for the baptism of infants,"§ and I was brought to agree with them in that fact, and hence I dismissed the subject as not belonging to Bible studies.

Thus I took up also the several doctrines of church government, regeneration, repentance, sanctification, and others. I was unable, of course, to consider those doctrines in their natural order, or to have a very definite understanding of their relations to each other. I pursued those studies with regard to doctrines in about the same arrangement of order that I have referred to them in this chapter; yet, however rudely those doctrines were arranged in my mind, I became well established and settled in my views in regard to most of them, with very little help or influence outside of the Bible. For some months, every hour and moment I could spare, and

* Acts xvi : 14. † Acts xvi : 31. ‡ Acts ix : 18. § Bishop Morris and Henry Ward Beecher.

some that I could not very well spare, were given to the study of the Scriptures.

I was thus not only set at rest in regard to many doctrines, but the exercise greatly strengthened me in spirit, and gave me such a familiarity with the Word of God that I could repeat chapters and verses from memory until I would be weary. I now look back upon that time as one of the best spent seasons of my past life. I have often felt the benefit of it since, and perhaps will to the end of my days.

In studying the model New Testament church, it was clear to my mind that these were some of the conditions under which it existed:—

1. Its members had all repented of sin.
2. They were true believers in Christ.
3. After believing they had been baptized.
4. They had been baptized by immersion.
5. They endeavored to live holy lives.
6. They were a missionary people, and gave labors, prayers, and money to send the gospel to every creature.

In the spring after my conversion, I learned that several persons were to be baptized a number of miles off, in the Des Moines river. I did not know what denomination of people was to hold the meeting, but having never witnessed the ordinance, I went, and after a sermon I saw, with most happy feelings, several converts buried and raised from the watery grave. I had heard that baptism by immersion was an "unpleasant spectacle," but I then thought I had never witnessed anything more scriptural or more appropriate and beautiful. When I first began to think about water baptism I was most inclined to favor sprinkling or pouring, for the simple reason that it seemed most convenient; but as the Scriptures encouraged no such argument, I thought it ought not to be consulted, and I thought that if I should still have seen any force in the argument of convenience it would now have vanished as I witnessed this appropriate and beautiful sight. The minister announced an appointment to preach in two weeks from that time at the same place and dismissed the assembly. I then introduced myself to the minister and began to ask him what his church held in respect to various doctrines, when he gave me a copy of its articles of faith, telling me to look them over carefully and compare them with the Bible.

I saw from the title that they were of "the Regular Baptist Church." During a number of days which followed, I gave much time to the examination of those articles, and compared them with the Scriptures. The quotations marked in them gave me new assistance in searching the Word of God, and I was very much benefited in the exercise. As soon as I examined them, I found that the views they held forth bore a striking resemblance to those doctrinal outlines which had been formed in my mind by previous study of the Bible, and I was so well pleased with them that I at once resolved to present my unworthy self at the next appointment as a candidate for baptism and membership in the Baptist Church.

I went to the meeting and made known my desires. The pastor requested that I should tell the church my Christian experience, before they voted on my acceptance. This I essayed to do, but was so much embarrassed, I could not tell half I wanted to; yet those Christian people saw that I loved Jesus, believed me to be regenerated, and voted unanimously to receive me. My heart was touched and melted at the kindness and readiness with which they accepted me; and the thought that I, who was once so vile, should be given a home among the dear people of God! All then repaired to the "river side, where prayer was wont to be made," and after a brief but impressive address by the man of God, upon the solemnity and importance of the sacred ordinance, during which tears stood in many eyes, and after a prayer was offered, poor unworthy I was led down into the Jordan, and in the presence of many witnesses, on the eighth day of June, 1843, was gently laid into the mystic grave.

Oh! the joys of that hour! I shall never forget it in time or eternity. My soul was filled with peace; and as I thought upon the great things God had done for me, I was lost in wonder, love and praise, and I journeyed home with a light heart, trying to sing—

" How happy are they,
Who their Saviour obey!"

Ever since that time, though my short-comings have been many, I have had an undisputed place in the church of Christ.

Reader, before closing this chapter, let me offer a reflection. It is too common a thing in these days, that when a convert is seeking to know truth and duty, there are many ready to lend him a book of discipline, or a catechism, or other prints of sectarian production, doctrinal or controversial; and many persons are ready to become catechists to proselyte him to their cause. The result is, that his mind is turned one way or the other, according to the personal views of the authors whose arguments he may read or to whose counsels he may listen, when he ought to be studying the sure Word of God. My candid opinion is, that he should be encouraged and urged to "search the Scriptures," and to take the Bible as the man of his counsel.

A certain young man in the West, who had professed a hope, was asked by a minister if he had not made up his mind to join a church.

"No, sir," said he.

"But have you not been trying to find out your duty in reference to it?" asked the minister.

"Yes, sir," said he; "I asked brother B——'s opinion, and he thought his church was the right one. I asked brother H——, and he thought B—— was wrong, 'For,' said he, 'my church is the right one;' and I asked brother E——, and he said that those other brethren were both mistaken, and he tried to show me that his church was the right one—and I can't decide."

"Was not Deacon M—— over to see you to-day?" asked the minister.

"Yes, sir."

"What did he advise you?"

"He urged me to study the Bible on the subject."

"That," said the minister, "was the best and wisest counsel of all, and I do hope that you may follow it. Remember that men may be mistaken, but the Bible cannot be. 'Search the Scriptures, for in them ye think ye have eternal life, and they are they which testify of me.'"

The convert took the deacon's advice, and in due time had a mind of his own, and knew what to do. This is the course I recommend to my brethren. Point the convert to the Bible; let it be first and last, and we shall have less heterodoxy as the result. Too much, however, cannot be said to the inquirer upon the importance of reading the Bible with a prayerful spirit, and an unbiased mind.

"HOW READEST THOU?"

LUKE x: 26.

'T is one thing, now, to read the Bible through,
And another thing to read, to learn, and do:
'T is one thing now to read it with delight,
And quite another thing to read it right.
Some read it with design to learn to read,
But to the subject pay but little heed;
Some read it as their duty once a week,
But no instruction from the Bible seek;
Whilst others read it with but little care,
With no regard to how they read, nor where!
Some read it as a history, to know
How people lived three thousand years ago
Some read to bring themselves into repute,
By showing others how they can dispute;
Whilst others read because their neighbors do,
To see how long 't will take to read it through.
Some read it for the wonders that are there,
How David killed a lion and a bear;
Whilst others read, or rather in it look,
Because, perhaps, they have no other book.

Some read the blessed Book, they don't know why,
It somehow happens in the way to lie;
Whilst others read it with uncommon care,
But all to find some contradictions there!
Some read as though it did not speak to them,
But to the people at Jerusalem!
One reads it as a book of mysteries,
And won't believe the very thing he sees;
One reads with father's specks upon his head,
And sees the thing just as his father said:
Another reads through Campbell or through Scott,
And thinks it means exactly what they thought.
Whilst others read the Book through H. Ballou,
And if it cross his track, it can't be true.
Some read to prove a pre-adopted creed—
Thus understand but little what they read;
For every passage in the Book they bend,
To make it suit that all-important end!
Some people read, as I have often thought,
To teach the Book, instead of being taught!
And some there are who read it out of spite—
I fear there are but few who read it right.
So many people, in these latter days,
Have read the Bible in so many ways,
That few can tell which system is the best,
For every party contradicts the rest!

CHAPTER VIII.

COURTSHIP AND MARRIAGE—LEARNING THE DRILL IN GOD'S ARMY.

You may think, dear reader, from the heading of this chapter, that you will get a little romance. Well, this brings us to the romantic period of life; but whether my matrimonial conquest would afford grounds for a novel by Charles Dickens, you may judge. I hope, however, that you do not read romances; and, above all, I hope that if you are a professor, you do not take that trashy sheet called the "New York Ledger." I have to my sorrow seen it in some instances in the families of professors, and if you read it, or have it about you, or any of those yellow-covered novels, or any fictitious stuff of that character, I hope you are ashamed of it, and very sorry for it, for you have promised better things.

The preliminaries of our marriage were few, and the account will be short. I did not intend to marry, at least not so soon; but—I always insisted that it was Sister Pickard's fault, and yet she blames me for it all. While teaching school in —— county, Iowa, in the winter of 1843, she was one of my scholars. In autobiographies the author usually comes out successful; but I must confess that in this school I was thoroughly beaten by one of my own scholars.

There were two or three gleeful, mischievous young women, including Miss More, who, though they made fair progress in study, were, as I thought, too full of mischief. Being but a young man, I felt a delicacy in correcting them, and I was put to my wits' end as to how I should keep them under proper command. After I thought I had shown sufficient toleration, I gave them a severe lecture, in which I told them that if they expected to still attend the school, they must be more sober—otherwise I would prefer that they stayed at home. At this they took offence, and all left the school. In a few days, however, Miss More returned, as I supposed repentant, took her place, and remained through the term.

It was not long until I saw many elements in her character that I liked. She seemed so teachable and happy, that I began to feel a partiality for her. In the mean time she became a Christian, and I thought she was one of the best scholars I ever had. Finally, I don't know how it came, but somehow, almost unconsciously, a strong attachment grew up between us. Suffice it to say that preliminaries were arranged, and on the 3d of August, 1843, about two months after our baptism, we were married by the Rev. S. L——, the man who baptized us both.

This step, as well as that of my baptism, was a grave offence in the eyes of the Quaker church. According to its rules, by getting married outside of the church or without its consent, I, like Esau of old, forfeited my birthright.* But love hazards all,

* Gen. xxv : 33.

and the die was cast. I was so happy in my choice, however, that I did not nor have I found occasion, like Esau, to seek with tears a place for repentance.

We stopped at my wife's father's until we could drum up a few things for house-keeping. In a few weeks we succeeded in this, and rented a cabin about five miles distant, where I had taken another school and moved in. Having but one bed we thought it necessary to have an extra one for company. To meet this demand I bought material for a straw tick, which Mrs. Pickard made up and we filled with straw. I then built a bedstead in one corner of the room, by boring holes in the logs and driving in timbers to form a support. As a substitute for a bed-cord we used boards, and soon had a bed. Thus we were established in life, and lived right ahead. In those days we knew nothing of such fine wedding tours as are often taken by the newly married in these more improved times, but I believe that among the cabins and wild prairies, as Col. Crockett said, "we used to love as hard as any people in the world." Many are the pleasant hours I have spent while living in a log cabin.

We were now living about twenty-five miles from the Quaker church. I expected they would discipline me, but they deferred it for nearly a year. A committee of "Friends" was then sent to see me on the subject.

They informed me that the requirements were, that I should confess that I was sorry for having married out of the church contrary to its discipline;

and secondly, that I should make the same confession for having joined another religious society.

We had quite a lengthy controversy. I urged that I had violated no law of the land, nor of God or the Bible. To this they agreed, but said, "Thee knowest thee hast violated the discipline, and thee knowest that every church must have a discipline;" but I could not feel sorry.

They visited and labored with me several times, to reclaim me from what they thought was the error of my ways, but all to no purpose; and in about a year from the time of their first visit they gave it up, and threw me overboard. I have always, however, regarded their efforts to reclaim me as very Christian-like and commendable, and I suppose I ever shall feel great respect for the Quaker people.

Though I had now become enlisted as a Christian, I soon found that it was no small matter to learn the drill in God's army.

Reader, are you a feeble Christian? Do you dread the cross of your Master? If so, I know well how you feel. I would sympathize with you and offer words of encouragement. It may be of some benefit to you to hear of my humble experience in learning the drill in God's army. When Sister Pickard and I began house-keeping, I had never made a vocal prayer in a family or any other place, though I had been a professor several months. I had often felt it my duty, but shrank from it. I did not receive such encouragement in that matter as most new converts do now; there were but few Christians around me, and as the duty was not urged upon me I had excused myself with praying in secret; but now that I was the head of a family I felt strongly condemned in the neglect of a family altar. You know, perhaps, that the Bible threatens those families that call not upon God. "Pour out thy fury upon the heathen that know thee not, and upon the families that call not on thy name: for they have eaten up Jacob and devoured him, and consumed him, and have made his habitation desolate." Such are the words of inspiration, and it is a solemn matter for Christians to neglect family prayer.

It seemed to me that I never could bear such a cross, and I deferred it from time to time, but the longer I neglected it the greater did the task appear. Cross-shunning Christian, is it not the same with you? I tried hard to think up excuses, such as want of time—incapacity—I would pray more in secret; but it was no use. I saw clearly that my neglect was bringing coldness and dearth upon my soul. The excuse to which I clung the longest was, that I thought I could not pray; but this did not ease my conscience.

After some weeks of inward conflict, in which I lost much peace, I one day determined that when that night came I would pray in my family, though earth and hell should mock me. "Yes," thought I, "I will do it if it kills me." As soon as my mind yielded to do the duty, my distress about the matter was gone, and I was filled with such peace as I had not enjoyed for many a day. I longed for night to come that I might pay my vow unto the Lord.

When night did come it seemed ordered that Satan should have another trial at me, and that my resolution should be put to the severest test. A very joking, fun-loving young man came that evening to spend the night with us. I thought I would rather have prayed in the presence of any other person on earth, but I stood firm to my vow. I read the Scriptures and prayed. I was so confused I never knew what I said in my prayer; I supposed it was a very poor, stammering one, but I afterward felt peaceful and happy. After this the cross grew lighter, and much of the time the duty seemed light and pleasant. I counsel all halting Christians to take the same course, believing that if they do they will obtain the same victory; for, as says a poet,

> "Satan trembles when he sees
> The weakest saint upon his knees."

I now lived happily and pleasantly for some months, being in fellowship with my brothers and sisters, enjoying the comforts of religion, feeling at peace with God and all mankind.

> "Not a cloud did arise
> To darken my skies."

The church with which I was connected was a young and feeble interest, and before I had belonged one year, the members elected me church clerk. So far as I know, I filled the office with approval.

Elder Elmore, our pastor, would come around once in four weeks and preach to our little band. Frequently before preaching he would call upon some of the members to pray. I loved to hear the brethren pray, and enjoyed the meetings very much, but the pastor began to urge me to take up the cross also, and pray in the congregation. I told him that there were other brethren who could pray well, and he must call on them; "I have not the gift," said I, "and can't do it." He urged that I had the gift, if I would only improve it—that I could pray in public, and that I should. He insisted that as I was now an officer in the church the people expected it of me. I felt it my duty, but hesitated; yet he urged it upon me at different times, until I resolved to attempt it. I concluded, however, that I should never try to pray extempore, for I thought if I did I should make such a ludicrous blunder that I would mortify myself and shame the cause. So I sat down and wrote out a prayer—looked it over carefully; and thought it would sound very respectably. I then committed it to memory as thoroughly as possible, and, to make sure of it, I repeated it a number of times before the next meeting occurred. "Now," thought I, "if the Elder calls on me to pray I shall make a prayer that none of us will be ashamed of."

It so happened that at the next meeting the house was crowded, and before I was expecting it the Elder spoke from the desk in a loud voice, saying, "Brother Pickard will lead in prayer." I felt as if I were thunderstruck! Every nerve within me seemed to tremble. I fell upon my knees, thinking to say my prayer; but to my utter confusion, I had suddenly forgotten it all! I wished the floor might open and let me out of sight; but there was no escape, and I tried to pray from the spur of the moment. I scarcely knew what I prayed, but after the attempt I felt much relieved. I was so scared that I did not think of my written prayer for a number of days; but the ice was thus broken, and after this I soon felt it a privilege to pray in public. I often felt much inward joy in the exercise, and realized that it was conducive to my growth in grace.

There are many brethren and sisters who by reason of their refusal to pray in their families, or in religious meetings, are suffering leanness of soul. In conclusion, let me exhort all such who may read this book, to arouse from that condition and bear the cross at all hazards. I have now labored and traveled many years in Zion, and I do know that this Christless, prayerless way of living among many of the members, is bringing dearth and death upon the churches.

CHAPTER IX.

CALL TO THE MINISTRY.

In the summer of 1844, while at meeting one evening, I was strangely, as I thought, possessed with the idea that it was my duty to preach. The feeling was impressed upon me with great power, but I thought that such a calling was so contrary to my tastes and feelings, and so much above my capacity, that I endeavored to banish the idea. This I could not do. The feeling continued and increased in force. My mind almost constantly brooded upon the subject, and yet it was contrary to my desire—I did not wish to think of it. I tried to flatter myself that it was but a notion I had fallen into, and would finally pass off; but contrary to this, the feeling so grew upon me that I became distressed.

I argued to myself that there were old and experienced ministers now preaching—they were loved, talented and useful; that with my feeble gifts I never could stand in their places, and that it was folly to think of such a thing; but this was all to no purpose. I strove to keep my feelings a profound secret, lest I should be made a butt for ridicule. This, however, only seemed to increase my trouble, and as time wore on I began to murmur against

God. My rebellious heart urged that God was chastening me uselessly in pressing such troubles upon me, and thus rendering me miserable; while by talent, temperament, and inclination I was altogether unfit for such a calling. When my mind rebelled against the Lord I finally lost the comforts of religion, and became most wretched.

One day, while grieving over my troubles, I received the startling intelligence that my beloved pastor and friend, Elder Elmore, was dead! Himself and wife lived about eight miles distant from our place, and we had not known of any sickness in his family until I heard of his death. In much sadness we went to attend his funeral, and on our arrival we learned, to our astonishment, that his wife, whom we had hoped to comfort, had died a few hours after her husband. They had died suddenly, of congestive chills, which were then prevalent, and the remains of both were in the house, prepared for the tomb. This was sad news to our little church, for they were a father and mother in Israel, and Brother Elmore was a guide and counselor for all.

We buried this faithful pair side by side in the same grave, and many were the tears shed on that mournful occasion. While I stood looking upon the process of burial, my mind was wrapt in thought upon the strangeness of the providence that had cut down this faithful servant of God in the midst of his usefulness. Thought I, "he was a man of piety and talent, and was really more useful to society than any other person in the country; yet he is taken, while I, and many others of little use, are spared.

Why was not I taken and he left in the world to do good?" While thus musing, my attention was abruptly called, and my soul startled, at what seemed to me a voice from heaven, exclaiming; "HE IS DEAD! NOW WILL YOU PREACH?" These words seemed to me to be spoken so loud that I fancied that every one present must have heard them. I went home from the grave much excited in feelings, and somewhat alarmed. I thought myself the most unhappy of mortals, because I could have no peace on earth or be let alone from heaven. I felt, however, that I could not yield, and in a few days the exciting effects of this occurrence left me.

I had exhorted two or three times in meeting, at the urgent request of the pastor, and had enjoyed tolerable liberty. Now that the pastor was dead the brethren urged me more than ever to publicly talk to the people. I attempted it once or twice, but finding that the exercise strengthened my convictions and revived my troubles about preaching, I afterwards firmly refused. Moreover, from some cause, the brethren began to think I ought to take a license to preach, and they pressed the subject upon me. With this I finally became so annoyed and provoked that I disliked to be in their company. In one instance, while at meeting, I saw that they were expecting me to exhort, and to avoid it I left the meeting and went home, leaving my wife behind me. I was ashamed of my conduct, yet I felt so crabbed and hateful that I could not help it. It seemed as though the devil possessed me. I wofully backslid—neglected the family altar, and became as sensitive and passionate as a fool. Much of my time I was so morose and sullen that I could scarcely treat any one decently.

About this time a Brother T., a young man, commenced boarding in my family. He was a kind Christian, and one of my warmest friends. One day he said to me, "Pickard, what's the matter with you lately, that you look and act so strangely?" He evidently spoke with friendly feelings, but I instantly became enraged, and heaped upon him a tirade of abuse! He took all in a meek, Christian spirit, but I saw that his feelings were hurt. I was sorry and self-condemned in an instant for what I had done, but I was too obstinate to show repentance. I noticed that he went to his room alone. As I passed by his door, which had swung slightly ajar, I listened, and heard him, in a suppressed voice, praying for me.

This circumstance acted powerfully upon my spirit. I hastened away with feelings of the keenest remorse, and lamented my folly in bitterness of soul. I heartily despised myself for what I had done, and felt that I was deserving of all the reproaches that could be heaped upon me.

I have always regarded the conduct of this young man as exhibiting some of the highest Christian graces—meekness, forbearance, and prayerfulness. I recommend his example for the imitation of all Christians in times of similar trial. Nothing so effectually confuses and defeats the tempter as to show him the meek, forbearing spirit, and take the

Saviour's way of heaping "coals of fire" upon the heads of offenders.*

One thing that had much influence on me against being a minister was, that while I was poor, having forfeited my birthright by my marriage and by joining the Baptist church, my brothers, who were now married, had good farms and a fair start in life; and I had formed the determination to accumulate property enough to claim position with them. To give up the earthly prospects which seemed to open before me, and consent to the life of poverty consequent upon the calling, and, worst of all, to have my family in poverty with me, and oftentimes in want, seemed to me more than I could possibly endure.

The force of such thoughts were far greater then than they would be now, for in those days a preacher was expected to labor abundantly with no remuneration. But these excuses gave no relief to my mind. During this long season of rebellion I was so tormented that I was often troubled with dreams.

One night I dreamed that hell was open before me, and that I stood upon its brink. A voice said unto me, "Look!" I thought I looked, and saw a wide expanse. Dark clouds of smoke and offensive vapors hovered over it, amidst which there flashed most fearful lightnings. In every direction were huge volcanoes, which were incessantly bursting and heaving up immense volumes of melted lava. Here and there were frightful precipices, immense black rocks, and yawning chasms. Beneath all were deep basins, in which rolled the surges of liquid fire. In

* Luke vi : 27 ; Rom. xii : 20.

these I saw countless fiends and lost spirits, which were yelling and screaming, and clutching each other in wild agony, while they were dashed about upon the fiery billows, or were overwhelmed in the roaring surge; while, ever and anon deep, fearful thunders joined the horrid chorus, and shook the dreadful region from center to circumference. I thought that while I gazed upon the hideous scene my knees smote together, and my soul and body were paralyzed with fear. Then the voice spoke again, saying, "WILL YOU PREACH OR TAKE YOUR PORTION HERE?" I exclaimed, "Oh, my Lord! I will preach, or do anything, rather than be lost in this place of damnation." At this another frightful thundering burst upon the air, making the region to tremble again, and I awoke.

On first recovering my senses, I was much concerned and affected by what had occurred. But I soon argued to myself that it was simply a feverish dream, which had resulted from a disordered fancy, and therefore amounted to nothing, and I still felt as determined as ever that I would not preach.

I yet had darkness of spirit and hardness of heart, and I felt an obstinate bitterness toward God for thus afflicting me in my poverty, when I was first making a start in life, while there were many others who, I thought, were better prepared for the ministry, and could enter it with less sacrifice.

Soon after my frightful dream I had another, which was its opposite. I dreamed that I stood upon the verge of heaven, apparently not more than an arm's length from the point of admittance, and I looked and saw its glories. It appeared to me far more beautiful than I had ever been able to conceive. Landscapes of the most rapturous beauty and variety stretched out in every direction, clothed in verdure of the finest tints, bearing delicious fruits, and watered by crystal streams which flowed to the river of life. Upon the banks of the river stood the tree of life, towering up in unspeakable greatness and beauty. The whole scene was made resplendent by the great white throne, from which proceeded light of an unearthly glory, which seemed to increase the otherwise enchanting beauty of every thing my eyes beheld. The throne was far whiter than marble, and seemed to be a living element shining by its own will. Upon it sat the Saviour, presenting an appearance of inconceivable magnificence. Companies of shining angels and redeemed ones, arrayed in rich garments, were floating upon the gentle zephyrs or walking amid the bowers.

Withal, music of unearthly sweetness, now rolling up to a pitch sublimely grand, then dying down to delicious softness, fell upon my ear. But words would fail to tell the delights that opened to my view. I thought I would gladly give all the worlds in the universe, if I owned them, to enter in at once and there make my final home.

I looked longingly upon the scene and wept, when a voice said to me, "THIS IS THE HOME OF THE RIGHTEOUS. WILL YOU PREACH AND ENTER HERE, OR WILL YOU REFUSE AND BE SHUT OUT?" I thought my tears flowed afresh as I exclaimed, "O Lord! I will preach, or do anything, that I may not miss of heaven." I thought that, somehow, I then received the assurance that I should be admitted when my task on earth was done, and I awoke, shouting with such ecstacy that I awakened all in the house.

When I saw that it was a dream, I felt very sad and disappointed, and soon relapsed into my former obstinacy. I had a number of dreams of a similar character, but these things did not reconcile me to the will of God.

By my backsliding I had for some time refused to attend our Sabbath meetings and prayer meetings, yet I remained clerk of the church, and had attended regularly the monthly meetings of business; but now I refused to attend even these.

One church-meeting day my wife inquired, "Are you going to meeting to-day?" I sullenly replied, "No." She said no more, and went alone. I sought something to busy myself, and soon found business in chasing hogs out of the field. Backsliders always have plenty of business on church-meeting days. Covenant-breaker, haven't you noticed that fact? Well, it might be a mercy to you if, every time you tried to steal half a day from God, when you ought to be at church meeting, you would have an experience like the one I am going to relate.

While I was chasing the hogs, every thing seemed combined to provoke me. The hogs were contrary, and the dogs were lazy, and I could do nothing with either. My anger became so aroused that I tried to kill both dogs and hogs. While chasing them at the top of my speed, with my soul boiling with rage, I suddenly saw, or thought I saw, an open grave, not more than two steps before me! A coffin was suspended over it, and a few feet above it. I stopped instantly, and thought I had very nearly stepped into the grave. When, with excited feelings, I had viewed for a moment this appalling vision, a voice said, "GO NO FARTHER OR YOU ARE DEAD, AND THIS IS YOUR GRAVE." For an instant I stood riveted to the spot, when the voice said again, seemingly as loud as thunder, "YOU ARE NEEDED AT CHURCH!" I wheeled round instantly, and fled for the church in the utmost fright. Before I got to the meeting, it being about half a mile distant, I slackened my speed, and began to think that what I had seen was only visionary, and the result of my previous excitement, and that it was cowardly in me to be scared to meeting. Moreover, I was dressed in very ragged clothes, which made me ashamed to enter the assembly. While thus reasoning, I hesitated, halted, and finally turned back for home. I had gone but a few paces in that direction, when the voice came louder than before, saying again, "YOU ARE NEEDED AT CHURCH!" I then ran for the church with all my power, and did not stop until I entered the door. Opportunity was offered to speak, and I made part of a confession; but did not tell the great trouble which was upon my heart, and I obtained no relief.

I continued two weeks more in the greatest trouble. My mind was much distressed through the day, and often affrighted in dreams of the night. I certainly felt the full force of Paul's expression "Woe is unto me if I preach not the gospel!"* I

* 1 Cor. ix : 16.

was finally induced, by the earnest solicitations of my wife and friends, to attend a regular meeting of the Des Moines church, about six miles from our place.

On coming near the church, I felt such a dislike to enter it that I left the company and went to the woods, where I roamed about all day, and went without dinner. We were to have night meeting. As it grew dark, I went into the church slyly, and took a back seat, not wishing to speak to any one, for, just as David said, "The pains of hell gat hold upon me."* I was in the deepest misery, and feared that I should not live to see another day. The long torments of mind had so affected me that I had lost my appetite, and become weak, lean, and peevish. The preacher commenced singing,

> "Oh when shall I see Jesus,
> And reign with him above."

"Alas!" thought I, "I shall never see him, I fear. I am upon the brink of hell, and if I do not obey him soon, I shall be lost forever!" I saw my folly in resisting, and yielded inwardly to the Lord, saying, "I will preach, though I suffer poverty, humiliation, shame, or death itself. Lord forgive my rebellion, and fit me for thy work!" When I had thus fully yielded, sweet peace flowed into my soul, such as I had been a stranger to for many long weeks. I was filled with holy ecstacy, and longed to begin the work of preaching, and fulfill my vow. My feelings were entirely new and surprising to myself. I

* Psalm cxvi : 3.

wanted to commence warning sinners that moment! Though I once thought that to be a minister was to live the most pitiable life, I now felt that it was the most exalted position a mortal could enjoy, and a calling that an angel might covet. Though I thought my talent small, I felt that God knew all about me, and could best decide as to my adaptation to the work, and I felt ready to obey, and leave the result with him.

The minister's text was, "I have found no fault in this man."* This was the testimony of Pilate concerning Jesus. As soon as he had finished his discourse, I went to the front of the desk, without waiting for an invitation, and poured forth the feelings of my overflowing soul with such liberty as I never before enjoyed. The Holy Spirit fell upon the congregation, the brethren rejoiced and wept for joy, and five or six ungodly sinners arose for prayers. A revival of religion thus commenced, which resulted in a general awakening throughout the community, and the conversion of a goodly number of souls. The joys of that meeting I shall never forget; it seemed that heaven and earth were met together. I continued to exhort with much liberty throughout this entire revival season.

I knew not what opportunities for doing good would open before me, but I now resolved to cast myself loose from the world as much as possible, and hold myself in readiness for any work Providence might assign me. This course I have at-

* Luke xxiii: 14.

tempted to follow, though with many missteps, until this day.

In respect to the dreams, visions, and voices of which I have spoken, I should not be misunderstood. As to whether they were real, and came from God, or from natural causes, I do not here venture an opinion. I speak of them simply as circumstances connected with my call to the ministry. As to their reality, each who reads this account of them must judge for himself. Of this much I am certain, they seemed real to me, and hastened my decision on the question of preaching.

I will close this chapter with a word of warning to young men who truly feel called to the ministry. If you are impressed with an intelligent conviction that it is the will of God that you should labor in the ministry, as you value your soul's peace do not dare to fight against him—the contest will be unequal. Do not attempt to run from him, as Jonah did—the race will be vain, and judgment will overtake you. Though you flee to the uttermost parts of the earth, or build your nest in the stars, God is there! Doing the duties the Spirit impresses upon you is the only way of comfort.

Brother M——, an intimate acquaintance of mine, and a young man of promise, felt deeply impressed that he ought to enter the work. Dreading its crosses and trials, he went to another State, several hundred miles distant, hoping that by getting away from the influence of his Christian friends for a time, his concern on the subject would leave him. But it only increased; and he vowed to the Lord that if he would only spare him to return to his friends in Iowa, he would obey the call. He did return in safety, but in a short time he took the gold fever, which was raging in 1849, and against the earnest solicitations of his friends, he started for California. I pleaded hard with him to remain and commence his work, but he urged that he was poor, and could do more good when he got means; and, besides, he had no library or outfit for the ministry, and no way of supporting himself in it, until he first raised the means to pay his way.

He had some fears about breaking his vows, but persuasion was of no avail. When I bade him farewell, I told him that I never expected to see him again, because he was trying to run away from God. At this he wept, but was resolved. He got along well until he was within thirty miles of Salt Lake. There he and a comrade climbed a mountain to view the country. He was apparently in good health, and before he left the top of the mountain he sang:

"Come let us anew,
Our journey pursue," etc.

He then kneeled down and prayed God to prosper him in his errand, and on his journey home, and vowed anew, that if the Lord would permit him to return in prosperity and safety, he would then preach the gospel. He went from the mountain down to the camp, took the cholera that night, and died upon the spot! It is far better that we trust and obey.

CHAPTER X.

COMMENCES TRAVELING—ELDER MORE—MEETING AT THE "DEVIL'S RIDGE"—DREADFUL DEATH OF A SINNER—RAISING A SKELETON.

Soon after the events of the preceding chapter, I commenced traveling with Elder James More, my spiritual father. Our plan was to travel and hold meetings through the fall and winter seasons, and each till a small farm through the summer, to support our families. The demands of the people, in a literary point of view, were less exacting then than in these days. There were no colleges then in the West, nor education societies to encourage and help candidates for the ministry, as there are now. There were no well-educated ministers, except the very few who came from the East. The church could not wait until colleges were built, and men were thoroughly fitted and polished for the ministry. Hence the Spirit took men from the plow, and from the various avocations of life, and thrust them forth. We pursued our theological studies in Brush College.

What may now be learned from books, we were compelled to learn by experience, at much greater cost, or go unlearned. What we lacked in scholastic attainments we tried to atone for by experimental knowledge and practical tact. Though our clothes were coarse and our appearance rough, and though our purses and general outfit were poor—our libraries usually consisting of little more than a Bible and hymn book—we were well received by the people, and regarded as the messengers of God. When I began to travel, though my education was what would now be considered quite limited, it was, perhaps, much better than that of most of the preachers in Iowa at that time.

Elder James More became my professor of theology and general instructor. He knew little of high schools and colleges, such as have since been reared upon those foundations he helped to lay as a pioneer minister; but he had much native talent, was deeply pious, and well acquainted with the tricks of the adversary. He was well versed in the Scriptures, and when warmed up with holy fire, he was gifted in speech and sometimes eloquent.

Many were the valuable lessons and wise counsels I received from that good man, as we journeyed and labored together. I often recognized the wisdom of the Saviour in originally sending forth his disciples "two and two," we were so much comfort and encouragement to each other. At first Brother More would have me exhort after he had preached; but gradually, as my talents improved, he pressed me into the pulpit, until we finally adopted the habit of preaching and exhorting alternately.

The first fall and winter, we held a number of revival meetings, were permitted to witness a goodly number of conversions, and I was much encouraged in the great and good work. Before the season of our winter campaign closed, however, my family began to be in want, for I was poor in this world's goods, being only a renter, and when I left them I could make but slight provision for their wants. Though we met with good success, and saw scores of souls converted during our tour, you need not suppose, reader, that we were successful in getting temporal remuneration for it; for all our labor and travel that winter we did not receive a single cent! We carried on the warfare against Satan's kingdom at our own charges. The work then had to be done on such terms or be left undone. We did not get supplied with clothing—not even with a pair of socks. When we ended the tour, my clothes were well worn, and I was poorly clad. In my cabin, want was peeping in at every crevice. But I had counted the cost, and was not disappointed; pioneer preachers did not usually have any better fare, and we both rejoiced that we were counted worthy to endure these things for Christ's sake.

There were of course causes for this. In the first place, Iowa was then only a territory; and there were but few Baptists, or Christians of any order, within its bounds. When I began to preach there was but one Baptist association in the whole territory of Iowa. It was called the Des Moines Association, and embraced the whole territory. The entire body did not number one hundred members.

The churches were young and feeble, and able to do but little for the support of the gospel, and the unconverted part of the people were of the pioneer or squatter class, who knew but little of the wants of a minister, and cared less. But the greatest cause of our receiving nothing was, that the few Baptists who then composed the churches were generally Southern people of the anti-mission stamp, and would not pay a preacher anything if they could. They "didn't think a preacher ought to preach for money." They "thought he ought to preach for the good of the cause," and were very jealous if one would hint that he wanted money, "because it would hurt the cause for people to think that *that* was what he wanted." They put this in the mouths of outsiders also, and we, of course, rather than "hurt the cause," labored for them at our own expense, and usually went home worn and ragged, to look after our needy families. God bless the do-nothing, anti-mission Baptists! I hope that most of them are now in heaven—and I wish the rest were there, for they are of little use on earth. By these things, reader, you may see what it cost, in those days, to forsake our business and enter the ministry.

In the spring of 1844, when I resumed my work upon the farm, times were very hard. I sold corn at ten cents a bushel, wheat at from twenty-five to thirty-seven cents, heavy pork at one dollar and fifty cents, and other products in proportion. Postage on letters was twenty-five cents. I have often had to let a letter lie in the office some time before I could get money enough to pay the postage. The people in Iowa then lived very poorly, and knew little of the many comforts enjoyed in the same country to-day. I will here give one example to show the privations of the early settlers. Mr. G. M—— moved to Iowa, in what is now called Lee county, in the spring. Not being able to erect a good cabin and raise a crop, he built a booth, about twelve by sixteen feet. It was covered with bark, and the front was left open. It contained but one room, and it was used for kitchen, parlor, dining-hall, and bed-room. Here he lived with his family through storm and sunshine until late in the fall, when, having secured his crops, he built a rude cabin. His nearest mill was on Spoon River, Illinois, distant about seventy miles. In the following winter he went there with his ox team to mill; but on his arrival the mill was ice-bound, and he was compelled to leave his grist and return empty. During the three months following, the family lived upon buckwheat, ground in a coffee mill, with milk and wild honey, as their only subsistence. Their few neighbors were generally in the same condition, and were unable to help each other.

As soon as my crops were gathered in the fall, I started again in company with my old colleague, Elder More, on another revival tour. Among the places where we held meetings this winter was one called "The Devil's Ridge," a name given to the settlement by Methodist ministers, on account of its hardness and wickedness. It bordered upon the grounds of the notorious Abner Kneeland, who is extensively known as having labored very earnestly to establish infidelity in Iowa and Missouri.

We had no special inducement to hold meeting there, but seeing the exceeding wickedness of the place, we felt moved to warn the people of their sins, and make an attempt for the honor of our God.

We found a Baptist couple newly settled there, and they tendered us the use of their house for holding meetings. We made the announcement all over the neighborhood, that our meeting would commence on Thursday night; but not a soul came. We preached and exhorted to the man of the house and his wife the best we could, and announced meetings for several nights in succession, to be accompanied by prayer-meeting every morning at nine o'clock.

The second night there were two hearers added to our audience. At this rate the meeting continued through the week. On Saturday night another man and his wife were present. The case looked hopeless; but we trusted in God for victory, and preached and prayed with all our hearts. On Sunday morning, to our joy and surprise, the people came from every direction and filled the house to overflowing.

That morning we began to pray at nine o'clock; preaching was to begin at eleven o'clock, and before the hour there were many crowding about the door and windows, who could not get in. Brother More preached. He felt that much was pending, and his discourse was heart-searching and soul-awakening. To my joy, I soon saw tokens of mercy; and before the sermon was ended the crowd seemed to wave like a forest in the mighty wind. Many wept, some cried aloud for mercy, and others fell on the floor at full length, under the mighty power of God's truth. When they were invited forward for prayer, there seemed to be a general rush. Some who had previously fallen could not get there, and others fell on the way. Brother More and I prayed and coun seled with them until a late hour, and such an intense religious interest I had never seen before. After having had one or two seasons of prayer, we seemed to be in a perfect Babel. Some were shouting lustily for joy in hope of salvation, while others were crying at the top of their voices for mercy. Thirty or forty souls professed conversion that night, and yet it was the first sermon that most of them had heard for years. A few days from that time we organized a Baptist church of about fifty members. This meeting encouraged me very much in the work, and increased my boldness in the faith. I clearly saw what God would do in answer to prayer, for I knew that this mighty work was to be attributed in but a small degree to human agencies. *God had surely heard our prayers, and began to work on the people's hearts before they came to the meeting.*

A remarkable incident occurred at this meeting, in the case of a wicked young man. He had attended several evenings, and was deeply convicted. I talked with him on the subject of religion, but could not prevail upon him to submit to God; and though his mind was most severely wrought upon, he resisted the Spirit with most brutal obstinacy to the end. On the last night of the meeting, the devil seemed to possess him entirely. As soon as service closed he ran out, slamming the door, hallooing at the top of his voice, saying, "The Baptist distracted meeting is done, and now we will have a distracted meeting of our own!" Then he commenced dancing, yelling, and mocking. That night he went home and to bed as usual, and in the morning waked up a raving maniac; and thus literally fulfilled his own mocking declaration—"Now we will have a distracted meeting of our own!" He continued in this situation until his death, which occurred a few days after. In his ravings he would frequently exclaim in great distress, "Oh, that meeting! that meeting!" He died without hope! Thus it is, as God has said, "He that being often reproved hardeneth his neck, shall suddenly be destroyed, and that without remedy." * Five or six others who were under deep conviction at this meeting, and resisted God, died within six months of its close; so common is it for judgment to follow mercy refused.

In the spring of 1846, I was again on my farm, preparing for a crop. God had given us two children, and though we were poor we enjoyed domestic peace and heavenly consolation, and I shall perhaps never be more happy in this world than I was then. While conducting my farming operations, I usually preached on Sabbaths in adjacent communities. I had but little time to sermonize, and I preached mostly as I found utterance in an extempore manner, upon such topics as most readily presented themselves. Often in the pressure of my business I have been unable to find time to think about a sermon, until Sabbath, and then I was frequently compelled to hunt a text after I entered the desk, read it for a beginning, and trust to God and the inspiration of the occasion for a sermon. What studying I did was mostly done at night, commonly by the light of

* Prov. xxix: 1.

a bark fire. My book of study was the Bible. It constituted the larger part of my library. This was not such a chance as one should have to become a workman, "rightly dividing the Word of truth;" but it was the best I had, and I could do no better; yet God often blessed me and my hearers with happy spiritual emotions under this style of preaching. About this period of my ministry, I one day resolved to get up a regular good sermon. I thought that after I had preached so much in the scattered style, I would have it right for once. I took paper and pencil, and after a hard task I produced a "skeleton." I found it very difficult to get it near what I thought would be right; but I found it much more difficult to preach it right. When I attempted to use it, it seemed so defective and confused that I became badly embarrassed, and made such a miserable mess of it that I threw it away, and gave the people an exhortation. This for a long time discouraged me from any further efforts of the kind; though I have since learned that it was chiefly owing to my want of time and practice in the preparation of sermons and the use of skeletons. Want of time for study has, in fact, been to me one of the greatest sources of embarrassment in my ministry, more especially in the early part. This, I believe, is a common complaint of the ministry, and they not only complain of a want of time, but a want of books.

Oh, that our brethren of the laity did but realize how much we feel the need of study to qualify us to preach with power! How often ministers are embarrassed and distressed thereby, especially where they preach long to one congregation. A want of books, or means to get them, and time to read them, is a common reason why your pastors, O ye churches! "don't wear well," and have "so much sameness," that after a short stay your congregations "run down," and they are compelled to "resign." If you would see these things as we do, your pastors would be better sustained, and their whole time would be given to the legitimate work of the ministry. But so it is, that "he which soweth sparingly shall reap also sparingly."* Remember that it is contrary to Scripture to "muzzle the ox that treadeth out the corn."† It is wrong, my brother, or my sister, to permit your pastor, if you can avoid it, to be entangled with secular cares. "Who goeth a warfare at any time at his own charges? Who planteth a vineyard and eateth not of the fruit thereof? or who feedeth a flock, and eateth not of the milk of the flock?" "If we have sown unto you spiritual things, is it a great thing if we shall reap your carnal things?" Remember that "even so hath the Lord ordained, that they which preach the gospel should live of the gospel."‡

Perhaps you say as you read this, "Oh, yes; that's all true. I sympathize with our preacher and his family. I don't know but I ought to give him something." But let me tell you that your pastor is not suffering for want of sympathy; what he wants is JUSTICE. Pay him what you owe him—your proportion of his salary. He is not needy because peo-

* 2 Cor. ix : 6. † 1 Cor. ix : 9. ‡ 1 Cor. ix : 7-14.

ple don't "give" him more, but because they do not pay him his due; he does not receive what he has richly earned. The one great boon the ministry asks of those for whom they labor, and to whom they preach, is JUSTICE. First give them that, and then if you have any sympathy they will be thankful for it, but they cannot live on it; and if you will give them any presents they will gratefully accept them as a mark of love and friendship, but not as paupers who live on the pities and charities of the world.

CHAPTER XI.

REMARKABLE MEETING IN LEE COUNTY—A DREAM—A RIOT—TWO MEN DRAG THEIR WIVES FROM THE ANXIOUS SEAT—LIFE THREATENED—MIDIANITES—THE CONGREGATION PRAYS FOR SAFETY—AUTHOR'S ESCAPE—RIOTERS FALL UNDER THE POWER OF GOD—DREAM FULFILLED.

LATE in the fall of 1846, Brother More and I set out on our third revival campaign. We journeyed on foot, not knowing where we should stop; but we felt that our commission, "Go ye into all the world and preach the gospel to every creature,"* was a broad one, and did not fear of getting out of our field. It appeared, however, that Providence directed us to the neighborhood of Brother A——, in Lee county, Iowa, where there were three or four Baptist families. They were rejoiced to see us; for preachers' visits, like those of angels, in that new country, were few and far between.

We arrived late and were very weary with walking, but by the earnest solicitation of our host we agreed to preach that evening in his cabin. We soon had about thirty-five persons for a congregation, including the family of the house. But six of the hearers

* Mark xvi: 15

were professors; and as the audience was so small we thought the prospect was very dull, but I began to preach, taking for my text—"Come, for all things are now ready." After I had proceeded with my remarks for a few minutes, the Holy Spirit alighted down upon us in an unusual manner; my soul caught fire, the few professors present seemed to be electrified, and I was blessed with great liberty in preaching. It was really wondrous to see what solemn awe pervaded the company. At the close of the sermon I gave an opportunity for any person or persons present to ask the prayers of God's people by rising to their feet. To our joy, every unconverted soul in the room, twenty-nine in number, arose. After a season of prayer for their conversion, we appointed another meeting for nine o'clock the next morning. At a late hour, being very weary, we laid down to rest; but our hearts were so light and happy, that it was near morning before we slept. We were rejoicing in the thought that the angel of the Lord, as when the servant of Abraham was in search of the bride,* went before us, as Isaiah said "to make ready a people for the Lord," and we felt that we had been directed by the Spirit.

When I fell asleep I had a peculiar dream, which I will relate. I do not think I am inclined to be superstitious, for I don't believe much in whims; but I have had a number of dreams in my ministerial experience, which were so impressive and so literally fulfilled, that I am almost compelled to believe that

* Gen. xxiv : 7.

there is something in them, though in rare instances, which cannot be accounted for by natural causes. "And it shall come to pass in the last days, saith God, I will pour out of my Spirit upon all flesh: and your sons and your daughters shall prophesy, and your young men shall see visions, and your old men shall dream dreams."* I think that those last days are that period of the world that began at Pentecost and will close at the Judgment. God's servants of old had revelations in dreams of the night, and why may not we of the present day?

But I will leave this question for others to discuss, and tell my dream. On this first night of my stay in the community, I dreamed that a great cloud gathered over the place, from which burst forth a furious storm. The thunders boomed in an awful manner, and the forests were swayed to and fro in the mighty winds. But, above all, the lightnings were most appalling; they struck in every direction, so that it seemed that nothing could escape them: they skinned or peeled every tree that I could see in the forest in any direction, from top to bottom, and the people were all terrified. The storm finally passed over; the heavens were cleared, the stars shone forth beautifully bright, the fields were green and delightful, the birds sang sweetly, and all nature smiled. When I awoke the scene was still impressed upon my mind, though I thought it was but a dream. Yet the sequel will show that "it was not all a dream."

* Acts ii: 17, and Joel ii: 28, 29.

At a late hour in the morning our brother and host aroused us, saying, "It will soon be meeting time." We bestirred ourselves hastily, but had only just finished our breakfast when the people began to come in for meeting. The news of the last night's doings had been circulated, and the crowd was now considerably increased. Every one who had attended in the evening was also present. I preached again; and after this second sermon, every unconverted person in the house came to the anxious seat! This included all who had attended the previous night, and all those who were then present for the first time. We had truly a Pentecostal time, praying for them; and we continued the exercises of praying, singing, counseling, and praying again, until two o'clock in the afternoon.

The meeting, from this, went on with some conversions every night. In a short time the people assembled in such numbers that the crowd could not possibly get into the house, and every night, after the house was filled to its utmost capacity, scores of people would stand around the doors and windows outside.

When reformation's fire was fairly under way, the devil, as he usually does on such occasions, got angry. He instigated certain lewd fellows of the baser sort to stir up the wicked people to mob us. We had preached very plainly, telling them boldly of their wickedness and corruption, and warning them that if they did not repent they might expect the judgments of the Almighty sooner or later to fall upon them. With this the scamps pretended to be insulted, and having laid the plot, and supplied themselves with clubs and jugs of devil's tea, they came on one night in a most tumultuous manner, using many oaths and curses, and making dreadful threats. Apprehending their design, we instantly closed the doors and windows. This appeared to increase their rage; they rushed up to the door and about the windows like a pack of wild Indians. They yelled and screamed like fiends; a regiment of catamounts could not have produced a more frightful jargon. They threatened to tear the house down upon our heads. At this the women and children screamed, and we had confusion inside and out. For a moment our chances looked dark and perilous; but, thought I, God has sent us here to preach to these sinners, and we have done our duty as He has required; most surely, if we ask it, He will deliver us from this drunken mob. I then quieted the congregation, and requested that all would kneel with us before God, and that each one would pray aloud unto the Lord, that he would have mercy upon those wicked men, defeat their purpose, and save their perishing souls. We all kneeled, and such loud and earnest petitions as went up from that assembly within a few minutes, I suppose the world has seldom heard. When we arose from prayer, an aged woman exclaimed aloud, "I know that God will answer those prayers, for it seemed to me that I could see them go right up through the roof."

The noise still continued outside, but from some cause, I never knew exactly what, they were quarreling and fighting among themselves in such a manner that, in the new issue they had raised, we were for the time forgotten, and we attributed it to Divine Providence, with which we thought we had been favored in special answer to prayer. It forcibly reminded me of the defeat of the Midianites which occurred in the days of Gideon, by the direct interposition of God.* I quieted the congregation, had them take their seats, and finished my sermon. On inviting the penitent forward for prayers, as usual after preaching, a couple of women, who were the wives of two of the principal rioters, came up, with others, and kneeled at the anxious seat. They were in great distress of soul, and pleaded most earnestly for divine mercy. One season of prayer had been offered for them, and we were just commencing another, when the door was forced, and their husbands rushed in from the outside with clubs in their hands, and in a brutal manner caught them from the anxious seat and commenced dragging them out of doors, threatening to kill them.

All was now terrible confusion. The poor women screamed for help. Some were shouting, "Stop them! Stop them!" others, "Knock them down!" Some were rushing forward, pell-mell, to the rescue, crying, "Hold! hold!" while the noise of the children and the dogs joined in the general uproar! But, in spite of all we could do, the women were dragged out of doors. They were scarcely out when a tremendous fight began between two of the men outside, and in less than one minute half a dozen or

* Judges vii : 22.

more joined the fray, and a number of broken noses and bloody faces was soon the result.

We then closed our exercises in the house, thinking that we would let the people get home as soon as possible, and make our own escape. As the crowd began to go out, we were told privately that several men stood by the door outside, with clubs in their hands, determined to kill us when we went out. Thinking it unsafe to remain, we retreated through the rear of the house, and, like the Saviour, hid ourselves and passed by.*

Having concealed ourselves in the woods for some time, the mob thought we had left for other parts, and finally dispersed. We then returned to our lodgings, and slept in safety. After consultation in the morning, we resolved to trust in God for safety, and go forward with the meeting.

The next evening the crowd returned, but the roughs did not have so much whiskey. They were more quiet, and a number of them stood in the house during service. They looked, however, very sullen, and we thought they were bent upon some new deviltry; but I looked to God in faith, and began my sermon, taking for my text, if I remember right, "O full of all subtlety and all mischief, thou child of the devil, thou enemy of all righteousness, wilt thou not cease to pervert the right ways of the Lord?"† They at first stared at me in a hard, brazen manner; but as I proceeded with my subject my soul became filled with the power of God,

* John vii: 59,

† Acts xiii: 10.

thoughts and facts of alarming interest opened to my mind, my tongue was loosed, and opened the batteries of God's truth, and poured the red-hot gospel right upon them. God's Spirit attended the effort with power, and it was not long until one of the wretches, who the night before had dragged his wife out of doors, and who was standing but a few feet from me, suddenly turned pale and fell headlong, measuring his whole length upon the floor! He groaned and cried for mercy; but I let him lie, showing him no attention, and continued preaching. Soon another fell in the same way, and another — until some half-dozen of the rioters were rolling and groaning on the floor under the mighty power of God! Thus was the devil defeated in his designs on God's kingdom.

This broke the ice. The meetings continued, and the work went on, until *every responsible soul in that community, who, so far as we could learn, had attended the meetings, made a profession of religion!*

Thus my dream was fulfilled. In the midst of a great storm every tree was peeled! The spring time of rejoicing came; "the singing of birds, and the voice of the turtle"* was heard in the land, and the barren desert was made to bloom and blossom as the rose. God's name was honored, and out of those rough ashlars from Nature's quarry did the God of protracted meetings hew out living stones for His spiritual temple, and establish a living Church.

* Sol. Songs ii : 12.

CHAPTER XII.

EARLY PREACHERS—SUDDEN LOSS OF HAIR—PRAYING A MAN OUT OF MEETING—INCIDENT OF CRAZY JOE.

As I have stated, when I first began my labors in the ministry, there was but one Baptist Association in Iowa, and all its churches did not contain a hundred members. Soon after this, however, we received some valuable additions to the ministry. They were of such men as Fisher, Post, Sperry, Ball, Elliot, Johnson, Jewett, and others worthy of note. They were all noble, self-sacrificing men, who had the cause of God at heart, and traveled and labored earnestly and actively for the establishment of churches and the salvation of souls. They were generally poor in this world's goods, and were called to endure hardships as good soldiers, often traveling on foot from one settlement to another, and at times lying upon the bleak prairies in the wild woods at night. Yet they were noble men of God, and under their labors hundreds of precious souls were converted, and many of the scattered sheep gathered up. Scores of other able ministers have since come forth to do battle for God, such as Griffith, Childs, Leonard, Lee, Edwards, Edminister, Eggleston, Cochran, Starkweather, Sutton, Gunn, Wood, Eberhart, Bush, Bates, Walton, Warren, and a host of others, many of whom I do not know, neither have space to mention. Many churches have been organized and ministers raised up. Baptist doctrines have been spread through the State, and our denomination has moved forward with surprising force and energy. Many of the first pioneers have gone to their reward, and others are filling their places. "God buries His workmen, and carries on His work." They had to contend with much opposition, and endure many trials; but the little feeble sect that was "everywhere spoken against," as the disciples of old, is now numbered in its ministry by hundreds,* in its laity by thousands, and is still increasing. "Behold, what hath God wrought!"

Yet those pastors and people who have the care of the Iowa churches, and enjoy a home among them, ought to bear in mind how much it has cost of self-denial, labors, cares, and tears, upon the part of their predecessors, to establish them, and defend and sustain them with a jealous care, and labor to promote them with zeal and fidelity. If apathy and worldliness are allowed to prevail, and your church meetings, covenant meetings, prayer and Sabbath meetings, are neglected and your discipline slighted, the spiritual building will soon fall to ruin. God forbid that this shall be the case; but may our Zion still be enlarged and strengthened.

Many incidents might be related of the early ministry which are of a laughable and of a serious character. Brother J. M——, a man who was just enter-

* Who in point of talent will compare favorably with those of any State.

ing the ministry, and who was uneducated and very timid, was called upon to lead a prayer meeting which was held one evening at a neighboring cabin. It was his misfortune on this occasion to have long, dry, bushy hair. The candle by which he read a chapter was placed near the window curtain. The chapter being read, all kneeled down for prayer. He prayed very earnestly for the descent of the Spirit, and that all might be fired up to start anew in the good cause. Forgetting his timidity in his earnestness, his prayer became quite lengthy, and in the mean time the window curtain caught fire from the candle; the string by which it hung was burned off, and while he was at the very height of prayerful interest, to his sudden amazement the blazing fabric fell upon his bushy head, set fire to his hair, and in spite of his active and almost frantic efforts, shingled his head as close as would a barber. The result of the affair was so laughable, that the solemnity of the meeting could not possibly be maintained; and he took so much to heart the frequent jokes he received about it, that he came very near leaving the ministry.

In the fall of 1847, after my crops were secured, a Baptist Brother S—— urged Brother More and myself to hold a meeting together in his cooper shop in L—— county. In addition to the community around, he had a number of coopers in his employ who lived with their families near the shop. The people of the community were generally wicked, especially the coopers, and Brother S—— was anxious to have something done for their souls.

Getting on the ground, we circulated an appointment, and prepared the shop with seats for the people. The meeting opened with very dull prospects, but we resolved to do all in our power to arouse the community before we gave them up, and appointed a sunrise prayer meeting in connection with the other services, to which we invited the attendance of sinners. The Lord finally came to our aid, and among the first converts were the wife and some of the children of one of the most wicked of the coopers. On hearing of this, he threatened to kill either one or all of his family that went any more to the meeting, and the following night, to show his determination, after getting about half drunk, he went himself to the meeting for the first time, that he might know if any of his family came. They, however, fearing his brutal disposition, especially when drunk, did not come. Brother More preached that night. As the shop was very long, we had our stand in the centre of one side. We had left open an aisle the whole length of the shop; and while Brother More was preaching, the scoundrel kept walking back and forth, up and down the aisle, pausing occasionally as he came near the preacher to listen a moment, when he would call him a "d——d liar!" and pass on. This he did in a loud voice, and continued his impudence through the whole sermon; though sometimes changing his phraseology, he would say in reply to some remark in the sermon, "That's a d——d lie, sir!" This was as trying to Brother More as anything could be, and under this annoyance he closed his sermon with embarrassment. It was my turn to exhort; and having made up my mind as to what should be done if he called me a liar, I began the exhortation with all my might. But his impudence, if possible, now increased, and coming up close before me, he shouted, "You are a G— d—— liar!" I then paused, and told the people that this disturbance, if allowed to continue, would break up the meeting, and that it must be stopped. The man now evidently thought he was going to be gratified with a row, this was what he wanted; but I continued and told them how wicked this man was, how he had insulted the Word of God and those who preached it, and that he had even threatened the lives of his poor wife and children, because they wished to attend the meeting, and in a free country at that. I told them that he was then under the effects of liquor, and near to the gates of hell, with a fair prospect of being lost forever; and then requested all who were in the congregation to get down upon their knees, and that every one who could would pray that God would either convert this man, or otherwise get him out of the way of the meeting.

Such tactics he did not expect, and was not prepared to meet. I led off in prayer, and he did not open his mouth. The moment the season of prayer was closed he quietly left the congregation, and immediately went out of the settlement. We heard no more of him during our stay. Where he went I never learned, but good order was restored for the remainder of the meeting. His wife and children came out in religion, and a goodly number of others.

In this case the devil would have been pleased to

havo a row. We could have forced the man out—the crowd would have helped us; but God was our best and present help, and in Him we chose to trust. "For the weapons of our warfare are not carnal, but mighty through God to the pulling down of strong holds,"* while "the wicked flee when no man pursueth."†

At the close of the meeting above mentioned, we were urged to hold another in a deserted dwelling several miles distant. We sent forward an appointment, and in due season were in the neighborhood; but on the night when the meeting was to have begun the rain poured down in torrents, and as we supposed that not a soul would be out, we did not go. Yet, in our absence, one of the most novel meetings did occur of which I have ever heard. There was a young man living in the vicinity who was a licentiate, by the name of T——. For the reader to understand what I am about to relate, he must remember that the mind of Brother T—— was somewhat enfeebled by poor health. There was another man, who was not a professor, by the name of D——, who was remarkable for having large, white-looking eyes. He was about middle-aged, and about the same height as Brother T——. These and a number of others, who were very anxious to hear the preaching, got in before the rain began, where they remained some time waiting for the preachers. There was a Baptist brother who lived a considerable distance from this place of meeting,

* 2 Cor. x : 4. † Prov. xxviii : 1.

by the name of Thomson. He was a pious man, but his mind was such that when it was affected above a certain degree of religious interest, it would become deranged; and in this derangement he would often fancy that he had a call to preach. On account of this he was called "Crazy Joe." He had attended our meeting at the cooper shop, and was not altogether satisfied, because he thought we had not given him a proper chance to preach and exhort; but being thoroughly waked up, he followed us to our new meeting. In crossing a field on his way, he cut a cornstalk and took it with him. While it was raining heavily without, he made his appearance in the meeting, dripping wet, with the stalk in his hand. Scanning the company and finding that the coast was clear of ministers, he resolved to go forward at once, and set the ship in order; and without invitation or ceremony he went to the preacher's stand, set his cornstalk by the wall, and opened out on the people with a strong exhortation.

He was very tonguey, and being a stranger to most of the people in the company, they supposed he was some minister who had been sent on to fill our appointment, and listened to him with close attention. For a time he talked well, but as he attempted to draw his remarks to a focus, they were something like as follows: "Brethren, a great work of salvation is needed here. Sinners are perishing around here by scores. But there is something wicked in the way. It 's hypocrisy! There 's rottenness in the camp! God can't and won't convert sinners among so many hypocrites. They must be got out of the way. They must make deep and thorough confession of their secret sins, and get out of the way of sinners, or God will put them out of the way by a shorter method. I used to be a hypocrite myself!" Here he confessed to some wickedness he had done when down in Missouri. "But," continued he, "I am not the only one; there are others here, right in this crowd, and they will soon be found out; God will detect and expose them before another morning. Their doom is close at hand!" As he was a stranger, and had so strangely introduced himself, this close cutting opened everybody's eyes, and some even had their mouths open with interest. Said he, "Yes, it's awfully true; if they don't confess and repent, they will be dead and in hell before morning. God told me so to-night! I can find out who they are, for I can tell a hypocrite the minute I set eyes on him; and I am going to find out some of them to-night." Here D——'s big white eyes looked like dogwood blossoms. "But," continued Crazy Joe, "there is one man here in particular, for whom there is no mercy. I can find the man. Here is his measure," said he, holding up the cornstalk. Here Brother T—— trembled and sighed; D——'s eyes were as large as they could get. "Here is the measure, brethren! Look at it! This is your measure!" All eyed the cornstalk, some of them with almost breathless interest. It was about five feet and nine inches in length, and there were four or five in the room, among them D—— and Brother T——, who

"'Here is the Measure, Brethren. Look at it! This is your Measure.' All eyed the Corn-stalk: some of them with most breathless interest. It was about five feet and nine inches in length, and there were four or five in the room about that height. Among them were D**** and Brother T****."

were about that height. It was an awful moment! Several felt guilty, but brother T—— could stand it no longer. He arose trembling, and said, "Sir, I think I am the man!" "Yes, yes," said Crazy Joe, approaching and measuring him with the cornstalk, "this is just your length;" and grasping him by the hand, "you are the very man. I could know that you were a hypocrite, just by shaking hands with you. Your hand feels like a poking stick!" Joe now stood shaking him by the hand, and exhorted him with the most intense interest and haste to get ready for death instantly, for die he must. He declared that there was no hope that he could live, and that if he had anything to say before he died he must say it soon, for not a moment was to be lost. In the midst of this Brother T—— fell sprawling on the floor, bellowing at a great rate, and tried to die. Some who thought they understood the case now gathered about Brother T——, and tried to comfort him by telling him that they thought the preacher was crazy, but T—— would not be comforted. They got the cornstalk and measured him as he was stretched upon the floor; some insisted that their lengths were not equal, though in fact there was not half an inch difference. T—— begged to be prayed for; Joe declared it was no use; yet T—— begged so hard that prayer was offered for him. Joe now declared that the devil was in the house. Said he, "I know he is, I won't stay here," and away he ran through the rain, when it appears that he attempted to hide at some distance in an old corn-crib. But the night was very dark, and a large black dog, which he could not recognize, was sleeping there, and pitched on him. He tore loose from the dog, and running back to the place of meeting in great alarm, he said, "Brethren, the devil is all around here. I found him in the corn-crib as big as a mule! I had a fight with him there. See how he has wounded me!" holding up one hand, which had been bitten by the dog, and was bleeding. Said he, "It's dangerous to stay here." At this, a boy about sixteen years of age, who was at meeting, and who lived about a quarter of a mile distant, ran home in great fright. On getting there he found that the family had gone, and for security he hid himself under a bed. In the meantime Crazy Joe, who still exhorted all to leave because the devil was all around there, could not be persuaded to remain, and ran off again for safety. It so happened that the first house he entered was the one in which the boy was secreted. Finding no light, he went to the fire place, took the poker and stirred up the coals, and immediately began to look around to ascertain whether there was any devil there or not. The boy, who had begun to be afraid of the man as well as the devil, kept very quiet, but he was soon found under the bed, and Joe, supposing him to be the devil, threatened to kill him at once. The boy yelled awfully, and begged for quarter; but Joe was resolved that the devil should not fool him in that way, and he seized him. After a short tussle, however, the boy managed to escape; when he ran back to the meeting and told what had happened. By this time poor Brother T—— had been brought to his right mind, and every one understood the case. Crazy Joe was soon cared for, and all went home. We afterward held a meeting at that place, though with small success.

CHAPTER XIII.

MINISTERS' WIVES—MEETING AT R * * *—PASTOR CONVERTED—DRIVEN FROM THE MEETING-HOUSE—THE POOR WOMAN'S MITE—REFLECTIONS—A THOUGHT ON REVIVALS.

UP to the fall of 1848, Mrs. Pickard had never been satisfied for me to give my time fully to the ministry. She had no objection to my preaching on the Sabbath, or spending a week day occasionally in holding a meeting, but to cast myself on the altar, and sacrifice my time for weeks and months together, and exhaust my strength, without any remuneration, as I had been doing, she insisted was not my duty. She thought we were too poor to endure it, and that the condition and wants of the family could not righteously allow it. I felt, however, that the scarcity of ministers, the destitution of gospel labor among the perishing, and the wants of Zion, demanded it. Besides this, I was so eagerly beset with entreaties to hold meetings here and there, by persons who would take no refusal, that I could not, in the opinion of the people, do credit to the ministry without much sacrifice of time; otherwise I would have been thought too worldly: such was the sentiment of the people. This fall, I once agreed to go with Brother

More, and be gone a few days at a meeting in a very busy time. My wife felt hurt about the matter. She blamed Brother More for coaxing me off, and rebuked me for what she thought my folly in promising to go. She insisted that, promise or no promise, I should not go; for, as she claimed, the promise was unjust, therefore I had no right to keep it. No more was said for the present, but when my colleague came along and called for me, I felt that the Master's business was so important that I must go. I hastened to the house to change my clothes, but lo, they were gone, and not to be found! Mrs. Pickard had concealed them. I, however, slipped out quietly, and went to the meeting in my dirty ragged suit, in which I had worked on the farm all the week. On my return she was so mortified at what I had done, that I really felt sorry for her; but she never tried the plan again, nor has she tried in any way to prevent my absence from home, as often as I have chosen to go. Her ambition for us to obtain an earthly competency was broken; she lost all hope of worldly success, became resigned to our thriftless fortune, contented to live in poverty, and gave me up as an offering to the church. She has never been disposed to murmur at our sacrifices, but has always given me encouragement to go as duty seemed to call, and she has often urged me to go when she knew, and I knew, that I was badly needed at home by reason of our necessities.

Many were the shifts and turns which she made in the earlier days of my ministry, to keep the wolf from the door. Often she has taken in sewing and knitting, and other kinds of work, to aid in the support of our family, while the wives and daughters of many of those whom I served without pay, would have been ashamed to have done the same things. I do not speak of this experience as a precedent, which some may think ministers' wives ought now to follow, but rather as a memory of the past. I am aware that it is not yet past with the wives of many of them; they are yet often compelled to make all sorts of shifts and turns to live. Fortunately, however, they usually become very ingenious in those things. I knew one of those dear women who, while her husband was off preaching, attempted to raise a garden. She had a good sized patch of potatoes, which, after much hard work in hoeing, she feared she was going to lose by the bugs. Finding, at last, that the bugs were of such a kind that they made good blister plasters, and would command a good price, she took some water in a large pan, which she moved along under the vines, and with a stick thrashed the bugs into it, where they were drowned. She then dried them in the sun, and sold them to a druggist for nearly twelve dollars. Being freed of the bugs, she raised a fine patch of potatoes and a good garden, and in the mean time took in knitting, by which she earned eighteen dollars, and when her poorer half returned, with a still poorer purse, she could show the most money. Reader, you must not think that the good things I have said about Mrs. Pickard come simply from that partiality which arises from conjugal feeling, for it is not so. I do declare to you, that if I have been useful and successful in the ministry, I am indebted to her for it, more than to any other person living.

In the fall of 1848, I shouldered my bundle and started on a campaign in Illinois. I walked on, not knowing the precise destination of my journey, until by some providence I stopped at the town of R * * *, in the county of S * * *, distant from home about seventy miles.

Learning that there was a small Baptist church there, and that it had not enjoyed a revival for several years, I circulated a notice that I would preach in the community the next evening. In the mean time I learned that they had a pastor, but both church and pastor had fallen into such an indifferent state, that they had not had a single meeting of any kind for six months past.

A few came out the first evening, and gave such good attention that I told them that if there was no objection I would preach again the next evening. To this there seemed a general agreement, and by the time of the next meeting the news was better circulated, and the congregation much increased.

I talked to them in my usual plain and bare-handed style, and preached up doctrines and duties to the professors which were very offensive to some of their backslidden hearts. The pastor, above all, seemed to be very severely hit, and as soon as I closed my sermon he arose and asked me to show my credentials. I did not have them by me, and scarcely knew what to do; but, fortunately, after some embarrassment, a man who was present reported himself, and told the congregation that he knew my reputation very well as a Baptist minister, and that my standing was good. This appeared to be satisfactory to all but the pastor, who seemed to bear the rebuff badly, and took his seat, where he maintained a sullen silence the rest of the evening. I then took a rising vote of the congregation, that they might decide whether they wanted meetings there or not. I told them that, if they saw fit, I would continue the meetings there a number of evenings more. Strange to say, only one man voted for it, and he was not a professor. Yet, from some cause, no one voted against it; I suppose they were ashamed. I felt satisfied that God had a work there for me to do, and as the chance was gained, although it was only by one vote, I announced that I would begin a regular series of night meetings. Some one now spoke up, and said that the meeting-house could not be used for meeting, as it was rented for a school-house. At this, the school-teacher, who happened to be present, arose and said, "Gentlemen, I pay rent for this house, and have charge of it. It is entirely under my control, and this minister can hold meetings in it as long as he wishes." This settled the question ot the right to use the house; but thus was I tried at every point. Every effort was made to discourage me. The church had just enough religion to oppose religious efforts and quarrel with God's ministers; but I gave notice that I should hold meetings a number of nights more, before I dismissed. No person in the vicinity offered me the hospitality of his house—not even so much as a bed, or a bite to eat. I had the fortune, however, to find an acquaintance, the only one I knew in the whole country, who lived three miles from the place. With him I was welcome, and I walked that distance back and forth, to get bed and board.

On the third night of my meeting the house was well filled, and the audience was very attentive. People were pricked in their hearts, and a score or more of them came to the anxious seat. The ice was now broken. The work went on from that time with power, and souls were converted every evening. Old hopers began to see themselves as "weighed in the balances and found wanting," and began to make confession of their sins.

One evening, while sinners were pressing forward to the anxious seat for the prayers of Christians, whom should I behold among them but the old pastor of the church! He had attended the meeting at first as a matter of policy, and though it was repulsive for him to be there, he thought that as he was a minister he must frequent the meetings for prudential reasons. As the work progressed, he became satisfied that he had never been regenerated, and that he had deceived his own soul and had been a deceiver of others. He earnestly besought us to pray for him, and he plead for the salvation of his soul in downright earnest. After a season of deep grief, in which he had many struggles, he rejoiced greatly, and professed the hope that he was happily and soundly converted to God.

After this he was one of my warmest friends, and helped me faithfully in the meeting, during the remainder of my stay. What is better, he was ever after a devoted and useful minister of the gospel.

The crowd that now attended the meetings had become so large that only a part of them could get into the house. Some Methodist brethren said to me, "Our house of worship is only about a quarter of a mile from here, and it is larger; come and hold your meetings in it." I gladly accepted their kind invitation, and took my congregation there.

The house was crowded there also, but the accommodations were somewhat larger, and prospects appeared better. It was not long, however, before I found that with the willingness to turn the Baptist meeting into the Methodist house, there was also a willingness to make a Methodist meeting of it. On the first night I called for the anxious after the sermon, and there were fifteen came forward, all young gentlemen and ladies. As these seekers kneeled at the anxious seat, the Methodist people began to be very noisy. As there was a railing about the altar, I got the anxious inside, to prevent them from intrusion by the pressure of the crowd, but the Methodist brethren and sisters crowded indiscriminately inside the railing, to help the seekers get religion and have a loud time. Some of them locked hands in a half circle, and stood swaying back and forth and shouting. Others kneeled among the seekers, and, amid short ejaculations of prayer, pounded them on the back. Some who were tobacco-chewers carelessly spit on their clothes. Others trod on them, and in the midst of the excitement some were pushed clear over them, by those who were shouting and pressing up from behind; and withal, the rowdies who stood upon the benches took the occasion to laugh and talk, and halloo "Amen" to each other back and forth. In short, we had confusion to perfection. I could do nothing to control it, nor could I do anything for the anxious. All I could do was to look on and take it as patiently as possible. In about half an hour from the beginning of this excitement there was a partial lull, and I began to think we would have order once more, that I might counsel and pray with the seekers. But I was doomed to disappointment. One of the brethren, who was a local preacher, determined on a desperate effort of eloquence, as it appeared, to raise it again. He saw that the tide was falling, and that if some stirring movement was not made it would soon die out.

Mounting the pulpit, and opening his mouth very wide, he raised his voice to the highest pitch and gave us eloquence about as follows: "Brethren, I thank God that I am aboard the old ship of Zion. I am glad that I have come aboard. I feel like taking a fresh sail in her to-night. Brethren and sisters, loose the cable and let her swing out. The gales are blowing from heaven; hoist her canvas and let her sail. Glory to God!" Here he began to jump and slap his hands, and shout "Glory to God!" Amens and shouts were heard all through the house, and in a moment the preacher's voice was almost drowned in the general noise. This state of things continued until about eleven o'clock, when, having despaired of restoring order, I dismissed the meeting with as little ceremony as possible.

The next day I went about to visit those who had been at the anxious seat. Some of them declared that they were actually sore from the pounding they had received while they were kneeling for prayer. They felt so mortified at the proceedings and the way they had been used, that they had resolved to go forward no more. The dresses of some of the young ladies were in a wretched condition, and it was with difficulty that I could pacify them. But I urged that these things were nothing compared with the loss of their souls, and promised them all that if they would still go forward and continue to seek religion at the meetings, I would be responsible for keeping everybody outside the altar except such as were invited there to labor and pray with them, and, setting life and death before them again, I exhorted them to go forward.

The next night I told those brethren of the confusion the night before, alluding to the way in which some of the seekers had been pounded on their backs, had their clothes torn, soiled, &c., and told them that they might make as much noise as they pleased, but that I now requested them to keep outside of the altar unless they were invited to go in for the benefit of the mourners. After this there was general quiet, and for the remainder of the meeting I never saw a more orderly assembly. They generally seemed to receive the new order of things kindly, and they worked and prayed with us in harmony until the meetings closed, and about forty had joined the Baptist church. Besides these, a goodly number of the converts had joined elsewhere, or were still holding the question of their church relation under advisement. The work was still going on; we had frequent conversions and baptisms, and it seemed that the whole country was going to turn to the Lord. The Methodist brethren generally worked with us in harmony, and rejoiced with us in the salvation of souls.

Finally the Methodist circuit-rider came around, and on seeing what had occurred his jealousy was awakened. Taking the stand, he expressed his dislike of Baptist influences, spoke of the dangerous tendency of Baptist doctrines, said he did not believe in building meeting-houses for their use, and forbade my using the house any longer.

According to Methodist rule, of course the preacher was the highest authority; and besides this, his movement was encouraged by two or three of his brethren who were leading spirits in the society, and very sectarian in their feelings; and although I felt that it was a great disappointment, I thought it would be best, for the sake of the new converts, to avoid any show of retaliation, and as quietly as possible I closed the meeting.* Notwithstanding all the hindrances of which I have spoken, a glorious work of God was done in that meeting. A Baptist church, worse than dead, was aroused and reclaimed; many good members were added to it, so that it was made a strong church; and besides this a man claim-

* This circumstance, and many others of a similar character, forcibly remind me of a remark I saw in the biography of a Methodist minister by the name of Cartright. He says, "I have never to this day found out what a Baptist means by a union-meeting."

ing to be a minister, and who was doing much harm, was truly and soundly converted to God, and made to be a light in the world.

The preacher who was so determined that the Baptists should not hold meetings in his meeting-house, is, I am told, yet living, and is now somewhere in Iowa. I have no doubt that as often as he has thought it profitable, which has been often enough, he has preached very warmly on the loving beauties of harmony and fellowship among all denominations of Christians, and I wish him success in that work.

Before I left the friends in R* * * a collection was taken for my benefit. This collection was meager, but the liberality of one sister is worthy of a notice in this book.

She had been a poor backslider, and had been renewed at the meeting. Being very poor and having no money to give at the collection, she went to the woods and gathered a quantity of wild grapes which she took to market and sold for twenty-five cents. On the night of the collection she gave it all. Having heard the facts in the case, I went to the poor woman and urged her to take back her twenty-five cents, but she would not receive it. She declared that she felt such gratitude to God for her deliverance, and such thankfulness to his servant, that it was a happy privilege for her to give it, and that she only regretted that it was not many times as much larger in amount.

I have often thought, with pleasure, of the Christian liberality and godly spirit of that sister; and I doubt not, that if she now lives to read this book the Lord has returned to her "good measure, pressed down, shaken together and running over.* Her example teaches one good lesson, and that is, where there is a will to support the gospel there is a way. This incident often reminds me of another: "And he called unto him his disciples, and saith unto them, Verily I say unto you, that this poor widow hath cast more in than all they which have cast into the treasury. For all they did cast in of their abundance, but she of her want did cast in all that she had.†"

I shall here offer a reflection on attempting revivals. There is, perhaps, no true Christian who will not desire a religious reformation in his church or neighborhood, yet there are members and there are churches that very seldom or never enjoy them. I believe that in a great measure the reason for this may be found in the fact, that such churches and people have a kind of impression that a true revival must always be preceded by certain signs and divine indications of an unusual character, such as "the sounds of a going in the tops of the mulberry trees," &c.; and that until such signs or indications do occur they feel that it is not their duty, and often that it is positively not right, to make special or unusual efforts, such as the holding of a number of night-meetings or day-meetings in succession, to promote a revival. As I shall deal with this subject at greater length hereafter, I shall not discuss it now,

* Luke vi : 38. † Mark xii : 43, 44.

but ask you, reader, to apply the doctrine just stated to the origin and history of this meeting at R* * *. I could hear of no favorable signs or indications; there had been no movings of the Spirit, the church was so dead that they had not held a meeting of any kind for six months. They did not want a meeting after I went there and had preached two nights. Only one man voted for it, and he was not a professor. The pastor or others tried to defeat and discourage from beginning to end. The very fact that the church was in a dead and shameful condition, was the strongest reason why I began the meeting. It is true that the meeting was not what it would have been, had I met with less opposition, yet, you see, the result was glorious. I do not believe that any special indications of a revival moved the spirit of Paul when he "stood in the midst of Mars-hill, and said, Ye men of Athens, I perceive that in all things ye are too superstitious." Evidently the contrary was the fact, for it is said that "his spirit was stirred within him when he saw the city *wholly given to idolatry.*" Yet he enjoyed a revival, and witnessed a reformation, for it is said that "certain men clave unto him and believed;"* and I am confident that if many of our churches and ministers would quit waiting for special indications, and do as Paul did on that occasion, they would witness similar results. Indications of a revival are cheering to pastor and people, and when they occur they should be improved; but it is certain that if we do but little more than wait for them they will never come.

* Acts xvii: 16–34.

CHAPTER XIV.

CONVERSATION WITH A BACKSLIDDEN DEACON — RETURN HOME — THOUGHTS ON THE SPIRIT — GOES BACK TO LYTTLETON — WICKEDNESS OF THE PLACE — HOLDS A MEETING — GREAT REVIVAL — INCIDENTS OF THE POWER OF GOD — DANCING-MASTER AND HIS CLASS CONVERTED — REFLECTIONS.

HAVING learned that there were thiee or four Baptist families in the town of Lyttleton, which was about twelve miles from the place of my last meeting, I concluded to go and hunt them out, and give them some preaching. Being directed to the house of Deacon W * * *, as the man who it was thought would probably give me the most information and encouragement, I called upon him. As I entered the house, he was writing some vendue notices for the sale of some property which had belonged to his son, lately deceased. After the common civilities, I said:

"Mr. W * * *, was your son a Christian?"

"No," said he; "he was a blacksmith."

"I was told," said I, "that there were some Baptist people in or about this village."

"There were some," said he, "who were Baptists, but I guess they are nothing now."

"I am a Baptist minister," said I, "and I have come to hunt them up, and hold some night meetings with you." Here he eyed me very closely. "What encouragement can you give me?"

"None at all," said he; "the people here care nothing about such things."

"But," said I, "can we not persuade them, by God's help, to care something about them?"

"No," said he; "you could not get them out to meeting."

"I should like to try it," said I.

"It is no use," said he, "it would be very inconsistent, for there is no place to hold a meeting, and besides that there is no place in the village where you can get kept over night."

It did not seem to occur to him that his own house was not more than a mile from the village; but I saw that he was wofully backslidden, and did not want a meeting, but was inclined to do all he could to discourage it. I thought that as he who was known as a deacon could show no encouragement, not even so much as to keep me over night, or do anything but really oppose the idea, I had better start home, and home I went.

The roads were so very bad that the journey of seventy miles made me very foot-sore and weary, and it took me several days to recover from the effects of the trip.

I believe that I was pretty thoroughly converted from Quakerism, but in one respect I am something of a Quaker yet. I do not believe in waiting at all times until we feel that we are moved by the direct agency of the Spirit; yet I do believe that if we live spiritually-minded, and breathe a praying atmosphere, with an earnest desire to do the will of God, we shall be often led by the Spirit to do what God will have us do. Says the Scripture, "For as many as are led by the Spirit of God they are the sons of God."* My own experience in the ministry has often proved this, and kindred passages, to be literally true; and I am satisfied that Christians and Christian ministers would often be much more useful if they would seek to follow the leadings of this heavenly Counselor. When I returned from my last revival meeting, I thought that the wants of my family and myself required my attention at home for the rest of the winter, and that I should stay at home.

But I had not remained there long until my mind began to run back to the village of Lyttleton, from which I had been scared by the backslidden deacon.

A feeling that I ought to return and preach at that place grew upon me until I finally felt that it would be wrong for me not to go. There appeared no earthly reason for such a feeling, for I had decided that there was not a more unpromising place for meetings to be found. Yet I was now unable to banish it from my mind, and felt that I must return. In a month from the time I left L * * * I went, "led by the Spirit," as I thought, back to the same place. The first thing I did was to put up at the village

* Rom. viii : 14.

hotel, where I engaged my board and lodging for an indefinite time. I then took a more complete survey of the place. The village contained some two or three hundred inhabitants. There was no meeting-house in the place, nor had there been any preaching, or even a prayer-meeting held for months past. There was a dancing-school which was well attended, and for which they had a building on purpose.

The most honored dignitary in the place was the dancing-master. There were also two or three dram-shops, doing a driving business in the drinking and gambling line. The people were very profane, and, in short, the entire village and surrounding community seemed wholly given over to sin and hell.

Thought I, this is a godless, hopeless-looking place, sure enough; but I will plant my batteries and throw some shells into the devil's kingdom at all hazards.

The best place for holding meetings that could be obtained was an old dirty school-house. Having secured this, I circulated a notice about the place that I would preach there that night. I then bought some candles and lighted up, and sat down to wait for a congregation. After a while I began to think that none would come; but finally, at a late hour, six persons came in and I preached to them. The second night twelve persons were present, and the third night the house was filled. I felt that I was in the line of duty, and God blessed my soul greatly in preaching. I prayed for the people, sang, preached and exhorted with my utmost energy. That night clouds of mercy began to appear in the deep feeling manifested, and from that time to the close of the meeting, the house seemed but as a nut-shell to the throngs of people that gathered from every quarter. God visited the meeting in great power. Every night the number of anxious was increased; and in many cases persons for whom we had the least hope were found among the seekers. In some instances strong men would suddenly fall prostrate under the power of the Spirit. One night while I was exhorting, there were four young men who were termed "hard cases," who had been crowded up by the press until they stood close before me. They were all standing up, and locked together with their arms over each other's shoulders. In some way my soul became powerfully aroused, as I looked upon them and saw their God-defying countenances, and I had the boldness for a few moments to address my exhortations to them personally. Under almost any other circumstances my movements would have been imprudent; but I felt that the Spirit's presence was awful, and in my earnestness I shook my hands within a few inches of their faces as I poured out upon them the threatenings of God to the guilty. At first their countenances fell, then they began to sway from one side to the other, then to reel and totter, and finally the whole pack fell headlong upon the floor together crying for mercy.

One circumstance occurred which shows that the wicked are not so indifferent to the prayers of Christians as they often pretend. Having gone into the back part of the congregation one night to invite sinners to go forward for prayers, I made the request of a young man while he was sitting in his seat, and he gave me a very saucy reply to the effect that our prayers were all nonsense, and that he cared nothing for them.

Said I to him, "Young man, do you *really believe* that?"

"Yes sir," said he, "of course I do."

"Are you willing, sir, that I should put the matter to a solemn test in your case?"

"How do you want to test it?" said he.

"Why, sir, by your consent I will test it now, right on the spot. I will kneel down and pray God to take your life instantly." And I began to kneel.

It was a solemn matter, and an awful moment. Why I felt and proposed as I did I do not know, but I was certainly in earnest and would surely have made the prayer; but as I was in the act of kneeling he exclaimed in great excitement, "O don't! I beg of you don't do it!" said he.

"But, sir," said I, "if prayer is nothing but nonsense, it will not hurt you," and I insisted on praying as I had proposed. But his pleadings finally dissuaded me from making the attempt, and he was soon broken in spirit and bowed at the anxious seat.

The religious interest in the community became such that people, of their own accord, hauled timber from the woods and built large log-fires outside of the house, around which those who could not get in would gather, and stand in mud and snow, half-shoe deep, to hear the gospel and witness the progress of the meeting. To accommodate the large numbers which gathered around the house, a platform was erected by one of the windows, on which I afterwards stood and preached to the people.

After the meeting had been in progress some time, the village dancing-master was converted, and after this occurred nearly his whole class of pupils, which was about fifty in number, came out in religion. It was a most searching time upon the hearts of the people. False hopes were exposed, false hiding-places uncovered, sandy foundations were destroyed, and souls everywhere throughout the neighborhood seemed to be shaken by the mighty wind.

The crowd was so dense that the convicted could not all get to the anxious seat. There were many of that class whom I could not get to speak with personally, and I had to exhort them publicly, and leave them to themselves and to the mercy of God; yet many of them were converted, and the tide of salvation rolled over the community.

I continued the meeting for about three weeks, having conversions and baptisms every few days, and before I left we organized a church of one hundred and twenty-five members. Beside these there were many professed religion who at that time did not join the church. There was a wagon road running through Lyttleton from M * * * to B * * *, and quite a number of travelers, who would halt for the night and attend the meeting, went away some convicted and some converted, most of whom I have never heard from, but hope to see at the great protracted meeting in heaven.

Such strange and unexpected conversions took place at the meeting, and so many "hard cases" were slain by the Spirit, that it was said that some of the teamsters on the road actually became afraid to stay in the place over night, lest the "influence" should come upon them and set them to weeping and praying.

During the meeting there were many instances of the power of the Spirit, a couple of which I will yet relate.

A very wicked man, while standing by one of the log-fires and looking at some others who were groaning on account of their sins, commenced swearing and cursing in a terrible manner, and declared that he could not be so overcome as to act the fool in that way. He had scarcely closed his mouth, when he was suddenly seized with such an awful conviction of his guilt that he acted as one distracted. Fearing that he would be damned instantly, he screamed and ran to the door and tried to get in where the circle of prayer was, that he might be prayed for. Finding the door so pressed by the crowd standing inside that he could not open it, he ran to a window, climbed in, and tumbled over the heads of the people, regardless of bonnets or anything else, and fell upon his knees near the preacher, begging, in a very loud voice, for the preacher and everybody else to pray for him. He continued in great agony and supplication until near morning, and declared that he was afraid he was going to fall into hell head-foremost. He almost despaired, but finally God had mercy on him, and he was filled with great joy.

There was quite an intelligent man living near the school-house, who had considerable wealth, and was somewhat prominent in the community. He had been raised a Catholic, and was then a member of the Catholic Church. He was a very wicked man, and feigned to have an utter contempt for the religious manifestations and the meeting. In one of our morning exercises he became convicted; but feeling mortified and unwilling to yield, he, for the lack of something better to spend his rage upon, became very angry at the preacher, and sought to break up the meeting. He swore that he would rather go to hell and be damned, than disgrace himself at the anxious seat. He went from the house in a great rage, and having a pen of hogs near by, he went to pounding them for the purpose of disturbing the services. Becoming weary at that, and thinking it slow work, he determined to butcher his hogs. It was not far from butchering time, and he thought it would afford a good pretext for disturbing the meeting by the squealing of the hogs. With this intention he went to the timber to get some poles which he wanted in making his arrangements but on getting to the woods, his mind became so agitated and confused that he got lost, and spent the rest of the day wandering about and did not get back until after dark. He then came to the night-meeting in great distress, pleading for mercy. His soul was set at liberty before I invited the seekers forward, but as soon as the invitation was given he presented himself at the anxious seat, avowing that his reason for doing so was, that he had determined to break all promises he had ever made to the devil, and one was that he would never go to an anxious seat. This man became an interesting Christian. When the church was organized he was chosen a deacon, and has held the office with honor and usefulness ever since.

In a few months, an excellent house of worship was built at L * * * and a good pastor settled. One year from that time I visited them, and found nearly all the converts faithful to their profession, and growing in grace; and that church has remained a flourishing one unto this day.

I think that taking this example for a basis, I may prudently offer a plea for protracted meetings. I do not believe that we ought to place our dependence entirely upon such means of grace for church extension, and Christian growth. All scriptural means ought to be used: but I do feel confident that among those means, the holding of protracted meetings by pastors and churches is one of the most efficient and successful ways of working for the upbuilding of churches and the salvation of souls.

As some of my views upon this subject are ably set forth in a lively essay which was lately read by one of our brethren at a Baptist ministerial conference in Illinois, and as I think our churches ought to see it, it shall constitute the next chapter.

CHAPTER XV.

ESSAY ON REVIVALS.

DEAR BRETHREN,—The subject you have chosen for me to discuss is one of extraordinary importance. It opens such a wide field for thought, that in a brief essay we can make but a mere introduction. We trust that no more than this will be expected.

What is a revival? The term has various meanings; but in this essay we will consider it to mean just what Christians commonly mean when they say, "A revival;" and define it thus:

An unusual demonstration of the power of God in any community, to awaken saints and convert sinners.

I shall confine myself, chiefly, to what I consider the question of first importance.

How can we promote revivals?

I premise, in the first place, that—

If we would have revivals we must believe in revivals.

"What!" says one: "Do not all orthodox people believe in revivals? especially Baptists. Do not all Baptists believe in revivals?" I answer, No. Granting the truth of our definition, they do not all believe in revivals. They may all say that they wish the churches to grow and prosper, but they wish them to be watered with dew. They are afraid of those big showers that have thunder and lightning in them, and set everybody and everything in commotion. They prefer to see the work go on gradually, and to see one or two born at a time. This would not be a revival, although they prefer it. A revival is an "*unusual* demonstration of the power of God," while they prefer the *usual*. Then they do not fully believe in revivals. This class of brethren, whether in the ministry or laity, do not encourage these unusual demonstrations, and commonly never make special efforts to promote a revival. Nay, they frequently discourage such a work. They seem very much afraid of "excitement," just as though it were possible for a soul to be converted without being excited—for a person's eyes to be opened to see himself trembling on the brink of hell—exposed to eternal ruin, and immediately raised to a hope of heaven, without being excited! We hear such persons say, frequently, that they are afraid of "fox-fire," in these special efforts; yet in their concern about this, they forget, that without some special efforts there is much greater danger that they will have no fire at all. They are afraid that the converts will not be genuine—forgetting that the Saviour has likened the Kingdom to fish in a net, from which, when the fishermen drew it ashore, they selected the good and threw the bad away. They are afraid that these revivals will turn out badly in the end, by cultivating ultra views and establishing wrong precedents among the churches; yet as big a dunce as Artemus Ward has been capable of telling us, that "If a man's views are right he cannot be too ultra; and if they are wrong he cannot be too conservative." But there is a long list of petty objections: their name is legion; those who harp upon them do not believe in real revivals; and it will be unto them according to their faith—they will not be troubled with them. I do not say but that some of the fears alluded to are often realized—many of the converts will backslide, and many will be spurious. There may be things done which are better undone, and things may be said which are better unsaid: yet under these special efforts, multitudes will believe to the saving of their souls. If we will look at the statistics of those churches that have grown up without protracted meetings—and how few there are of such—we will find that they show as great, if not a greater number of exclusions, in proportion to the number of converts they receive, than those that have. If any one doubts this, let him refer to the pamphlet produced by Deacon Wilbur, of Boston, on the labors of Elder Knapp,* and he will see that there is no chance to doubt it. If those brethren who borrow so much trouble about the frequent apostacy of protracted meeting converts, would be equally troubled about the fact that by the working of their policy there are seldom any converts to apostatize, and that their churches have to be kept alive by immigration or die out, it would be better for Zion. Where there are converts there will be apostates, whether they have been brought in by protracted meetings or otherwise. The Word of God foretells it, and we may expect it. There were plenty of such under the wise and holy minis-

* See Appendix.

try of the Apostles, and we cannot calculate on conducting things better than they. Those who urge that fact as a weighty objection to special revival efforts, and on account of the objection do not make such efforts, or encourage them, evidently do not believe in revivals; and I say again, it will be unto them according to their faith.

If we would have revivals we must make special efforts for them.

We must watch the most favorable seasons for these efforts, and then hold protracted meetings. The church and pastor must devote themselves to prayer and Christian labors every day and every night, for days or weeks in succession. It is a stubborn fact, that in the West the great majority of converts have been born in protracted meetings. Most of our churches have had their birth, and the principal part of their growth, under God, through protracted meetings. I think it was at a meeting of the General Association of Iowa that a minister, while speaking upon this point, requested all the professors present who had found their hopes in seasons of protracted meeting to rise up. The congregation was large, and two or three hundred arose. He then requested those who had found their hopes under the usual means of grace to arise, and out of the multitude only nine persons arose! Of these the speaker also observed, that if they would look back carefully, he thought that some of them, at least, would find that their first serious convictions began from protracted meetings. It should be remembered that this congregation was not of the illiterate class, but consisted chiefly of ministers, deacons, and respected representatives from churches in various parts of the State; and it cannot be said, in the face of that rising vote, as it is sometimes said, that protracted meetings draw in only the light trash of the community.

Facts undoubtedly show that nine-tenths of the Baptists in the West have been brought into the churches under the influence of protracted meetings. In view of this I am astonished that such meetings are not of more common occurrence among the churches, and that there are many pastors and churches who live from year to year, for many years in succession, without making a single protracted effort.

I remarked that we should watch for the favorable seasons in which to hold these meetings, but I do not mean that we should always wait. There are times when we see spiritual indications, and have unusual encouragement. In such times we ought to be found ready; but if such times do not come, go forward, at all events, and hold meetings.

Said I to a certain pastor, "You don't believe in protracted meetings, do you?"

"Not much," said he.

"Do you believe," said I, "that it would be right to follow your Sabbath evening service by another on Monday evening?"

"Yes," was the answer.

"Then," said I, "it would be no harm to follow that with service on Tuesday evening, and another on Wednesday evening, and so on through the week, would it?"

"Oh," said he, "it would be well enough to hold such meetings, perhaps, if we saw good indications to begin with; but otherwise, they do more harm than good."

This pastor has been settled about eight years, and I believe has never yet seen any "indications" which he thought warranted him in holding a protracted meeting. Sometimes some of his brethren's children attend revivals at other places, become converted and join his church; occasionally a new member moves in, and thus the church lives, and thus only; and he may vainly wait all his life for "indications," unless he grinds his sword and goes at it in earnest. The Testament does not say much to us about waiting that I can see. The Saviour has said, "Ask and ye shall receive," without specifying any time in the future to which we shall wait before we can receive the blessing; but we are taught that we should go forward in God's work with earnestness, and he will bless our work speedily.

There is good reason why protracted meetings are successful above other means of grace. If a sinner hears a good sermon on the Sabbath and is partly awakened, he has, under the usual means of grace, to wait a week before he will hear another; and thus he has a long space of time in which to stifle his convictions, drive away his serious thoughts, and listen to the tempter. But when one stroke is followed by another and another, he has less time to maneuver—is driven to the wall, and feels compelled to surrender to God.

On the same principle, the people of God are kept in working order. They may attend one meeting, and before they have time to lose the ardor of their feelings they enjoy afresh the most powerful means of grace.

If we would have revivals, the laity must be trained to work for them.

This responsibility must lie with immense weight upon the pastor. It is a trite saying, "Like priest like people." He must show the revival spirit in his preaching and conversation, for the people will become more or less assimilated to his character, whether it be good or indifferent. His preaching should be direct, earnest, pungent, and as searching as he can make it. He should be careful not to spend too much time in polishing his sermons, but bring out the stirring, convicting truth, if he has to let the drapery go. He should give backsliders and luke-warm professors no peace, but tell them that they are dead-weights to the church, stumbling-blocks to sinners, and clogs to the chariot wheels of salvation. He must strive to show all Christians that it is impossible for them to please God without working for him, and he must get them, if possible, to make personal effort every day with the unconverted for their salvation. He must get them, if possible, to leave their homes, take up the cross, and visit, exhort, and pray from house to house among their neighbors. If the work of personal effort and visiting be left for the preacher alone, he cannot begin to do it. But let the deacons, and as many of the brethren and sisters as possible, go out in every direction, day after day, and talk with sinners. Let each one become a home missionary, and religion will soon become the all-absorbing theme in the community for miles around; believers will be strengthened, and sinners brought to God.

I have never yet known of a church becoming in earnest in this work without souls being converted. The reason why such work is blessed is evident; it is because it is God's arrangement. The book of Acts says, that after the death of Stephen the disciples were all scattered abroad through Judea and Samaria, and they (that is, the disciples, not the apostles) "*went everywhere preaching the Word.*" What was the result? We read that soon after this believers were added to the church, and still a little later, "believers were multiplied." In those days, when the laity worked, fear laid hold upon the wicked, and they were converted by hundreds and thousands. But in these days it is a common thing for the laity to attend the Sabbath service when convenient, hear the pastor's sermon, pronounce it good, bad, or indifferent, and go home to assume no farther responsibility in the matter; and if their pastor should wish them to spend a day, or less, in missionary work among their neighbors, they would think the idea a novelty. Brethren, if the churches could control the latent power that is now slumbering in them, and have it wholly sanctified to God, we would see the hosts of Zion march forth to victory, "clear as the sun, fair as the moon, and terrible as an army with banners."

If we would have revivals, we should try to sustain genuine evangelists.

In doing this we fall in with the divine arrangement, and if we follow God's plan we shall succeed. He has called some to be evangelists, and has bestowed upon them special gifts. Says Paul, "There are diversities of gifts." He tells us that some have gifts for pastors, and some for evangelists. Now, if God has called this class of men he has a place for them; but, for some reason, it appears that many of our people are almost ready to say that evangelists have no place in the churches, and that they ought to be nowhere. It is true that there are some who ought to be nowhere, but it is just as true of pastors, and we ought not to discourage evangelism because unworthy men are sometimes found in the work. There are evangelists who are available to the churches, and they are good men, who are favored of God, and prove a blessing wherever they go. For the fact that this class of men is in no greater demand among the churches, the pastors are perhaps as much to blame as anybody else. The evangelist commonly selects a few of his warmest, choicest sermons, and preaches them as often, and repeats them so much, that he can make them more effective than a pastor whose old stock is exhausted, and who usually is obliged to try a new subject when he preaches. With this advantage the sermons of the evangelist will he more powerful than those of the pastor, although his gifts may be inferior. For this cause a pastor will sometimes get jealous, make the trouble himself and throw the blame on the evangelist. If the meeting proves successful, the pastor will be apt to hear some silly brethren giving all the credit to the evangelist, and he will perhaps hear it intimated that the stranger would be just the man for a pastor, if the pastorate was only vacant. Under such trials the pastor needs prudence and humility; but if, through his own folly and jealousy, he stirs up division and loses his place, it is his own fault. I believe that if the pastor has shown himself an earnest, godly man, and has the love of his people, he has little to fear in those things; but if such is not the case, and he has but a frail hold upon their regard, it will be no damage to him or the cause if he does lose his place.

Brethren sometimes object to foreign aid, because, they say, it takes money to pay for it, and they can scarcely sustain their pastor—hence they have nothing to spare. But I believe the pastor will find, in most instances, that the more there is raised for this purpose the more he will receive himself; for his flock and the financial strength of the church will commonly be increased more than enough to make amends.

The advantages of evangelism are easily seen. The pastor, however good and talented he may be, after a lengthy settlement becomes an old bell to the careless, and there is a large class of this kind who must be called out and arrested by something that is novel. They seldom attend church unless something new brings them out. Let the new preacher come in with his warmest sermons, and let the pastor be active in getting the careless out, and they will come from every direction. The pastor will feel at greater liberty to urge people to come out and hear a stranger than he would to have them come out and hear him. There are those whom a pastor never can reach, while an evangelist can. Thus scores of the careless are brought under the means of grace who otherwise would not be; the house of God is thronged; the members are encouraged. The ministry is doubled in strength for the occasion, so that the pastor is not over-taxed, and the effort may thus continue for weeks, and religion be the common theme among saints and sinners, in the field or street, on the road or in the shop, and thus many will be brought to Christ through this union of strength. Let the pastor and evangelist understand each other before they commence laboring together. Let the pastor keep his throne, and let it be understood by all that it is not the evangelist who is holding the meeting, but it is the pastor, and that the pastor has the meeting under his control, while the evangelist is only helping him. Let the pastor steer the boat, and the stranger pull the oars. Let them love each other, and put down jealousies, as Christians ought to do. See that the foreign help remains until the revival is done, and not allow him to go off saying that it should continue right on just when it is ready to die, and then leave it to die on the hands of the pastor; and my opinion for it, if pastors and evangelists will thus work together in harmony, we will see more revivals in our churches.

Finally, if we would have revivals, we must exercise faith in the reality and attainableness of the blessing.

We must have faith in the specific thing, not a vague, general notion of something, we know not what. We often treat the subject of a revival as sinners commonly do the gospel, as something to be believed in, in some way, they know not how, and by somebody else, but not by themselves. We are apt to begin a series of meetings, and say we will try for a revival a few evenings, and if we can't make it go we will close the meeting; but such efforts will most surely fail. This is experimenting with God, and he does not want us to experiment on his promises, which are yea and amen in Christ Jesus: he wants his people to be in *earnest*, and take him at his word. Christ has said, "Ask and ye shall receive," and he expected us to *believe it.* If we would have revivals we must believe that God will grant them, and that in answer to our prayers and labors we will have them, and that we *must* have them. We must hang to the divine promises with an unyielding grasp—if necessary, in the night watches, or until the dawning of the day—and wait before the throne of grace in that spirit which prompted the prayer of John Knox, when he said, "O, Lord, give me Scotland, or I die!" We are too doubtful in our prayers and labors. If one brother can get hold of the arm of the Lord by faith, the community will be shaken as a forest in the mighty winds, and the wicked will quail before God and cry out, "What shall we do!"

When Jesus went to raise Lazarus, he commanded

them to take away the stone from the sepulcher. Brethren, sinners are dead, and *our unbelief is the stone on their sepulcher!* Let us roll away the stone and we will hear the voice of Deity saying to the sinner, "Arise, and come forth from the dead!"

CHAPTER XVI.

GOES TO RUSHVILLE—LOANS A MEETING-HOUSE—RELIGIOUS VISITS—A FIDDLER CONVERTED—IMPUDENCE OF A SINNER—A TUMULT AND THE RESULT—SPREAD OF THE REVIVAL—HOW IT CLOSED—DISAPPOINTMENT OF TWO MINISTERS—PERILOUS VOYAGE AMID THE ICE—PROVIDENTIAL ESCAPE—LABORS IN A MEETING—THOUGHTS ON DIVINE PROVIDENCE—RETURNS HOME—SUCCESS OF THE TOUR.

HAVING bidden the newly-formed church at Lyttleton an affectionate farewell, and received many a "God bless you," I went to Rushville, Illinois. There was a small Baptist organization, which held meetings occasionally, about two miles north of the town, and the brethren wanted me to hold a meeting in the town. The place then contained about five thousand inhabitants. It had a seminary of learning, and there were in it several denominations of Christians, among which there was a church of Cumberland Presbyterians. The religious interest in the town was said to be unusually dull. The attendance at the places of worship was very small. The Cumberland Church had so nearly died out that they seldom had meeting; but they owned a large meeting house, and we tried to rent it. We could not persuade them, however, to rent it, but they consented to loan it for an indefinite time.

This offer we accepted, and I began a meeting in their house. It was soon evident to me that something was required beside preaching, to awaken a religious interest among the people; and having announced that some of the brethren and myself would visit the families through the town as much as possible, by calling at their houses, we commenced visiting on the first Monday of my stay. We went out two and two, taking it street by street, to canvass the town. This proved to be one of the hardest and happiest day-works I ever did. A good deacon went in company with me, and we spent the whole day, from early morning until late, exhorting and praying from house to house with the utmost diligence. The Lord seemed to go before us and open the way. Occasionally some of the members of a family would be seized with conviction during a season of prayer. Five persons declared themselves to have found peace in believing during this day's visits. In one instance we called at a place where the man of the house was within, playing on a violin. Said the deacon, "It's of no use to go in there, is it?" "But," said I, "we must go in and redeem our pledge." We ventured in, and he received us kindly. He laid by his fiddle, listened very respectfully to all we had to say, and appeared to take a deep interest in our remarks. It finally turned out that he went to hear the preaching, and was the first one who experienced religion that night. This incident may be an encouragement to those who will attempt a similar work for the Master. To any such I will here say: fear not to enter the house of any one on so good an errand; "for thou knowest not whether shall prosper either this or that."* This visiting proved to be just what was most needed in that place. It was new tactics to the unconverted, and produced a general stir. On Monday evening the house was filled. This had not before occurred while we were there. The spirit of God rested upon the congregation in an unusual degree, and quite a number present were concerned for their souls. I invited the anxious forward for prayers, and as was sometimes my custom, I went back into the congregation to entreat individuals personally to go up to the altar of prayer. Among others, I saw two young ladies who were deeply penitent, and who desired to go forward for prayers; but when they attempted it, a young man who was with them, and who I afterwards learned was a brother of one of them, posted himself between the slips, and would not allow them to go. Thinking that my presence might release them, I went to them and said,—"Young ladies, don't tarry—move right out." At this they took courage, and attempted again to pass him; but as they did so, he laid hold upon one of them to detain her. Seeing this act of meanness, I could not endure it. Seizing him by the arm with a strong grip, and looking him sternly in the eye, I said to him sharply, "Release that lady, sir!" At the same time I gave him a push backward, and the lady went forward. I suspected that he would grapple me for a fight—he seemed half inclined to do so, but for some reason he did not, and I moved

* Sol. Songs, 11: 6.

on and engaged in counsel and prayer for the seekers.

We had three stoves in the room, and I had been occupied but a short time at the anxious seat, when this fellow, who doubtless felt humiliated in the eyes of the lookers-on, and greatly enraged withal, caught hold of one of the stoves and turned it over, spilling the fire upon the floor, knocking down the stove-pipes, and filling the house with soot and smoke. Soon all was confusion. Some ran for water to extinguish the fire. Some carried the stove out of doors, and others took out the pipes. In the meanwhile the offender ran out of doors, and himself and two or three others yelled about the windows like wild Indians, determined, if possible, to complete the disorder by breaking up the meeting. Order, however, was restored, and the meeting continued.

Such occurrences do often dishearten the people of God in protracted efforts; but I would here remark that I have commonly seen them overruled for good. It was so in this instance.

In using this desperate fellow Satan overshot his mark. The occasion was improved to show the people the unmasked deformity of sin. But this was not all; the next day, although it was very cold, this young man and one of his companions in iniquity, were found alone in an old, deserted wagon-shop, each one being in a corner by himself, weeping over his sins. Their own wickedness had corrected them.* Soon after this they went to the meeting as meek and quiet as lambs, and sought

* Jer. ii : 19.

and found the favor of Him whose mercy knows no bounds. Thus does God often make the wrath of man to praise him, while the remainder of wrath he will restrain.*

Our place of worship became so crowded, and the religious interest so general, that I requested the other denominations to open their houses of worship and hold meetings also. The Methodists and New-School Presbyterians did so, and although they had good crowds, our congregation did not seem to diminish. So general was the interest that religion was the chief topic of conversation among saints and sinners all through the town, and it seemed that the awakening angel had knocked at every door. After we had witnessed about sixty conversions, and while our meeting was in full blast, one of the elders of the Cumberland Presbyterian Church informed me that a couple of their ministers had come to preach to them, and that they must use their house of worship. As they had not been using the house for some time previous, and had not expected to use it soon, this move was unlooked for, and I was much taken aback; but the house was theirs, and thus suddenly ended our meeting. Under these embarrassing circumstances a good number of our converts were lost to the Baptists; but even thus the result was happy. We organized a good Baptist Church, which soon after built a meeting-house of their own, employed a regular pastor, and have sustained worship and prospered ever since.

The two ministers who took the meeting off our

* Psalm lxxvi: 10.

hands, I afterward learned had been sent for a distance of seventy miles. They and their brethren had hoped to improve the opportunity which seemed presented in the large awakening to strengthen their church, but they were disappointed. When they commenced the house was filled with people, but though they preached every night for two weeks, public feeling was against them, and they finally closed their meetings with a congregation of twelve persons on Sabbath, and their church was in a far worse condition than when they began.

Leaving Rushville, I set my face homewards. On getting to the Mississippi, I found the river so full of floating ice that the ferry could not run. The chances of getting across seemed small; but long absence from my family made me anxious to hasten home, and I resolved to get over if possible. After some inquiry, I found a man who, for the sum of one dollar, agreed to attempted the passage in a skiff. I accepted his offer and we shoved out. The wind was blowing unfavorably against us from the western shore, but we thought that with proper caution we could work our way between the floating cakes; but our difficulties increased as we went, and when we were about half way across the skiff became so hemmed in with ice that we could not advance. We attempted to clear away the ice, but with all our efforts we were soon so completely locked in that we could neither advance nor retreat, and we found ourselves hopelessly floating down the river. To complete our troubles night soon came on, the wind increased to a strong gale, and it became bitterly cold. The raft of ice about us was constantly increasing, and apparently making our imprisonment more sure. We renewed our efforts, and struggled our utmost to escape, but finally gave it up as hopeless and useless.

It was now terribly cold; such intense cold I had seldom felt. We very much feared that we should freeze to death! I thought it dreadful that we should perish in such a condition, beyond the reach of human aid, but committing myself into the hands of that God whom I loved and had tried to serve, I was resigned to wait patiently the issue, and abide it with Christian fortitude, whatever it might be. The gloomy aspect of either shore, the outlines of which we could but dimly perceive through the darkness as we floated on, together with the dismal sounds made by the grinding and crushing of ice-floats against the points and islands, served to make our condition appear more terrible.

Thus we were carried down helplessly upon the broad stream.

After we had floated about eight miles the wind providentially crowded our travelling prison into a bend of the river, on the Illinois shore, and as it struck the bank it was separated into several pieces. Seeing our prison doors thus thrown open we renewed our struggles for liberty, and after several efforts we stood once more in safety upon *terra firma.*

We were now not far from the town of W * * *, to which we hastened, and found a hotel as soon as possible, where we had a good fire and were soon restored to comfort.

I soon fell into conversation with the landlord, who was a very agreeable man, and I told him of my late adventure. He said that it was next to impossible to cross the river then, and that it was dangerous to attempt it. He told me that I might as well try to be contented, for I might be compelled to remain there several days. As we went on in conversation I found that he was a warm Baptist brother, and when I told him that I was a Baptist minister he was perfectly pleased. Said he, "God must have blown you here on purpose to help us in our meeting, for we are holding meetings in the Baptist church in town; and now I want you to go with me to the meeting immediately, for you are needed there;" and without further words we went. Though the church had no pastor at that time, a visiting brother had been with them several evenings; a good interest had begun, and all were pleased to see an accession of help. My visit was seasonable, for the church was weak, and they did indeed need help. I was ice-bound for eight days, during which time I labored diligently with the minister and the brethren, and saw about thirty souls added to the church. I then crossed the river in safety and went on my way home rejoicing, feeling the firm belief that the landlord's remark was true when he said that God must have blown me to W * * * on purpose. Experience, as well as Scripture, has taught me to count much on special providences. This is only one among many instances which have occurred in my ministry to confirm me in the belief. Many times have I felt the force of these almost inspired lines of Cowper:

"God moves in a mysterious way,
His wonders to perform;
He plants his footsteps in the sea,
And rides upon the storm.

"Ye fearful saints, fresh courage take;
The clouds ye so much dread
Are big with mercy, and shall break
With blessings on your head.

"Judge not the Lord by feeble sense,
But trust him for his grace;
Behind a frowning providence
He hides a smiling face.

"His purposes will ripen fast,
Unfolding every hour;
The bud may have a bitter taste,
But sweet will be the flower."

As I neared my home, and thought back upon the gracious dealings of God to myself and many others, during this campaign against Satan's kingdom, my soul was inexpressibly happy.

Though I had been out less than three months, I estimated that not less than two hundred and thirty souls had professed to have found hope in the various meetings in which I had been engaged. Besides this, the Presbyterian and Methodist churches in Rushville had been aroused by our meeting there, and they in turn had been instrumental in the conversion of a considerable number. It had been truly a season of the right hand of the Most High. Though there are many of the converts whom I have not since been permitted to see, and years have passed since we wept and rejoiced together, my heart yet warms in remembrance of them, and I look forward with hope and comfort to a happy reunion, which I trust we shall enjoy in the fair climes of immortality,

> "Where congregations ne'er break up,
> And Sabbaths never end."

CHAPTER XVII.

GOES TO MISSOURI — MEETING IN THE TOWN OF W * * * — INCIDENT AT THE BAPTIZING OF A NEGRO — THE NEGRO'S POETRY — RELIGIOUS INTEREST AMONG THE SLAVES — A NEGRO SITS DOWN ON THE HOT STOVE — THE RESULT — MAKING AN AGREEMENT WITH HELL — WARNINGS — A STINGY COLLECTION — APOLOGIES — RETURNS HOME.

HAVING remained at home about two weeks after my last return, I set out on foot for the State of Missouri, and the first night from home I stopped at the town of W * * *, distant about twenty-five miles. There was a Baptist church there, of about two hundred members, some of whom were quite wealthy. I was informed that the money and property among them was worth not less than three hundred thousand dollars. They were very anxious for me to stop and hold a meeting with them, and I thought, as I had labored so much in destitute places where I received little or no pay for it, that in view of my poverty I had better do so; for in the first place the church had no pastor at that time, and my help was much wanted; and as the people were abundantly able, they would perhaps give me a good remuneration, which I very much needed. I accordingly held a meeting with them, in which I labored very hard for about twenty days. It pleased God to give us the victory, and we had a powerful revival. Fifty-three persons were baptized, and a good number professed conversion besides, who were not baptized. Many backsliders were reclaimed, the members were renewed in spirit, and a general reformation of feeling was produced throughout the community. Among the converts were some very interesting colored people. One of them, an old negro man, when being led into the water for baptism, requested permission to repeat a hymn he had learned. Permission being granted, he repeated it in the hearing of the people, greatly to his satisfaction. As I think it contains some good and plain gospel instruction, and is well worth the reading, the reader shall have it. It is as follows:

"Go read the third of Matthew,
And read the chapter through;
It is a guide to Christians,
To tell them what to do.
In those days came John Baptist,
Into the wilderness,
A preaching of the Gospel
Of Jesus' righteousness.

"Then came to him the Pharisees,
For to baptized be;
But John forbade them, saying,
Repentance bring with thee;
Then I 'll baptize you freely,
When you confess your sin,
And own your Lord and Master,
And tell how vile you 've been.

"When John was preaching Jesus,
The all-atoning Lamb,
He saw the blessed Saviour,
And said, 'Behold the man
Appointed of the Father
To take away your sin,
When you believe in Jesus,
And own him for your King.'

"Then came the blessed Saviour,
For to baptized be:
He was baptized in Jordan,
The Scripture reads to me;
He came out of the water—
The Spirit from above
Descends and lights on Jesus,
In likeness of a dove.

"The heavens then were opened,
As you may plainly see;
A witness to the people,
That thus it ought to be.
A voice from heaven proclaimed,
'This is my only son;
And I'm well pleased with Jesus
In all that he has done.'

"All you who say you've Jesus,
Come, prove you have the Lord;
Come, follow his example,
Recorded in his Word.
Take up your cross as freely
As Jesus did for you.
I leave you all to Jesus,
And bid you all adieu."

When the old negro had finished repeating this hymn, he was baptized and came up out of the water very happy.

There were thirty or forty slaves owned by the membership of the church, and they were remarkably fond of attending the meetings. They seemed to think it a sad misfortune to miss a single night. Those who professed religion showed a warm and sincere attachment to the cause which it would have been well for some of their masters to imitate. They were good natural singers, and when they were at meeting there was never any lack of music. Some of them had a good share of native wit and talent; but being unlettered and unschooled, they made a great many ludicrous mistakes. During this meeting they often tested my gravity severely, and in some instances entirely overcame it.

One evening, just before preaching, after the room had become well filled, and everybody seemed unusually quiet and solemn, a large, dull-looking negro man came into church. The seats were all full, and the space about the stove was occupied with those less fortunate hearers who were standing. The negro, seeing no seat, pressed his way through, and took his position among the standers near the stove. Here he stood for a minute or more staring about the room, and, as I suppose, his attention was so completely absorbed in looking about at the people that he forgot himself and sat down upon the hot stove! His presence of mind returned instantly. I had no idea that he was active; but, O dear! "Tell it not in Gath." He excelled any puppet show or ballet-dancer that could be found, for he was so active that it was as much as a bargain for the house to hold him. The crowd about him was suddenly set into a jostle, a space was cleared, and for one or two minutes he jumped up and down, hallooing at the top of his voice, "Lor' a mercy! O Lor' a mercy!"

The whole affair was so peculiarly ludicrous as to defy the most determined gravity; and people and preachers were so overcome with laughter that it drove away all seriousness of feeling for the entire evening. The poor fellow was no doubt in some pain and much alarm, but the affair was so laughable that pity and prudence plead in vain.

Some occurrences connected with that meeting were of the most solemn character. I labored a great deal in the congregation, and through the community in conversations with individuals at their homes. In this way there came to my notice two young ladies and two young gentlemen, who, as I believe, made "a covenant with death."

On learning something of their circumstances, it appeared that both couple were keeping company with prospects of marriage. I saw that they were convicted of their sins, and that I ought to press upon them the vast importance of seeking the mercy of Christ while it might be found, and the great danger of grieving the Holy Spirit forever away; but they were much inclined to levity and pleasure-seeking, and felt such a strong aversion for my interviews that they tried to avoid me. For this purpose they sought to disguise themselves by changing hats or bonnets, and various articles of dress. I still sought them out, however, and pleaded with them to yield to Christ; but so determined were they to live on in their folly, and resist the influences of the Spirit and the Word, that they covenanted together that rather than go to the anxious seat they would go to hell! This was an awful covenant, and having heard of it I went to them again, and earnestly endeavored to show them its wickedness and folly, and besought them not to dare thus to trifle with God; but in spite of my utmost persuasion they continued obstinate.

In a few weeks from that time the two young men were on their way to California, and while one of them was taking his gun from the wagon, its hammer caught against the side of the wagon-box, discharging the contents of the gun in his chest, and he died in few minutes. In a few days from that event, the other young man fell with his head under a wheel, and was killed instantly!

On the last Sabbath of the meeting, while I was preaching, a messenger came into the congregation, and walking up to the pulpit he whispered to me that Miss * * *, who was one of the young ladies who had made the dreadful covenant, was dying, and wanted me to come and pray for her. I whispered to one of the deacons that he had better go immediately, but knowing the circumstances he begged to be excused, saying, "I would go, but somehow I have no heart or faith to pray for her." I dismissed the meeting and started upon the solemn errand as soon as I could, but when I arrived she was a corpse! In something over three months from this, the other young lady sickened and died also.

Thus, in less than four months from the time they made the rash vow together, they were all in their graves, and every one died without hope! They had made "an agreement with hell," and a "covenant with death," that for the uncertain promise of a life of liberty in sin and folly, they would dare to brave the dangers of delay, and hazard the highest interests of their souls!

Reader, are you an impenitent sinner? Beware! Do not dare to trifle with offered mercy! Let these sad examples teach you a lesson never to be forgotten. Hear what God has said to such covenant makers: "Your covenant with death shall be disannulled, and your agreement with hell shall not stand; when the overflowing scourge shall pass through, then ye shall be trodden down by it."*

They banded together and strengthened each other in their rash purposes to drive off conviction, but says the Bible: "Though hand join in hand, the wicked shall not be unpunished."†

You may wonder, reader, that the deacon did not go and pray for that young lady, and I confess that his refusal was strange to me. I thought it a solemn matter for him to refuse, yet it was no more solemn than these words of John: "There is a sin unto death; I do not say that ye shall pray for it."‡

But I will now return to my personal narrative. As the time of my departure from Missouri drew near, there were many expressions of sorrow among

* Isa. xxviii : 18. † Prov. xi : 21. ‡ 1 John v : 16.

the people that I must so soon leave them. Frequent allusions were made to the prosperous and happy hours we had enjoyed together, and the faithful manner in which I had labored and preached the gospel among them; and, indeed, I felt sad in prospect of leaving the place, as I always do where God has given me converts. It is natural for me to feel a warm attachment to those for whose salvation I have labored and prayed.

On the last night of the meeting there was a general turn out to hear my farewell sermon, and all seemed to feel that we had the best of the wine at the last of the feast. I preached, gave them my parting counsel, and sat down. There was present with us that evening Brother C* * *, who was a minister, and a man of good sense and talent. When my discourse was ended he arose, and in a happy style alluded to my earnest and successful labors among them. He then spoke of my poverty, self-denial, and the destitution of my family, and told the congregation that he hoped these things would be remembered when the hat was passed around for Brother Pickard. Finally he said: "Brethren and friends, you are able to contribute largely, for God has blessed you in the concerns of both earth and heaven, and I hope you will show your gratitude to God, and your kindness to Brother Pickard, by giving generously." The hat was then passed around while a hymn was being sung. The collection was counted, and lo! it amounted to two dollars and thirty cents. I felt somewhat disappointed that this should be the reward of three weeks of hard labor, but said nothing.

When the money had been counted, Brother C * * * ordered the congregation to stop singing. He then told the people the amount of the contribution, and openly said that they ought to be ashamed of themselves. Said he, "Brother Pickard is here by your solicitation. He has labored hard, and has honestly earned one hundred dollars. You justly owe it, his family needs it, and he ought to have it." From this he struck fire, and poured it out upon them for several minutes, with wit, satire, and eloquence, rebuking their parsimoniousness, until they were so completely flagellated that I thought if I had wished for revenge for my treatment, which I did not, I should have been more than satisfied. I fancied that every one present was ashamed that he was there. I never heard an appeal before or since, of a similar character, so full of sarcastic power. I really felt sorry for the brethren, and was glad when he stopped.

One brother then arose, blundered out a few apologies, and concluded by saying that he did not know that Brother Pickard was preaching for money. These apologies Brother C * * * answered in short order, and starting around with a subscription paper he urged every one to sign it. When this effort was done, he handed me the paper, which footed up seven dollars and twenty cents. This I returned to the people telling them that it was of no use to me, as I should be out of the State before another night. The next day I was left to plod my way home on foot. This ill-usage cut keenly upon my feelings at the time, for I was very needy. My only decent pantaloons had been worn out at the knees at that meeting, in laboring and praying for the anxious. My hat had become seedy, my boots leaky, and my scanty purse exhausted. My sorrow, however, was of short duration; my mind turned from this to think of the many mercies of God toward me. I fell to singing spiritual songs, became extremely happy, and went home rejoicing.

I relate this circumstance to show how sorely ministers are sometimes tried, hoping that if any should read it who have niggardly habits in respect to supporting the gospel, it may cause them to think of their duty to those servants who labor for their highest welfare. In justice to the Baptists I must remark, however, that there are few such churches. This one was an exception. I believe that there are as many noble, generous spririts among the Baptists at the present time, as there are in any order of Christians in our country; and though there are others who may be equally good, I love my brethren better than any other class of men on earth.

CHAPTER XVIII.

MEETING AT A* * *—DULL PROSPECTS—REVIVAL—SCENE AT A BAPTISM—A NOVEL WEDDING—WHO SHOULD HAVE THE MARRIAGE FEES—THOUGHTS ON BAPTISM—A DIAGRAM—CHURCH GOVERNMENT.

On getting home from my Missouri meeting, I was much worn by the labors of the winter, but the stern demands of want allowed no time for rest. I immediately set about gathering supplies for my family, who were destitute of wood, flour, groceries, and almost the necessaries of life. After working at home two weeks, to replenish our store, I went to the town of A* * *, the place of a county-seat on the Mississippi, to hold a meeting. There was no Baptist interest there at the time, and I obtained the use of the court-house, in which I preached three weeks. It was the breaking up of winter, and the streets and roads were very bad. The mud was so deep that I saw one team stick in the middle of a street. The bad going was thought by the people generally an excellent excuse for not coming to meeting; in fact, they considered it altogether impracticable, for that reason, to attend. For a week or more the prospect looked gloomy enough, but we managed to get a few out. To these we continued perseveringly to preach and exhort, and earnestly besought the Lord to give us victory. At length some of the few hearers began to seek for mercy. From this an interest went out through the town, and the people soon found plenty of ways and means to come in and crowd the court-room. The mud now seemed scarcely an impediment. Conversions occurred every day, the meeting went on gloriously, and finally resulted in the organization of a promising Baptist church.

On the occasion of our last baptism, as the audience were going to that noble baptistry, the "Father of Waters," to witness the ordinance, the first up-river steamer for the season hove in sight, and landed at the point where we stopped, with about three hundred souls on board, to witness the ceremonies. The captain requested all on the boat to keep the most respectful silence, which was done with an appearance of becoming reverence. The converts, about fourteen in number, were then laid in the watery grave. At the close of the exercises, the captain, crew, and passengers were remembered, with the rest of the congregation, in prayer. The morning was so clear and charming that it increased the solemn beauty of the scene, and made it delightful to witness. Some of the passengers on the boat were heard to remark that it was the most solemn and impressive sight they had ever beheld.

While I was at A * * *, a happy couple stepped up to the desk, one evening, just as I had dismissed the congregation, and requested me to unite them in marriage. They were taking rather a late start in wedlock. The groom was seventy-two and the bride sixty-eight years old. Their request surprised and confused me at first, but recollecting the substance of an old Quaker marriage ceremony, I pressed it into service, and

"Joined them in that silken tie
Which binds two willing hearts."

The groom, who seemed wonderfully pleased with his new state, generously gave me one dollar and fifty cents; which, for the times, was liberal indeed. Though I had been in the ministry a number of years, this was the first couple I ever married. People then commonly had the unfair custom of not only allowing the minister to preach, travel, visit sick beds and attend the funerals of the country, gratis, but of adding to this neglect the aggravation of sneaking off to the squire, or some other civil functionary, to pay him their marriage fee. I will just say here, that I am glad, for the sake of the poor ministers, that this way of doing is getting out of style. Ministers do more gratuitous labor than any other class of men, and a common sense of justice should certainly secure to them the marrying patronage.

At the close of the meeting an old lady gave me nine yards of calico for a dress-pattern for my wife. This, with the marriage fee, was the sum of my receipts for the three weeks' labor.

As the topic of baptism has been suggested by the impressive scene at the steamboat landing, I will here venture to offer a few thoughts and facts relative to it, though it may be at the expense of some digression.

The apostolic mode of baptism by immersion has an impressive solemnity to the spectator which no other mode can have. When some of the passengers on the steamer declared, of our last baptismal occasion at A * * *, that it was the most solemn and impressive sight they had ever beheld, they but repeated what has been felt and said thousands of times. I have seldom, if ever, administered the ordinance without hearing more or less declarations of that character. There are but few sights upon which the eyes may look which are so well calculated to affect the heart. Hundreds of living witnesses can testify, to-day and forever, that their first alarm for their souls occurred while looking at the impressive sight of converts being buried in the baptismal grave. Many cases of the kind have occurred under my own observation. In my meetings I have noticed that a baptism usually gives new interest, and I have often counted more upon such occasions, in arresting the attention of the careless, than upon a good sermon. God thus speaks through his own appointed ordinance. This fact highly favors the doctrine that immersion is the only scriptural mode of baptism, and is one of the very strongest of presumptive arguments, for the same cannot be said of other modes. Again: I have conversed with hundreds of persons who have been sprinkled or poured, who have been more or less dissatisfied with their baptism, so called, and I have immersed scores of such persons at their request, and received them into the Baptist churches; but never in my life have I known of a person who had received the ordinance by immersion and afterward doubted that he had been baptized. This shows very clearly which way the finger-board of conscience points, and is a fact which to me speaks upon the subject with convicting power. The sure and firm growth of the Baptist denomination for the last three hundred years is perhaps attributable in a large degree, by the blessing of God, to this fact, that when a person is once a Baptist he is satisfied with Baptist doctrines, and can seldom be persuaded to change them or change his church relation for another. On the other hand, the Baptist denomination in the United States has for a number of years back been receiving by immigration members from the different Pedo-Baptist churches at the rate of two thousand a year, and it has been receiving ministers from the same source, at the rate of one for every week in the year.* This is a church immigration which has never been heard of except in this instance. During one year of my ministry I kept an account of the number I baptized of those who had been previously sprinkled or poured, and it amounted to fifty-seven persons. I have baptized a greater or less number of that class every year since I was ordained. All these, of course, were received into the Baptist church.

Again: the fact that our Pedo-Baptist brethren have kept preaching so much on baptism is good

* History of Baptist Denomination.

evidence that they are conscious, themselves, that their theory on that subject is one of the weak points in their creeds. Hence their greater uneasiness about that point and their disposition to bestow upon it the more care. I will not suppose that there is such a want of charity on their part that they do it simply for the purpose or with the desire to tear us down. I believe that I may safely affirm, as the result of extensive acquaintance, that in the States of Illinois and Iowa there have been five sermons preached against our views on baptism, communion, etc., where there has been one preached for their support, and yet this immigration still keeps coming into our churches. The reason why Baptists now-a-days preach less on baptism than other denominations is, that they are so confident in the strength of their position that they feel more at ease.

I have not space to dwell upon the subject of baptism in this book, but I will simply point the inquiring reader to a few scripture passages, suggest a safe rule by which the different views on the subject may be criticised, and dismiss it with the recommendation that he "search the Scriptures," to know the will of God, not only in this but in all things.

If the word *sprinkle* or *pour* means baptism, it will make good sense if you substitute either one of those words for the word *baptism.* So of the word *immersion,* when substituted for the word *baptism,* if it be borne in mind that to immerse, according to Webster's Unabridged Dictionary, is to bury—to overwhelm—to involve, or to deeply engage in. The word baptism is often used in a figurative sense: for example—Matt. iii: 11—"He shall baptize you with the Holy Ghost." Where the word is used thus, one of the figurative words corresponding with immersion should be used instead of the word *immersion.* Thus: "He shall *overwhelm* you with the Holy Ghost."

To give a clearer idea of the figurative words which correspond with the word *immersion*, or which present the likeness of immersion by a different figure, we might say of a person that he is immersed in the affairs of life, deeply engaged in business, involved in the concerns of state, overwhelmed in sorrow, or that his name is buried in oblivion. It would mean the same thing if we should say that he is immersed in the affairs of life, immersed in business, immersed in the concerns of state, immersed in sorrow, or that his name is immersed in oblivion; yet, according to modern taste, the former mode of expression, by preventing repetition, would be more elegant, and hence is more used. This is enough to show that these words do present a figurative likeness to the word immersion, and that they may be used interchangeably with it. I shall so use one of them in the diagram which I shall present. In reading the common translation of the New Testament on this subject, we are not accommodated with these words of figurative likeness, but the simple word *baptism* is used with reference to things literal and things not literal. It is comprehensive in its meaning and varied in its application, and it is left to the discriminating judgment of the reader to find its exact shade of meaning by the relative position which it occupies in any given place. By allowing the same liberty in the use of the equivalent word, *immersion*, it will make precisely the same sense as does the word *baptism*, if it should be substituted for it, in EVERY PLACE WHERE IT OCCURS IN THE BIBLE. This fact any one may know for himself by taking the pains to test it with the Scriptures. But the same cannot possibly be said of the word *sprinkle*, or *pour*. We will now try this plan of substitution in the following.

DIAGRAM.

	Common translation.	*The word* SPRINKLE *substituted for the word* BAPTISM.*	*The word* IMMERSION, *or its words of likeness, substituted for the word* BAPTISM.
Mark i: 4.	John did baptize in the wilderness, and preach the baptism of repentance, for the remission of sins.	John did *sprinkle* in the wilderness, and preach the *sprinkling* of repentance, for the remission of sins.	John did *immerse* in in the wilderness, and preach the *overwhelming* of repentance, for the remission of sins.
Mark iii: 16.	And Jesus, when he was baptized, went up straightway out of the water.	And Jesus, when he was *sprinkled*, went up straightway out of the water.	And Jesus, when he was *immersed*, went up straightway out of the water.
John iii: 23.	John also was baptizing in Ænon, near to Salem, because there was much water there; and they came, and were baptized.	John also was *sprinkling* in Ænon, near to Salem, because there was much water there; and they came, and were *sprinkled*.	John also was *immersing* in Ænon, near to Salem, because there was much water there; and they came, and were *immersed*.
Acts viii: 38.	And they went down into the water, both Philip and the eunuch, and he baptized him. And when they were come up out of the water, etc.	And they went down into the water, both Philip and the eunuch, and he *sprinkled* him. And when they were come up out of the water, etc.	And they went down into the water, both Philip and the eunuch, and he *immersed* him. And when they were come up out of the water, etc.
Col. ii: 12.	Buried with him in baptism, wherein ye are also risen with him.	Buried with him in *sprinkling*, wherein ye are also risen with him.	Buried with him in *immersion*, wherein ye are also risen with him.
Luke xii: 50.	I have a baptism to be baptized with, and how am I straitened until it be accomplished.	I have a *sprinkling* to be *sprinkled* with, and how am I straitened until it be accomplished.	I have an *immersion* to be *overwhelmed* with, and how am I straitened until it be accomplished.
Gal. iii: 27.	For as many of you as have been baptized into Christ, have put on Christ.	For as many of you as have been *sprinkled* into Christ, have put on Christ.	For as many of you as have been *immersed* into Christ, have put on Christ.
Matt. xx: 22.	Are ye able to drink of the cup that I shall drink of, and to be baptized with the baptism that I am baptized with?	Are ye able to drink of the cup that I shall drink of, and to be *sprinkled* with the *sprinkling* that I am *sprinkled* with?	Are ye able to drink of the cup that I shall drink of, and be *immersed* with the *immersion* I am to be overwhelmed with?
Acts xix: 4, 5.	Then said Paul, John verily baptized with the baptism of repentance. When they heard this, they were baptized in the name of the Lord Jesus.	Then said Paul, John verily *sprinkled* with the *sprinkling* of repentance. When they heard this, they were *sprinkled* in the name of the Lord Jesus.	Then said Paul, John verily *immersed* with the *overwhelming* of repentance. When they heard this, they were *immersed* in the name of the Lord Jesus.
Rom. vi: 4.	Therefore we are buried with him by baptism.	Therefore we are buried with him by *sprinkling*.	Therefore we are buried with him by *immersion*.

Having spoken of the steady success of Baptist principles, it is worthy of notice that the political revolutions which have been going on in the world for the past few years have not only called the attention of the people to consider what is the best and safest form of civil government, but, with this, more interest has been taken with reference to what is the true church government. The model of our present civil government was suggested to Thomas Jefferson while at a Baptist meeting, watching the administration of its church government.† The ordeal of the past has convinced Americans, at least, more firmly than ever, that the republican form of civil government is the only just and true one; and many are becoming convinced that the same is true of church government. Americans naturally love soul-liberty. This is bringing many of them into the Baptist churches, and will yet bring many more.

* I here use the word *sprinkle*, because sprinkling is more commonly practiced, but I recommend the reader to try the word *pour*, also, as a substitute, in the same way, or any words that may have a likeness to *sprinkle* or *pour*.

† See History of Baptist Denomination.

CHAPTER XIX.

HARD TIMES—MEETING IN A CABIN—THE OLD BAPTIST AND HIS DOGS—THOUGHTS ON BUILDING MEETING-HOUSES—REVIVAL AT S* * *—A HARD PLACE—DISTURBANCE—HOLDING MOCK COMMUNION WITH A BOTTLE OF WHISKEY—IMPUDENCE OF A ROWDY—CONFUSION OF A YOUNG SQUIRE—THE REASON WHY DONKEYS ARE SCARCE—THREATS OF PERSONAL VIOLENCE—MOVEMENTS OF A REVEREND SCHOOL-TEACHER—HIS BUILDING BURNED—A MAN THREATENS TO SHOOT—TESTIMONY RESPECTING IMMERSION—SAD AFFLICTION—FARMING.

On returning from the meeting at A * * * my family was in a poor condition. My wife was sick, and I was so much exhausted with revival labors that I was in a poor condition for manual labor; but the Lord recovered us both to good health and spirits. This spring I moved on the farm of Brother H * * *, who was to furnish me with a team, and give me one half the crop. During the summer I lived as usual, working six days in the week on the farm, and preaching once or twice usually each Sabbath, at some destitute place.

When my crop was raised the corn was worth ten cents a bushel, wheat fifty, pork from one dollar and thirty to one dollar and fifty per hundred, and I lived so far from market that it was more than it was worth to get the grain marketed. You may be sure we had hard times; but I gathered the crops, did the best I could with them, and prepared for another winter's campaign against Satan's kingdom. This was in 1849. In the fall a Brother T * * * came from Missouri in person, and earnestly urged me to go to a certain community in that State, distant about thirty miles, to hold a meeting. After he had helped me to get up a few loads of wood, we set out together on those old-fashioned chariots which have neither wheels nor horses. The first snow had just fallen, and the roads were so slushy and slippery that our tramp was very fatiguing. On getting to the Des Moines river we only succeeded in crossing with the greatest difficulty. At night we found a cabin near the river, where we gratefully received free hospitality. The next day we finished our journey, and stopped at the place where Brother T * * * thought that a meeting was so much needed. I thought it a dull prospect. It was a very rude cabin. The region was thinly settled, and the proprietor of the cabin, who claimed to be a Baptist, was the only one in the settlement from whom we might hope for any encouragement. These things, however, would not have been so forbidding to us if our host had been a warm Christian, but this he was not—he was a poor representative. He received us very coldly, and conducted himself during our stay as though he thought that preachers were a necessary evil. He had a couple of big, ugly mastiff dogs, which took a large share of his attention, and he seemed to think far more of them than he did of us. We circulated notice of a meeting, and preached in his cabin that evening to sixteen persons. I would have left the next morning but for Brother T * * *, who was still hopeful that we should do much good, and we decided that as we had taken such a hard tramp to get there, we would hold on a few evenings, at all events.

Our Baptist man could not allow us to hold meetings in the day-time at his house, because it made his dogs cross and would not answer. But greater ills were in store; for finally, on the third day of our stay, the man's pet dogs got to fighting, and when their affectionate master went to part them, one of them turned upon him and bit him severely. Instead of thrashing or killing his nasty dogs, as he should have done, he laid all the blame for the misfortune upon the meeting, and said that it brought so many strangers around that it was making his dogs cross and would be the ruination of them. After this, he was so crusty toward us that we gave up the meeting as hopeless, and left the next morning. I thought our old Baptist was treated right, for he was making an idol of his dogs, and was worshiping them more than he did his God. But his punishment worked no repentance, and by his unfaithfulness we had all our tramping and toiling for nought, and were obliged to leave him in as much coldness and poverty of soul as when we found him, to raise up his family without religion, amidst a Godless, Christless set of neighbors.

I have related this partly as an example of the

trials of pioneer ministers, but more particularly as a warning to any of our brethren who may now live in a churchless community, or who will hereafter settle in a new country. Had this professed Baptist but done his duty, and appreciated the day of his merciful visitation, a Baptist church would probably have been organized there which would have been a blessing to himself and family, and all his neighbors, as long as they lived—a blessing, the value of which dollars and cents could not estimate. There are now many places in the West, even in Illinois and Iowa, where there are two, or three, or more, Baptist families destitute of the blessings of church relation, who, if they were only awake, might hold prayer-meetings, employ some evangelist to hold a protracted meeting of two or three weeks, and joining with him in an earnest and faithful effort for God, might see a church raised up among them, and their neighbors brought to Christ. All the effort and expense it might cost them would make them no poorer: it would enhance the value of their property; it would be of inestimable benefit to their children; and, above all, it would make them richer for the life to come. If any such brother should read this book, I pray him to arouse and make an effort to build a Zion of God in his community. Many of our churches which do exist owe their origin and advancement, under God, to the piety and enterprise of some one family or one person who lived in the locality where they were organized. May God grant to raise up many more such brethren and such churches. Instances might be cited where even a sister has been the chief promoter of a church, and that not only of its organization, but the building of a house of worship. Spiritual stupor and a want of pious enterprise are the curse of some and a great impediment to the common cause. Pious enterprise is what the cause needs; without it we shall be as trees without fruit—with it we shall be "terrible as an army with banners."

Leaving my crusty brother to take care of his dogs, I pushed out for W * * *, in Missouri, where I tarried over night. In the morning I started for the town of S * * *, on the Des Moines river. A deep snow had fallen during the night, and the walking was slavish. I several times lay down in the snow with weariness, but I finished my journey, though it was too late to circulate a notice and have a meeting.

The next night I preached. Only five persons were present, but I was urged by two or three of them to remain and hold a protracted meeting. The town of S * * * contained only about eight hundred souls, but it supported a number of whiskey shops, and was a perfect devil's nest—a complete sink of iniquity. I held the meeting in the town school-house, a place which would seat about three hundred hearers. Few were out the second night, but every night after that the house was crowded.

The work of the Spirit was soon manifest. Believers were quickened, and sinners were made to seek for mercy. No sooner did sinners begin to inquire, than the devil, as he commonly does on such occasions, commenced his work of finding fault with the doctrines preached, the character of the meeting, and everything possible connected with the revival. He tried various expedients to hinder the work; but as wicked devices increased with some, religious interest increased with others. "Where sin abounded, grace did much more abound:" yet the wicked seemed determined to do their utmost to throw the meetings into disorder.

The roughs finally went so far with their insults that they brought a bottle of whiskey with them into the congregation, and held a mock communion with it during divine service. When the bottle was emptied, a young man, as if to complete the impudence, held it up and waved it about his head in the sight of the whole assembly. At this I gave him a sharp rebuke, and calling out to him, I said, "Put up that bottle immediately, sir, or I will arrest you." But he did not do it, and I threatened again. The roughs then became very disorderly; some of the people began to be clamorous against the insult, and I was obliged to dismiss the meeting as quick as possible, to prevent it from breaking up in a general row. On consultation with a few friends as to the question of arresting the disturber, they said that if I attempted it, it would be a profitless undertaking, for the reason that the magistrate and all the civil officers of the place were of the same character, and would privately sympathize with them. I then decided to make no prosecutions, but go on with the meeting and trust to Providence for a successful issue. As no arrests were made it encouraged them in their wickedness, and the next night they behaved as badly as ever.

There was a young magistrate present that night, and he was one who thought he knew about all that was worth knowing. He professed to be a Presbyterian, but I suppose he must have had a poor standing. However, after I dismissed, this knowing individual requested the congregation to tarry, while he asked the preacher a few questions. The people took their seats again, and he began thus: "I wish to know by what authority, sir, you say that these young gentlemen and ladies are on the road to hell?" I allowed him to proceed, and he asked several other questions in a disrespectful way, about certain doctrines I had preached. When he had exhausted his inquiries, I answered him by saying, "Have you no Bible, sir, that you are ignorant of these things? If you have not, some well-disposed person ought to give you one. In answer to your first question, I can tell you that if you should ever have a Bible and read it, you will see that the Lord Jesus Christ says to the Pharisees, 'How can ye escape the damnation of hell?' And, sir, in my opinion, you are the very man who ought to take a lively interest in that question, for how shall you escape?" This gave me good opportunity to apply the anathemas of the gospel. I took those words as a text, and preached a short sermon especially for his benefit. The Lord gave me good use of my tongue, and I told him of the threatenings of the divine law against the disobedient and guilty, with a vengeance; and referring to the manner in which, after having been chosen by the citizens to promote law and order, he had come into an assembly of free people with the avowed purpose of interfering with the progress of the revival, I warned him to beware lest judgment should overtake him, and soon show him more about hell than he really wanted to know. The tide of feeling was soon so turned against him that he went off enraged and mortified. After this the young squire was a target for the wit of all the wags and saucy boys in town, and whenever they would meet him upon the street they would ask him such questions as—"Squire, has no one given you a Bible yet?" Or, "Did you never own a Bible, Squire?" Or, "Squire, have you found out anything more about hell, yet?" Or another would call out, "Squire, they say you have had a call to preach; is that so?" "Where do you hold your next meeting, Squire?" etc. Thus the man was nicely caught in his own trap, and so completely bored that I presume he wished a hundred times he had minded his own business, and I will warrant that he never tried to show off in a similar way again.

He was nearly as badly done for as another certain squire I once heard of, who, I think, must have been some relation to this one. He was very fond of picking at professors and ministers. One day he fell in company with a minister, and, as usual, began to find fault with the ways of the church and kingdom.

Finally said he to the minister, who was riding a very fine horse:

"It seems to me that you preachers now a-days are getting so proud that you don't try to imitate your master."

"How is that?" said the preacher.

"Why," said the squire, "we read that Christ rode on a jackass, but preachers now must have fine horses."

"You are right," said the preacher. "It is a lamentable fact, but it can't be helped; for the truth is, the people in these days have used all the jackasses to make squires of!"

The next move made by the rowdies was an attempt to get out a writ to arrest me, on the charge of slander. This was because I had publicly told them of their wickedness and rascality; but, finding they could do nothing at that, some of them agreed together, as I afterwards learned, to attack me personally. This was to be done on a certain night, as I would pass out at the door; but before the time came for the attack to be made, the Lord magnified the hazard of the attempt in their eyes to such a degree, that the leading spirit of the clique declared that he would have nothing more to do with it. Said he to his companions, "You had better take my advice, and let the job go. That Pickard is a dangerous man to quarrel with; just notice the look of his eye and you will see it so. Just watch his motions and appearance: he is built from the ground up; and mind you, if we get into trouble with him he will not stop at trifles; mark my word for it, you had better let him alone." Though they might easily have overpowered me, they deferred, through fear of what might be the result, to take further counsel. In the mean time the leading spirit among them fell at the foot of the cross for mercy, and sought the Lord with all his heart. This gave a new turn to affairs, and took the rest by surprise. Soon another one of the number was convicted; better thoughts began to occupy their attention, and it was not long before every one of the clique that had thus threatened to do me bodily injury was hopefully converted to God! They generally became faithful Christians, and one of them is at this time a minister of the gospel. Thus did God maintain his own cause, and make the wrath of man to praise him.

The gospel, however, must ever work its way through opposition. When this difficulty was disposed of a new one came up. There was a kind of apostate Presbyterian minister in the place, who was trying to teach a high school. He was very much dissatisfied with the meeting, and gave lectures to his pupils every morning, to prejudice them against it, and prevent them from going to the anxious seat to seek religion. He took the position that the idea of regeneration was nonsense, and taught that infant baptism and a moral life were sufficient. He told them that it was a shame and a disgrace to go to an anxious seat, and that he very much hoped that none of his pupils would think of doing such a thing.

An old deacon, who was attending my meeting, having heard how the teacher was trying to impress his pupils, sent word to him that he would pay him twenty dollars for his trouble if he would attend the

Baptist meeting regularly every night while it lasted, and listen carefully to the preaching; but this he would not do. Though he could neither be coaxed nor hired to come near the meeting, he continued to work very diligently against the revival, especially among the young people, and caused us a great deal of trouble and uneasiness. We felt his evil influence so deeply that we at length prayed earnestly that God would either convert him, or otherwise get him out of the way of sinners, that he might not prevent their salvation in that community.

He had in his possession a fine school building, and was thought to be permanently located. Our prayers were not answered during the meeting, though they were not long after. This was done in a way we would not have chosen, and by a process we did not expect. His building took fire in open daylight, as was supposed, by sparks from a stove-pipe, which caught in the roof, and was not discovered until it was too late to save the building, which was soon burned to the ground. The poor sinner was insolvent, and ran away to escape his creditors. Whether or not this was a judgment of Heaven upon him, for fighting against the work of God, others may judge.

During the meeting a Mrs. M* * *, the wife of a wicked man, was converted and wished to be baptized. The husband sent me word that if I attempted to baptize his wife he would shoot me, and that I might fully depend upon it. This seemed a hard case, but I felt that it was my duty—that God commanded it, and that I should obey God rather than man. The woman was very anxious to be baptized, and I determined to do it if it cost me my life. I did not expect to get killed, for I thought upon the promise in the great commission: "Lo, I am with you always, even unto the end of the world."

On the next Sabbath I had about twenty persons to baptize. We opened a baptistry through the ice in the Des Moines river. The day of the baptism was beautiful, and as we gathered upon the bank the Spirit was present. During the introductory exercises of singing and prayer, I became so happy that I forgot all about the shooting business, nor did I think of it until after a part of the converts had been baptized, when, as I happened to look up the river, I saw the man walking up and down along the bank with a gun in his hand. The threat had been so positive that the sight somewhat confused me. I felt fearful for a moment; but I mentally prayed to God for courage and protection, and went forward with my duties. I baptized the rest of the candidates, including his wife; but he did not shoot. He went home angry and ashamed. This was the third company of converts I had baptized during the meeting; and although the water was cold, the man's wife was not injured, nor did a single one even take cold; they were the better for it, by their obedience.

It is a fact worth noticing, that while the lives of ministers have been threatened hundreds of times, they have rarely ever been murdered in America. In some instances they have received bodily injury, yet I do not remember having heard of more than one minister being killed in this country within the last hundred years, except in connection with the rebellion, for preaching too plainly to the wicked. One was killed, I am told, in an early day in Cincinnati. The statement is, that a Baptist elder, who had been preaching in a saw-mill, was struck on his head with a large stone and killed, while returning from meeting at night, by a young man who was enraged at his plain dealing, and who had concealed himself behind a fence and threw at him purposely.

After this baptism I was sent for by my wife to attend to a calamity at home, and thus suddenly ended the meeting. As I have an important testimony to give in regard to immersion, I will give it here. As you will see by this book, I have immersed hundreds of people. I have administered the ordinance in all kinds of weather—in cold, heat, and rain; and though the greater part of this has been done in the winter, often when the ice had to be cut, I have never known of a single instance where an individual's health has been in the least injured in receiving the ordinance of baptism by immersion. On the contrary, I have known several cases where feeble persons were improved in health by the watery burial. One most remarkable case of the kind will be found in this volume. There are some who often argue that to require baptism by immersion is unreasonable, because, they say, it often endangers the health; but facts are stubborn things, and to all such persons I will but say that the facts just given are my answer to their argument.

The circumstance which called me from the meeting at S * * * was an accident which befell one of my little boys, then about one year and a half old. He fell into the fire and burned his face horribly. It was a calamity, indeed, the mark of which he will carry to his grave. This affliction, combined with pecuniary embarrassment, kept me at home during the remainder of the winter. As no one had given me a shilling for the labors of my tour, I returned utterly pennyless to face doctors' bills and many other worldly perplexities. It may be supposed that it was in part my own fault that I so seldom received anything for my ministerial labors, because I did not demand it; but in those places where my work was most needed, and where I more commonly went, society had such an abhorrence of the idea of paying a preacher, that if he should say anything about it he would make ten enemies where he would get one dollar. Many would then take it for granted that he was too lazy to work, and had taken to preaching as an easier way to get money. It was almost necessary for him to labor for nothing, in order to convince them that he had the good of souls at heart. Ministers of all kinds were obliged to endure these things. There are yet some destitute places in the West of that kind, but the great improvement that has been made in this particular is truly wonderful.

During the following summer I remained on Bro. H * * * 's farm at the former terms, usually preaching at some place on the Sabbath as before.

CHAPTER XX.

VISIT AT R * * * AND L * * *—JOYS—MEETING AT M * * *—EXPERIENCE WITH THE DANCERS—VISITING—SEXTON WORK—CONFESSIONS OF THE BRETHREN—IMMENSE FEELING—A TIME OF POWER—THE COLLECTION—ABOLITIONISM—PREACHING IN A BAR-ROOM—RETURN HOME—TAKES THE SMALL POX—EXTREME SUFFERING—THOUGHTS ON JOB'S AFFLICTIONS—DOCTORS' BILLS.

Early in the winter of 1850 I visited my friends and acquaintances in the town of R * * *, in S * * * county, Illinois, where I had held a meeting two years before. Here I enjoyed a rich feast of soul with the converts. As evidence of their growth in grace, they had built a good house of worship, and the church was in a prosperous condition. Some of the converts, who were not there, I learned had died happy and gone home to heaven. Some had removed to other parts; but those who remained were steadfast, and greatly rejoiced with me in our reunion. As I heard them tell of their trials and triumphs, their confidence in God, and fair prospects of a happy heaven, my soul fluttered with joy. Sordid gold could not have purchased me such comfort as I felt with these spiritual children. O ye that labor for the meat that perisheth! Though ye increase in riches, I envy not your lot; for all your gains would not purchase a single hour of such felicity as was mine, when with these converts I thought and talked of Christ and heaven! I have often thought that as we are permitted to experience such joys as we sometimes do upon earth when we meet together, oh, what will be the bliss of heaven! Oh, what rapturous joy, what holy ecstacy will possess our souls, when in that final meeting whence we shall never part we shall taste of those things which "eye hath not seen nor ear heard, neither have entered into the heart of man!" *

After a short visit with the brethren at R * * *, I went to L * * *, where I had also labored two years before. There I preached in a good house of worship, which they had built since the revival. I stayed and preached several times to them, with a view to comfort and strengthen them in the work of the Lord, and was not a little comforted myself to find the church in such prosperity.

I then went to the town of M * * *, about twenty-five miles from Nauvoo, where there was a Baptist church and a small meeting-house. Here I fell in with my old yoke-fellow, Brother More. The church was in a miserable condition. Some two or three years before this, Satan had crept in among the brethren, through some difficulties about Mormonism. The church had attempted discipline, but the troubles increased and the infection had spread until it pervaded the whole body. For a long time they had held no meetings except once a month, which

* 1 Cor. ii : 9.

was on Saturday, and that was occupied in discipline and quarreling. The members had all back-slidden, and some of them had put their profession to an open shame. Though it was the only church in the region, it had become a by-word, and was hissed at, and was a standing reproach to the cause. Brother More and I felt our spirits stirred within us by the mournful state of the case, and resolved to make a trial in the place for the honor of God. We obtained permission to use the house, circulated our appointment for meeting, and after packing wood about half a mile upon our backs and warming the house, we swept it, lighted up, and waited for the people, but we could get no congregation. For the first two or three nights we could not get enough hearers for a corporal's guard. We appointed a morning prayer-meeting, but it seemed to have no more effect than the Pope's bull against the comet; not a soul came out. Brother More and I then held a council of war, and decided to divide our forces, go through the town, visit every family, and preach to them at their houses. We drew a line through the place to make an equal division of the work, and, he taking one side and I the other, we separated; agreeing to meet at the meeting-house, the Lord willing, at sunset, to make our report to each other, and talk matters over. During the day, I knocked at the door of a house, and was bidden to "come in." I saw no one in the room but an old lady, who was busily working at a spinning-wheel in one corner. I introduced myself to her, told her my object in calling, drew up a chair, and commenced a religious conversation with her. Suddenly some half-dozen young men and women entered the room. One of them had a fiddle, on which he immediately began to play, and the rest fell to dancing with all their might. I saw at once that it was a trick of the devil to bully me out of countenance; but paying them no attention, I exhorted the old lady to seek the Lord, reminding her that she was near the grave, and warning her not to delay. By my request she said I might pray for her, and, kneeling by her spinning-wheel, I besought the Lord in her behalf. For a time it seemed doubtful whether dancing or praying would take the sway, but the dancing ceased, and I commenced praying for the dancers. I told the Lord what they had done, and why they had done it, remarking in my prayer that they were evidently not Christians, and prayed God to open their eyes to see the folly of their ways, and prepare for the great judgment to come. When the prayer was closed, they were as quiet as kittens, and hung their heads as though they had been stealing sheep. I then exhorted them to mend their ways, and invited them out to hear the preaching. That night all the company were at meeting. In a few days every one of them was converted, and ever after treated me with the most cordial respect. I give this incident to show timid Christians that, so long as we have God on our side, there is no need of being scared out of countenance by the devil.

I made a number of calls through the day, but had the misfortune to go without my dinner; though in the evening I happened in a house just as they were

"For a time it seemed doubtful whether Dancing or Praying would take the sway."

sitting down to supper, and gladly accepted an invitation to eat. I had heard nothing of Brother More through the day, and at sun-set went to meet him at the church, as agreed on, but could find no Brother More. I began to be uneasy for him, but near dark he came, and on inquiry I found that the first place he had stopped at in the morning was a grocery, and he so much dreaded to visit that he remained there all day, talking with the customers. He said that their chief business was drinking, playing poker, and casting slurs at religion. That night the house was crowded, and Brother More preached a powerful sermon. There was weeping through the house, but sinners made no move. The next morning a number of the brethren came to prayer-meeting. I told them of the view of the church before the world, the tremendous interests pending, the fearful responsibility upon them, their backslidden state, and exhorted them with all my power and feeling to confess their sins and backslidings openly to the world. I told them that they were verily guilty of standing in the way of sinners, and that if they did not make their confessions we would not stay another day, but would leave them with their ruined church to die in their own shame. It was like pulling teeth to get their confessions, but they saw that it was that or death. Finally one man got up very reluctantly, and began to talk a long way from the point; then he came a little nearer, and began to warm up and came a little nearer still. I was afraid he would miss it, but at length he grew very warm and came up square to the mark. Said he, "Brethren, I am a poor, miserable, wicked backslider. It was *me* that stole the pig! I have been a trouble-maker in Zion, and I want the church and the world to forgive me!" Others then began to melt, and when he sat down there was a number who wanted to confess, and we soon had a regular breaking up and melting down. The ice was thawed out, and the spring-time came to their hearts. I then told them that this confession was well enough for the church, but that the world ought to hear it, and proposed to draft resolutions to be read to the public congregation from the desk at night, to the effect that the church would confess their short-comings to the sinners of the community, and ask their pardon. The resolutions were then drawn up and agreed to. At night I read them to the congregation, and dwelt upon them at some length and with much feeling. I then requested the people that as many of them as would freely forgive, would make it known by rising to their feet. At this there was a general rising. Tears flowed freely. It was a moment of deep interest. An awful solemnity prevailed. A certain doctor, who arose, fell down with emotion. The Spirit of God filled the place with mighty power; many cried aloud for mercy; and, seemingly in a moment of time, not less than fifty souls were brought under conviction. No preaching was done that night; there was no chance; but it was a time to pray, and all who could pray began praying for the anxious in downright earnest. The meeting went on with power for several days, and many were converted to God. The membership of the church was doubled;

backsliders were reclaimed; believers were renewed, and a new impetus was given to the cause of religion in that section.

The people did not allow us to go away empty. By previous announcement a collection was taken up on the last night of the meeting, for Brother More and myself, and when it was equally divided we had one dollar and seventy-five cents a piece to take home with us.

The leading trouble with this church was its antinomianism. The two leading spirits in the church were hyper-Calvinists. One of them had the peculiar belief that no church should have a settled pastor, and thought that no regular preacher should have a settled place of labor, but that all such should travel from place to place as circumstances would direct, and thus a church would hear new talent nearly every time it had meeting. But there was no need of a better argument against his doctrine than the condition of his own church, which was without a pastor. I would as soon think of raising a sweet family on wolf soup, as think of raising up a good church by feeding it with the doctrines of antinomianism. It is often called the "Two-Seed Doctrine," and I believe it is the right name, for if you plant it, one seed will grow up an Infidel, and the other a Universalist.

Brother More and I now went to the town of C * * *. On our arrival we stopped at a tavern, thinking that as we were tired we would get refreshment and retire to bed early; but the landlord, who was a Baptist, and had heard of our meetings, urged us to preach that night in the court-house. We told him that we did not feel able, and prayed him to excuse us. He then pleaded with us to allow him to gather a congregation in the bar-room, and have one of us preach there; but this arrangement we refused, and he left us. A short time after, as we were about going to bed, we noticed that the bar-room was being filled with people, and learned that the landlord had been spreading a notice about the town for preaching at the tavern. We saw that we could not well avoid the stratagem, and it fell to my lot to preach. The room was very warm, and crammed almost to suffocation.

While preaching, I was conscious of a strange, musty smell in the room, but I gave it no particular notice at the time, and finished my sermon as well as I could. That night it snowed heavily, and the next day we walked twenty-six miles, and finished our journey home.

My wife having fattened fourteen hogs, I took them to market, and sold them for one dollar thirty-seven and a half cents per hundred weight. The morning following I was taken very sick, and sent for a physician. When he came he said that I had the fever, and he blistered me and left medicines to stop its progress; but I grew worse. Finally, there was a strange breaking out of spots all over my body; and one who was acquainted with that loathsome disease, revealed to us the sad fact that I had the small-pox!

It appeared that I had caught it while preaching at the tavern in C * * *. The pestilence was brought there in the clothes of some of the people, and this accounted for the strange smell in the room during service. The news of my dreadful affliction ran among the neighbors like wild-fire; all took the alarm and shunned my house with fear, as though it were the plague-spot of death, and we could get no assistance. My condition was terrible. My wife had all the burden of caring for me.

So worn did she become in attending me in my helplessness that she often dropped asleep in her chair. I had never seen a case of the small-pox, and my impression of its fatality was such that as soon as I learned that I had it I despaired of life. My head became a hideous sight. It was so swollen that for two weeks my eyes were so tightly closed with the swelling that I could not distinguish daylight from darkness. There was scarcely a spot on my person where a pin's point could be placed without touching a sore. My whole body was a bloated, festering mass, disgusting to the sight and offensive to the smell. To add to our afflictions, two of our children caught the disease from me. Had it not been for the kindness of my wife's brother, who finally came to our aid, I believe we would all have died. He had not even been vaccinated, but came and waited upon us, and in every way he could ministered to our necessities, though he did it at the risk of his own life. I have since seen men braving danger on the battle-field; but I have never seen a nobler heroism than was shown by him in this instance. Nor did he suffer for his generosity, for he was permitted to pass through the exposure without taking the infection. There is much in the saying that "to the brave there is no danger."

I was confined to my bed nine weeks, but after this I was unable to move for two weeks more, only as I was helped; for my feet were longer in healing than any other parts, because the humors could not break through the thick sole-skin, or escape from under the nails of my toes; and before I could entirely recover I had to lose all my toe-nails, and about a quarter of an inch thickness of old flesh from the bottom of each foot. This might have been prevented, but the physician was not practiced in the treatment of the disease, and some of his appliances only aggravated it. In prospect of death my soul was full of bright hopes for the future, but my sufferings were so extreme that I begged for death to be sent to my relief; but God, who it appears had something more for me to do, restored me to health, contrary to every expectation. Our children were also spared; their sufferings, however, were much less than mine.

I have ever since believed that it was the small-pox with which the devil afflicted Job. His being "smitten with sore boils, from the sole of his foot unto his crown,"* his extreme misery, the loathsomeness of his person, his being forsaken by his friends, the distractions of his feelings, the length of his illness, and his scraping himself with a potsherd,† (a piece of broken earthenware,) presents as complete a description of a case of small-pox as any physician could give. When my boils were

* Job ii : 7. † Job ii : 8.

healing, and especially when the scabs we e coming off, the itching of my body at times was almost distracting. Concerning Job, "the Lord said unto Satan, behold he is in thine hand, but save his life." Satan had the privilege of afflicting him in the way which he thought the most trying, and I believe he chose the small-pox; for of all the diseases which are in the service of death it is the most horrible.

When I recovered, however, my general health was better than ever. I had formerly been troubled with the rheumatism, but the ulcerous exhalations carried off all the impurities of my system, and so rectified the fluids, that I came out from the furnace of trial like a new coin just from the mint.

When Job recovered his worldly goods were increased to "twice as much as he had before," in oxen, sheep and camels, but I was dealt with in a very different way, though, doubtless, none the less merciful; for the Maker of heaven and earth doeth all things well. My small stock of money had been paid out for necessaries in our sickness; my stock of hogs had nearly all perished for want of care; my doctor's bills had so accumulated that I sold all the cattle I had to square accounts, except one milch cow, and that cow died soon after, leaving us as poor and penniless as when we first began.

CHAPTER XXI.

LEARNING THE CARPENTERS' TRADE — LABORING AS AN EVANGELIST — THE STOOL-PIGEON — RETURN TO THE BENCH — A SHARPER, ALIAS SCHOOL-TEACHER — A COSTLY JOKE ON TWO BRETHREN — LABORS AGAIN AS AN EVANGELIST — MEETING WITH A STUPID CHURCH — WHO THE DEVIL DON'T WANT — REVIVAL AT COTTON-WOOD CREEK — BAPTISM OF AN INVALID — REMARKABLE RESULTS — REFLECTIONS.

JESUS was a carpenter; Paul was a tent-maker; Luke is supposed to have been a physician; Matthew and James the Less were tax-collectors; Peter, Andrew, John, and James the Great, were fishermen, and it is thought that the other six Apostles were also; and though farming has always been the most common employment, it is nowhere intimated that Christ, or any of the twelve Apostles, or seventy disciples, ever followed it. This is suggestive. I think that if a minister is obliged to unite other labor with his calling in order to live, there is no honest occupation which will embarrass him more than that of a farmer. By it he is more apt to be tied to his secular business and shorn of his strength. To be a mechanic, artist or physician, is better; for he will have more liberty.

I had always found it very difficult to unite the calling of a minister with the business of a farmer; and now that the small-pox had made my feet so tender that I had no hope of being able to pursue this employment again very soon, I found that some other was necessary. Thinking that the old trade of my Master would accommodate my calling as much as any other, I engaged with Brother M * * *, a Baptist minister in Missouri, to work for him one year as an apprentice to the carpenters' trade for one dollar per day and board. The brother with whom I worked was pastor of three churches, and he gave me plenty of preaching to do on Sabbaths; but we moved on happily, feeling that we were useful beings in creation, for we worked at the framing and building of the world six days in the week, and at the polishing of it on the seventh. As the winter came on, I was employed by the Wyaconda Association of Missouri to labor for three months among the churches as an evangelist. This association embraced Clark county and a part of Scotland and Lewis counties. I was to hold protracted meetings with such churches of the body as invited me, and spend the remainder of my time, if I should have any, laboring in destitute places. I was to receive twenty-five dollars per month. I gladly embraced this opportunity for usefulness, and this was the first labor I ever did in the ministry with the promise of any pay. I found it necessary to have a horse to travel among the churches, and succeeded in buying one with my claim of seventy-five dollars for labor in the Association. I then moved my family from

Iowa to Missouri, and began the good work. The Lord was with me, and in my meetings within these three months about one hundred and forty souls were converted, many backsliders were reclaimed, and one hundred and fifteen persons were baptized.

Many incidents of interest occurred during this time.

In one of my first meetings the daughter of a rich slaveholder came to the anxious seat with others, and wept and prayed for a change of heart. She was fully resolved to find salvation if there was mercy for her, and not obtaining a hope at first, she continued to go forward and bow at the anxious seat every night as long as the meeting lasted. We prayed with her and for her, and I gave her all the counsel and encouragement I possibly could, but all seemed of no avail. Many others who had kneeled in sorrow at the same time and in the same place of prayer had found peace and were rejoicing, but there seemed to be no mercy for her. She was in great despair, and nothing we could do or say seemed to show her any reason for comfort; and though she was still at the anxious seat, I was obliged to close the meetings and leave her without hope.

The next protracted meeting I held was in another part of the country, and after preaching a night or two in the new place, I invited seekers of religion forward, and to my surprise, the first one who came to the prayer-circle was this same young lady. She besought us not to forget her, but to pray on, for she felt that in her present state she would surely perish if she could not find mercy. I then renewed my exertions in her behalf, and tried to present the saving truths and gracious promises of the gospel to her mind in a new light; and as she kept coming to the anxious seat, I repeatedly tried to instruct and encourage her. She was willing to bear any cross, or obey any gospel requirement, and I could not see what was in her way. I prayed and plead for her; the people of God joined in my petitions, and she prayed for herself, but all appeared to be to no purpose whatever.

Finally, feeling that it was one of the unaccountable things in grace and past my finding out, I committed her to the mercies of God and dropped her case entirely. My mind somehow would not take any more interest in her, and as a seeker I paid her no further attention whatever. Yet the poor creature would come to the anxious seat until it perplexed me to see her there; nor did she stop until the meetings were closed.

I then began a third meeting in another place, and as I looked among the penitents who came forward, whom should I behold but the same young lady who had so long been the stool-pigeon. I wondered how she managed to follow me so closely, and found that she had a carriage and a black driver at her control, and was independent to go when and where she chose. By this means she had followed the meetings, and in the spirit of the importunate widow, she pressed her plea with a perseverance that could brook no refusal.

I took up her case again, and the thought came into my mind that there must be something yet unrevealed in her past history which would account for the fruitlessness of her search. I ventured to inquire more particularly about her former course of life.

She said that though she felt that she was a sinner, she had surely committed no overt acts of crime, but had sought to live a blameless life, and that she often prayed, and had given much thought to the subject of religion.

I asked her if she had ever really felt any delight in prayer. She replied that she had, and that when she was quite young she had often felt happy with pious reflections.

By following this channel of conversation, the fact was revealed to my satisfaction that in her early experience, at the age of ten or twelve years, she had been truly regenerated, but, for lack of gospel instruction and religious encouragement, she had neglected duty, lost confidence, and had since lived in fear, as the result. I then told her of the impossibility of a soul receiving the gift of eternal life the second time, and being born on earth the third time. I told her that her trouble was, that she had not improved the blessing God had given, and that if she would enjoy comfort and hope, she must take up the Christian's cross, and go forward openly and boldly in every religious duty. At last she grasped the truth, acted by the advice, and was blessed with abiding peace. Ever after this, as long as I knew about her, she was a faithful and happy Christian. Should this account ever be read by any friend under similar embarrassment, may it prove to him or her a blessing.

In the spring I returned to the carpenter's bench with Brother M * * *, completed the term of my apprenticeship, and worked on at the business until the next fall.

In the Baptist church at W * * *, of which my employer was pastor, were two brethren, one of whom was a deacon, and both men of considerable means. They were very much taken up with a young man who had come into town, wishing to start a high-school. He appeared like a young gentleman of high principles and superior culture, and withal was very modest in his behavior. He drove a fine horse and carriage with silver-mounted harness; and as his calling was a respectable one which promised to benefit the town, he was well received by the people generally, but more especially by these two brethren, who thought he was a young man of extraordinary promise, and became his warmest friends. He showed a marked appreciation of their good will, and spent considerable time in their company. As they were ready to help him carry out the enterprise he proposed, they built, at his request, a new addition to the already fine school-house. The young man said that he was from Kentucky, from which State he frequently received letters from his friends. He seemed to feel a great deal of concern about a suit which he had instituted in Kentucky, and which was still pending, relative to some matters of family estate, consisting chiefly of negro property, in which an interest of several thousand dollars was involved. He showed letters to his two friends occasionally, which he said were from his lawyer in Kentucky, in regard to the progress of his suit. While the school building was being erected, he began to get serious and show a deep interest in religion. He said that he liked the preacher very much, and attended the meetings regularly. Finally, to the great satisfaction of his friends, he expressed confidence of having found a good hope through grace, and requested to be baptized. A few days before his baptism was to occur he drove up to Deacon B * * * 's, and showed him a new letter from his lawyer in Kentucky, about the suit for the recovery of his negro property. Deacon B * * * read the letter, which stated that he had gained the suit, but there were three or four hundred dollars cost to pay, and that his client must send money for that purpose immediately, as he could not make a hasty sale of his negroes to a good advantage. As soon as they could be sold at a fair price, however, he would send on the proceeds.

After the deacon had read the letter, the young man told him in a modest way, that he did not happen at that time to have money enough by him to send his lawyer, and that if he would lend him one hundred and fifty dollars for a short time, it would be a great accommodation to him, and he would leave him his horse and buggy as security. Though the horse and buggy were worth more than twice that amount, the deacon told him he would not take the security; he would lend him the money without it; but his friend urged him to take them, and getting the money, he left them in his hands. He then went to Brother C * * *'s, and in the same way borrowed two hundred dollars; leaving his gold watch as security. Brother C * * * told him he did not want his watch, as he had no uneasiness about his friend's honesty; but the young man got him to take it by strong urging. Things went on again as usual. The young man told his friends that he was very thankful for their favors, and seemed quite contented.

In two or three days he went again to Deacon B * * *'s, and said he wanted to go to the town of A * * *, about ten miles distant, to solicit students for their new school, and post some notices concerning the terms and time it would open, and he wished he would lend him the horse and buggy. The deacon said that, of course, he could have it. He then drove by his equally confident friend C * * *'s, and with the same ease borrowed his gold watch. After that he started in the direction of the town of A * * *, but has never been heard of since. The brethren were so befooled that for several days they would not believe he had run away, and when, finally, they tried to search for and arrest him, no trace of their nice young man could be found, and they beheld to their loss and great mortification, that their friend, convert, school enterprise, and all the fond hopes and plans pertaining thereto, had

"Vanished in empty air!"

"Not every one that saith unto me, Lord, Lord, shall enter into the kingdom of heaven."

In the winter of 1852, I was employed again by the Wyaconda Association for three months on the same field and upon the same terms as those of the previous winter. A large portion of my time, however, was spent in laboring in destitute places. I held one meeting in a place called Wakentaugh, where I found a number of Baptists from Tennessee, who, I think, were a little the coarsest and most ignorant of our brethren I ever fell among. It was a place of great spiritual poverty, and there were just enough such brethren there to show the utter destitution of that poverty. I could not get them to do anything or say anything. After several nights of vain effort, I resolved to set the plow deeper and prepare for it. We had been troubled every night for want of lights, and when night came again, there was a full congregation, but there was not a candle in the house, and we were all in such darkness that we could not tell the negroes from the white folks. I apologized to the congregation, and told them I hoped we would soon have light, and requested that some brother would go immediately and get some candles. As no one moved I urged again, but still no one wanted to go. I then gave them some pretty plain talk, rebuking them for their neglect. At this, a brother who seemed to think he knew what ought to be done, spoke out and said, "Jest git some bark and put it in that are stove, and throw open the door and it will give light a plenty. That's the way we used to do down in Tennessee, and we used to have glorious times; fact is I can't see the use in a preacher havin to have a half a dozen candles to preach by anyhow, and if Ise you, I'de jest put in some bark an go on with the preachin."

I remarked that that would never do, because it would not give light enough to see across the room, and that besides it would smoke us out of the house in the bargain. Said I, "Can it be possible that there is no one here who will go and get some candles?"

At this, another brother spoke out, and said: "I keen't, for I haint got none at hum." Two or three others then spoke to the same effect and showed considerable tartness toward me, for they felt hurt because I pressed them so hard. The fact was clear that they were too mean and stingy to afford candles for the services, and after blowing them up right well, I cut everything short in righteousness, dismissed the meeting and cleared out. What will ever become of them I don't know. It is certain that unless they have mended their ways, God will not own them, and they are of so little account that the devil don't want them; but such is a specimen of much of the society, or "white trash," that is raised under the accursed influences of slavery.

During the winter I held a meeting on Cottonwood Creek, which resulted in a large revival and the organization of a Baptist church. A brother and sister W * * *, who resided there had a consumptive daughter, who became interested in religion during the meeting, but was unable to attend. After I closed the protracted effort there I went to other places, and having heard no more of the young lady for some time, by reason of the many acquaintances I was continually forming, the rememberance of her had almost passed from my mind; but in the latter part of March following I was sent for, by her request, to go on purpose to see her.

She sent me word that she was in the last stage of her disease, and that as she expected to die soon she was very anxious to see me before she left the world. The greatest reason why she wished me to visit her, was that she wanted to be baptized, because she believed that since the meeting I had held near her father's, God had forgiven her sins and that it was her duty thus to obey Him, and as the Saviour said, "Fulfill all righteousness."

When I went, her parents told me that she had often talked about being baptized, and wished them to send for me to administer the ordinançe, but they had repeatedly refused, because she was so very feeble they feared it would kill her. They had tried to dissuade her from it, but all in vain; they said that she would not be refused, but had begged and pleaded until they were wearied with hearing her, and they had felt compelled to send for me.

They had hoped, however, that when I came I might be able to satisfy her mind that baptism in her case was unnecessary; but in this they were disappointed. When I went to her room she was overjoyed at seeing me, and said she could not tell how glad she was that I had come. She then told me what great things the Lord had done for her soul, and repeated her request to be baptized. I inquired carefully of her in regard to her religious experience, and was well satisfied that she had truly become a subject of grace; but told her that the Lord did not ask impossibilities, and that in her present condition of body he certainly did not require her to be baptized; the Lord asks according to what a man hath, and not according to what he hath not. "Besides," said I, "if I should baptize you now, it might hasten your death and lay me liable. If such a thing should occur, the enemies of religion would use it to embarrass my ministry, and it might cripple my usefulness for life." Though she offered answers to all my objections, I felt that I certainly could not baptize her, for I feared she could not survive the shock. She had been confined to her bed a number of weeks, was a mere helpless skeleton and so weak that it was with much weariness that she conversed with me; but she kept pleading for baptism with such an intensity of desire, that I held a council with her parents and friends to consider thoughtfully what should be done. All felt satisfied that she would soon die at best, and finally decided, her parents in particular, that they would prefer to run the risk of having her baptized than that of her continual worrying and ultimately dying unsatisfied; and they agreed that she should be baptized the next day, if alive.

We then employed a carpenter to make a large box of sufficient size for the baptistry, and notified the neighbors that there would be preaching in the sick-room the next day. The invalid heard of these arrangements with the greatest satisfaction and rested quietly with her mind at ease awaiting the hour.

The next day she enjoyed the sermon very much. A watery grave had been prepared during the service within a few feet of her bedside—it was a solemn scene. After the dedicatory prayer, six brethren, three on each side, lifted her from her bed by the sheet on which she was lying and held her over the water. I supported her head with one hand while I repeated the ceremony, and when it ended with the solemn "Amen," she was buried in the water, and raised again. When she was laid upon the bed she showed no alarming symptoms whatever, and when her garments had been changed a few moments after, she said that she felt better than she had before for some time. To the glad surprise of all her friends, she really began to recover, and by degrees finally regained her former strength and spirits.

The last I heard of her she was still living, enjoying tolerable health, was the mother of three children, and I suppose she will read this book.

As I have already offered some reflections on the subject of baptism, I will say but little here. This is simply a fact presented which may be attested by living witnesses; and on the controversy, as to whether the apostolic baptism endangers health or not, the reader may apply it for himself.

It is certain, however, that some of our most noted physicians refuse to treat many chronic diseases unless the patient will submit to an occasional cold bath; and I believe that there are many timid, nervous people, who have been scared about the old-fashioned baptism, who would have better health if they were immersed in cold water once every week.

CHAPTER XXII.

BECOMES A MERCHANT—REPORTED AS AN ABOLITIONIST—FAILS IN BUSINESS—REMOVES THE STORE TO IOWA—PROSPERITY—BOATING—RAILROAD ENTERPRISE—FINANCIAL RUIN—THE DEACON'S WISH—ADVICE TO MINISTERS—REMOVES TO CHARLESTON—MEETING AT NEW BOSTON—PERPLEXITY WITH TWO MOCKERS—WHAT BECAME OF THEM—METHODIST LADY BAPTIZED BY MISTAKE—EFFECTS OF READING THE BIBLE BY TWO LADIES—INTERESTING CONVERSION OF MR. R * * *,—A REVIVAL MEETING IN KEOKUK—RETURN HOME.

In the spring I returned again to my jack-plane, but had not worked long when new prospects opened. A Baptist brother by the name of C * * *, who was an old acquaintance, came to the town of W * * * to set up a store and proposed to accept me as a partner. By selling my horse I managed to raise one hundred dollars. I then borrowed nine hundred dollars of my partner, and we commenced business with a stock of two thousand dollars between us.

This was getting all my eggs into one basket; but, thought I, "Nothing risked, nothing gained," and hoping for the best, we stuck out our shingle.

At first, things looked hopeful, but it was soon noised about by our rivals in trade that our firm were Abolitionists. This was thought to be a horrible story, and we soon felt its effects on our business. We undersold the other merchants, but to no purpose, the patronage was carefully withheld from us; and after a fruitless trial of about nine months we abandoned the place.

We then moved our store to the town of C * * *, on the Des Moines river, and increased the stock two thousand dollars more, which was done chiefly on credit.

Here our custom increased, and we prospered finely. At length we connected the grain trade with our store-keeping. We bought the grain, loaded it in keel-boats, and ran it down the Des Moines, where we sold it at a good profit. Our business became quite extensive, and we made money fast. I had not ceased to preach on the Sabbaths in the mean time, and enjoyed life pretty well, though my mind was evidently too much engaged in secular plans.

Finally we took a contract to get out and deliver a large quantity of railroad-ties, for building the Warsaw and Rockford Railroad, in Illinois. We employed a large number of hands to work on the job, and paid them in money and store goods.

We were to receive our dues from the company every month. They made several failures to pay us, but the company was thought to be perfectly reliable, and we were so confident of its solvency that we went on with the work. We rafted the ties down the Des Moines, towed them across the Mississippi by steam, banked them all on the Illinois shore above high water mark, and thus completed the whole contract before we stopped.

Here we made a dreadful mistake in putting all our eggs in one basket—nearly our whole capital was consumed in filling the contract, and the railroad company, after making many fair promises, burst up and left us in financial ruin!

We then went out of business, and, after settling all claims against the firm, and dividing what was left of our hapless fortune, the cash balance in my favor was only three dollars and fifty cents! About eighteen hundred dollars in old book accounts fell to my share, but of that I never collected more than fifty.

Before this misfortune I was in good circumstances and prospectively rich; but thus did our riches "make themselves wings"* and fly away, leaving us to the dreary comforts of disappointment, and the sober fellowship of our own reflections.

Says the Saviour, "Take heed and beware of riches, for a man's life consisteth not in the abundance of the things which he possesseth."

While a merchant I was pastor of two small churches, but was not expected to do much for them except to preach on the Sabbath, and it was my impression that the Lord was not pleased to have my mind so much occupied in worldly pursuits.

A good deacon of my acquaintance once said to his pastor, "I have often thought, elder, that if I had a million of dollars I would do a great amount

* Prov. xxiii: 5.

of good with it, in building churches, supporting missionaries and Sabbath schools, and the like. It grieves me that I have so little to give for the cause of religion."

The pastor remarked that the Lord knew his heart, and he believed that if his deacon would really have made such a use of that amount of money he would have been allowed to use it.

"Ah! that's the rub," said the deacon; "*I'm afraid the good Lord knows me too well to trust me.*"

Like the deacon, I thought I would do generous things for the cause, if the Lord would grant me the capital, but I suppose for the same reason he did not, because *he knew me too well to trust me.*

I warn ministers against making too large calculations on obtaining worldly wealth, for it is a fact that the Lord is not often willing to trust them with much money—he knows them too well.

The sons of Levi had no possessions among their brethren; they were so well fed and supported in their holy office that they did not need them;* their office was their riches, and God designs that their office shall be their riches still.† Also, "they which ministered about holy things, lived of the things of the temple;" and God often shows us, by providences such as I have related, as well as by his word, that ministers have no business in secular pursuits, but that their office should be their sufficient wealth, as "they who preach the gospel‡ should live of the

* Num. xviii: 21. † Matt. x: 9.

‡ 1 Cor. ix: 11—14.

gospel, and give their whole time and all their talents to the work.*

I now moved to Charleston, Iowa, and rented a house, paying $2.50, the first month's rent, in advance. I commenced preaching to the people and working at my trade. Moderate prosperity attended me. Through my trade I bought the house I had rented, and when I had lived in it for a year I sold it for double what it cost. But even here I was too thoughtful of the world, and had much coldness of soul, which was manifest in my preaching through the summer.

In the winter following, I held a meeting at New Boston, three miles from Charleston.

On the second night of the meeting, after nine persons had been received for baptism, two young men came up, requesting to be baptized on the following Sabbath. I asked them to tell their experience, but they would not even make any attempt. We tried to ascertain their feelings by asking them questions, but they did not make any replies. I thought it strange. Their cases were deferred, and a committee was appointed to wait upon them, obtain more satisfaction, and report to the church.

We hoped that they were children of God, though they seemed to be dumb ones, and I required of the brethren to find some better evidence of their conversion before they were baptized; but that night one of the most severe snow storms occurred that I ever knew. On Sabbath morning it was bitterly

* 1 Tim. iv: 15.

cold; the snow in places covered the tops of the fences, and when I attempted to get to the place of worship, I floundered along in the snow for about three hundred yards, but the cold was so intense I was obliged to return, almost perished. This put a stop to our meetings; and as the weather continued severe they were not renewed, and some of the converts were not baptized until spring. It was afterward found that those two young men who had requested to be baptized on the following Sabbath, were hypocrites, who had been hired by a certain man to feign religion, and attempt what they did. They might have gone so far as to have been baptized, but Providence prevented it. It was a bold, God-insulting mockery, and they doubtless chuckled over it among their wicked companions; but what was the sequel? It is one which ought to be a warning to all mockers. The next summer one of those young men suddenly took the cholera while at the plow-handles, dropped down in his furrow, and was soon a corpse! The other was put in the penitentiary for the commission of crime! Let the wicked beware! God is not to be mocked with impunity; for he has declared that the way of the transgressor is hard.* Those mockers both probably perished in their sins; so true it is that they who sow to the wind shall reap the whirlwind, and the hard-hearted and stiff-necked "shall suddenly be destroyed, and that without remedy."†

The same winter I was requested to hold a protracted meeting in Tuscarora, in Lee county, Iowa.

* Prov. xiii : 15 † Prov. xxix : 1.

It was a field which had been held for some time by the Methodists and Presbyterians; but their efforts had not been successful, and a couple of Baptist familes having moved into the place, they wished the Baptists to make an effort also.

We made the effort and enjoyed a glorious revival season. It resulted in the organization of a Baptist church of about fifty members, and some accessions to the other churches.

An incident occurred in connection with this meeting which was rather odd. A lady living in the vicinity, who belonged to the Methodist church, sent a messenger to me saying, that having been sprinkled she was not contented, and that she wished to be baptized. This was no unusual occurrence, but the oddity was that she wished to receive the ordinance at my hands and still remain in the Methodist church. The Baptist church was the church of her choice, but her parents were opposed to her joining it; and she wished to remain with the Methodists until such time as she could unite with us with less opposition. I sent her word that I had no jurisdiction over the members of the Methodist church, and had no right to molest them, and furthermore, that she would violate her church rules and make herself liable to discipline by taking such a step, and I would not baptize her. I heard no more from her for some time; but a few days after this I baptized a considerable number of converts. I knew how many were expected to be baptized, but having a very short acquaintance with the converts, and being very happy in singing and talking, I did not take particular notice, and baptized every one who stepped forth.

When the baptism was over, I got into a wagon, which was already well-loaded, to ride from the water; but I had not been in long until the laughing and talking of some of the passengers, in a sly way, gave me a hint that something odd had happened, and I inquired what it was, when they told me, to my surprise, that I had baptized that Methodist lady! I felt embarrassed about the matter, and went immediately to see her. It appeared that what led her to take the course she did, was her great anxiety, and this was her only apology. I then told her that as we held baptism to be the initiatory rite into the church, it followed that she had, by her own act in the step she had taken, come into the church, and that we were obliged to regard her as a member until her dismission, exclusion, or death. I told her, also, that as she only was responsible, she must take her own choice of the chances. But still, instead of regretting what she had done, she was tremendously pleased to find that she was a Baptist, and thus the matter was settled; she remained in the church, and made a good member.

I believe that I have already said that I have baptized as many as fifty-seven in one year, who had been sprinkled or poured, and so I have been baptizing more or less of those every year of my ministry. I might give many incidents concerning such cases. I will here relate one which just now occurs to me as I learned it from a Baptist minister of my acquaintance, and which shows the effect of studying the Scriptures on doctrine; and as it is not so long as the history of Theodosia, I deem it worth a place here. The incident occurred not long since under the brother's ministry, in a certain town in Illinois.

There was a Mrs. R * * *, an intelligent lady who had been sprinkled in infancy, and though she did profess to be a Christian, she had been raised, under Congregationalist influences, to look upon her infant baptism as a most sacred thing. While stopping with a Methodist lady in town, she attended a series of Baptist meetings, and was induced to give her heart fully to the Lord. She greatly loved those who had been instrumental in her salvation; but said to the minister, when he afterwards called at the house in which she was stopping, that however much she esteemed the Baptist people, she did not see how she could unite with them, as they would require her to be immersed, and she could not consent to that, because, in the first place, it was mid-winter, the river was filled with ice, and she felt that she could not endure the trial; she thought her constitution was not strong enough to bear the shock of the cold water; but this was not all. The most serious objection was, that if she should be immersed it would be treating her infant baptism with contempt; this she could not think of doing, as she held it as most sacred and binding. The minister then asked her if she was not willing to do anything which she was persuaded that the Lord required of her. "Yes, sir," said she, "I hope I would be willing, if necessary, to die at the stake."

He then asked her if she had ever searched the Word of God carefully, to ascertain whether he required her to hold to her infant sprinkling or not, and whether he did not really require her to be baptized. "I have not searched it closely," she replied; "for I have always been well enough satisfied without it; but I think, though, that I can find abundance of proof of my baptism in the Scriptures." The minister then told her that he would present no argument whatever, but that he wished her to give all her spare time for the next two days, in searching the Scriptures on the subject, and that if she found any passages which sanctioned infant sprinkling, or sprinkling of adults, for baptism, she would mark them down on paper, for as he would call again at the end of that time, he would like to see them. He also remarked that as her friend, the lady of the house, had been a Methodist for twenty years and had been sprinkled, she no doubt believed in it, and would aid her in finding the passages. This the Methodist lady consented to do; and expressing the hope that Sister R* * * would obey whatever the Scriptures taught her, the minister took his leave.

Mrs. R* * * was quite awakened to the subject, and searched the Scriptures diligently; and as the Methodist lady was a little piqued at the remarks of the minister, she searched very carefully, also, for the purpose of aiding her boarder to find infant sprinkling; and for two days they gave the Bible such close attention as they had scarcely ever done before. The result was that both of them were surprised and disappointed.

When the minister called again and wished to know the results of their study, Mrs. R * * *, with a hopeless look, pointed him to the passage which speaks of Christ blessing little children, and the baptism of the households of Lydia and the Philippian Jailer; but as she confessed that they afforded no real proof, there was little to be said. A brief outline of the Baptist views on Bible doctrine was then presented to her, in the hearing of the Methodist lady, and a list of scriptural references left, with the request that Mrs. R * * * would look them out, read them thoughtfully, and act so far as her conscience, enlightened by the Bible, should dictate.

A few evenings after this, as candidates were being received for baptism, Mrs. R * * * and the Methodist lady both came up, related their Christian experience, spoke of their confidence in Baptist doctrines, and on the following Sabbath were both immersed in the Mississippi river, while the ice was floating around them; nor did they show the slightest alarm in receiving the ordinance, but declared immediately after it was over, that they never felt better in all their lives, either in soul or body. Ever since then they have been respectable members in the Baptist church.

While I was pastor of the church in Charleston, in the year 1856, one of our deacons, who lived near the meeting-house, sold out his farm to Mr. R * * *, whose family consisted of himself and wife, and five or six children, who were old enough to attend to religion. Neither Mr. R * * * nor any of his family were professors, though they were very respectable people. The wife and one of the daughters, after they had been there a short time, became concerned for their souls, and one day they were induced to attend our covenant meeting. At that meeting the power of God was manifest; they sought religion, became hopefully converted, and before they left the house were both received for baptism.

The husband, who in the mean time was in the field sowing buckwheat, observed that the meeting was lengthy, and felt a presentiment that his wife and daughter were acting some part in it, and it gave him great uneasiness. As soon as meeting was out, he went home and asked his wife in regard to it. She then told him what she and the daughter had done. As soon as he heard this he was very much provoked, nor could his feelings be pacified. He knew well enough that they had done right, and yet he hated it with all his heart, and he became so unhappy over the matter that he tried to sell his farm, that he might move out of the country; but he did not succeed, and thus the matter ran on until the next winter. We then commenced a protracted meeting. To this Mr. R * * * came a few times, but it became too hot to suit him, and he grew very much displeased with it, as it revived his troubles of mind, and getting up his team he went off to a mill, a distance of twenty miles, and remained away a considerable time, visiting with some friends and trying to sell his farm. He became so anxious to move out of the country that he put down the price of his farm to a very low figure, and tried hard to sell it; but as he could not find a purchaser, he returned, after an absence of several days, hoping that at least the meeting would be closed; but on getting home he found, to his surprise, that it was yet in full blast, and what was more annoying still, nearly all his family had joined the church!

Being prevailed upon to attend meeting that night, he went, and tried to get into a back seat; but the devil had all the back seats occupied, and the poor man was pressed up pretty well forward into the warm atmosphere, where he was obliged to receive the full force of the sermon, without any whisperers around him to prevent it. When, finally, the sermon was ended and the invitation given, he rushed to the anxious-seat, exclaining, "I can't stand it any longer!"

He was afterward converted, and proved to be an excellent Christian. In a short time he was chosen to the deacon's office, to fill the old deacon's place, which post he has filled with usefulness to the cause, and dignity and honor to himself. This meeting lasted about six weeks, and many of the leading citizens were brought into the church, who remain there to the present.

It is truly wonderful how the Lord, by his providences, often overrules the plans of men for their own good and his glory, and it is no less surprising how men of natural hearts will try to run from their highest interests.

One dear brother, who belonged to a church in Illinois where I held a meeting, and who was one of the main supports of the church, sold out his possessions and started to Oregon; but he had not gone far on his journey, when sickness and other hindrances combined, compelled him to turn aside and make his home, for the time, in Iowa.

It was so ordered that the community in which he stopped was one in which there was no church or religious interest. He began a little prayer-meeting, invited the neighbors in, and prayed for them and talked to them the best he could; and after he had continued these efforts for some time, a revival began among them.

He then procured the assistance of a minister, who united with him in his efforts, and in a very short time they had a church in the vicinity which numbered over a hundred souls!

In the spring of 1857, some brethren who wished to maintain a mission interest in the city of Keokuk, about three-fourths of a mile from the First Baptist Church in that place, sent for me to hold a meeting at that point. I was so much engaged with cares at the time that I thought I could not go, and refused; but in about two weeks after this they came for me, bringing a carriage to take me down, and declared that they could not return without me.

Their request was so urgent that it could not well be refused, and I went with them. We began meetings in a private house, as it was the only available place, and the Lord soon gave us souls for our hire; but after we had preached a few evenings, the crowd which would come could not get into the house, and as some eighteen or twenty souls had already experienced hope, who had been gathered in by the meeting, the brethren thought that the interest demanded the organization of a church at that point, that we might work with more efficiency, and make better arrangements for the up-building of the cause. Keokuk was a growing city, and as it contained but one Baptist church, it was thought that another was needed in a different part of the place; but to this plan a strong opposition arose from a certain quarter which was unlooked for, and threw us into perplexity.

The source of this opposition, or its character, I need not mention, but suffice it to say that it defeated the plan for that time, and so discouraged our efforts that we ceased them, and I went home.

CHAPTER XXIII.

RETURN TO KEOKUK — A CHURCH ORGANIZED — ELECTED PASTOR — INTERESTING PRAYER-MEETINGS — "BRIMSTONE CORNER"—GREAT PROSPERITY—BAPTIST COUNCIL — PERSECUTION — STRUGGLES — SCRAPS OF HISTORY CONCERNING BAPTISTS — DEFENCE OF THREE MINISTERS BY PATRICK HENRY, AND HIS ELOQUENT SPEECH — REFERENCES — A NEWSPAPER ARTICLE.

In a few weeks from the time I left Keokuk the brethren sent for me again. They had resolved to go forward with the interest at all hazards, and had rented a hall in which to hold meetings that would seat three or four hundred hearers. We then renewed the attack on Satan's kingdom, and held a series of meetings in the hall which lasted about five weeks.

The Lord was pleased to hear the prayers of our little company, and set down the right foot of his power, and before the meeting closed we had baptized eighty-five converts. These converts, with the few other brethren, then organized themselves into a church. The newly organized body then elected me pastor. I did not wish to take the post, but the brethren would not hear a refusal; and as Providence seemed to point out my duty in that direction,

I moved my family into the city, and was installed bishop of the new church.

During the first year we received fifteen or twenty accessions more, and enjoyed a high degree of spirituality and prosperity.

The most marked feature of the church at this period was its large and interesting prayer-meetings. As the members were nearly all new beginners in religion, I gave particular attention to the prayer-meeting interest, and tried to get every one to attend regularly, and pray and talk as much as possible. We felt that they were the hope of the church, and tried to leave nothing undone that could be done to make them profitable and interesting.

These meetings were so lively and varied in their exercises that they became a popular place of resort for the careless on Sabbath nights, and the prayers and exhortations were so often full of warmth and fire, that the wags gave to our place of worship the name of "Brimstone Corner." The name, however, did us no harm; it only made the place the more noted and popular.

"Where are you going to-night, Lemons?" one would ask as he would halloo across the street to an acquaintance.

"I don't know," would be the reply, perhaps.

"Let's go down to Brimstone Corner, to prayer-meeting."

"Agreed," would be the answer, and off they would go the prayer-meeting of the Second Baptist Church.

Thus scores came in to hear and to see who, it was true, cared little for religion, but some who came only to see and to hear went away to pray and to weep, while the members greatly grew in grace and waxed bold in the faith.

A strong attachment grew up within me for my brethren, and I took such delight in laboring among them, that although I had commonly thought that my most useful sphere was that of an evangelist, I felt so much encouraged as to the prospects of building up a strong and useful church, that when they elected me pastor for the second year, with the generous promise of $1,000, I continued with them. During the next winter we prospered greatly. I held a great many night meetings, and we were permitted to visit the river and baptize every Sabbath, for eleven Sabbaths in succession. When the second year closed, the membership of the church numbered two hundred souls. In the mean time we had bought a good lot in the city, and got part of the materials on the ground for building a good house of worship. Though all this was done, under God, in the short space of two years, it is the more surprising that it was done in the midst of the most determined sectarian opposition. Every inch of the ground we gained was hotly disputed.

While I was laboring in Keokuk the First Baptist Church had an unfortunate difficulty with a heterodox minister, by which means it was badly perplexed; and after much embarrassment about the matter, it finally called a council. This council, which was a large one, and of which the Rev. N. Colver, D. D., was chairman, was composed of much of the first talent of the West. As the minister in question was non-fellowshiped, as such, by the council, for unsoundness in doctrine and practice, and also dismissed by the church, the opponents of our doctrines in the city, who had been wonderfully pleased at the manner in which the said minister, who was very popular with them, had been setting aside the old Baptist land-marks, claimed to have a strong sympathy for him, and were loud in their denunciations against the proceedings of the church and the council. We felt sorry that there was a necessity for his dismissal, but it could not be helped. It was truly urged by way of apology, that no denomination would be willing to sustain and nurse a minister to destroy its own doctrines; but this apology was not heeded, and when the council dispersed, it left us behind with the bear to fight. The Pedoes presented their charges against the Baptists with earnest declamations, and "piled them on and rubbed them in." The attacks upon us were so simultaneous, that it seemed that they were going to take us by storm. They fondled the man as long as they could use his case to create public prejudice against the Baptists; but when their new harp was spoiled and became useless, they forgot their sympathy and dropped him in the mud, which doubtless disappointed and mortified him more than anything the Baptists ever did.

While going up a street one day, I was met by a certain Pedobaptist elder, who opened his batteries upon me in a style about as follows:

"Good morning, Pickard."

"Good morning," said I.

"Pickard, that Baptist council you had here was a dreadful concern. The man who was chairman was the most corrupt and bigoted man I ever saw. In fact I consider that the whole body was a corrupt mess. Such persecution as they showed in their deliberations and decisions haven't a parallel in modern history."

"My dear sir," said I, "it must be then that you have not read modern history very closely; for if you had you would have read of some persecutions, with which these imaginary ones you speak of will bear no comparison."

"If modern history," said he, "gives any record of more bigoted religious intolerance, I would like to know it."

"Well, sir," said I, "as to the case of this minister, we have simply expressed our views of doctrine and practice, and have withdrawn ourselves from him, as the New Testament requires we should do, from all those who walk disorderly.* We have thereby merely sought to disabuse ourselves without abusing him, and have left him free to enjoy his own opinions, and unite with some other Christian body which will be more in harmony with his views; but, sir, history informs us that your Pedobaptist fathers have locked the Baptists from their places of worship, and forbidden them to enter at their peril. They have forbidden Baptist ministers to preach. They have banished them from the country. They

* 2 Thes. iii : 6.

have whipped them at the whipping-post. And *all this has been done on American soil, mostly within two hundred years!* But, sir, let me tell you what all this was for: It was simply for '*denying infant baptism, and the use of secular force in religious affairs!*' "*

This was turning the tables wonderfully, and the brother came very near collapsing. He flew into a splutter, declared he did not believe a word of it, and left me with his feelings very much riled.

As we received frequent assaults, more or less of this character, in public and private, which I thought were prejudicial to the Baptist cause, I resolved to stir up their pure minds by way of remembrance, and to this end preached a sermon according to previous announcement to a large audience, on Baptist history. My object was, inasmuch as the subject of religious bigotry had created considerable interest of late in the Gate City, to unmask it when and where it could be found, and show what it was, and whom it most concerned. In the discourse I related and read numerous historical facts, by which I showed that the Baptists, instead of being such intolerant bigots as some would like to make them appear, had from the beginning of American history and before, always insisted on liberty of conscience in all matters of religion, to all mankind; and that in our early struggles for deliverance from national thraldom, their views and ideas were the very vanguards of liberty; † and that instead of their having been oppressors of other sects, they had suffered the

* Backus.

† "Baptist Denomination," p. 333.

most bitter persecutions from other sects on account of their doctrines. As I think that two or three of those historical quotations may benefit the reader and enrich my book, I will here give them.

PERSECUTION OF OBADIAH HOLMES, IN BOSTON.

"Let us roll back the dial of the world to the month of September, in the year 1651, and place ourselves in imagination in one of the streets of old Boston town. See! there is a crowd passing along toward the place of public punishment and disgrace. In their midst is a man, bound and handled by the rude officers of the law as a criminal; but showing in his meek upturned countenance no tokens of guilt, and uttering with his lips the language of Christian exhortation and prayer. Who is he? What is his name? And what is the crime with which he is charged?

"He is a minister of the Lord Jesus Christ, a Baptist minister. His name is Obadiah Holmes, and his crime is, that he has dared to preach the same gospel and administer the same ordinances as those which have been maintained on the same spot by the beloved and venerated Stillman, and Baldwin, and Sharp, in succession, now for more than three quarters of a century. But see! his clothes are rudely torn from his person by the coarse and brutal executioner, and this minister of Christ is tied securely to the whipping-post. Hark! he speaks. 'Good people all, I am now about to be baptized in afflictions, that so I may have fellowship with my

Lord; and am not ashamed of His sufferings, for by His stripes I am healed.'

"His voice is silenced for a moment by the cruel thongs of the 'three-corded whip,' dashing the crimson gore from the quivering flesh of the man of God; and again he cries aloud, 'Though my flesh should fail, and my spirit should fail, yet God would not fail me!' 'And so,' to use the language of the meek sufferer, in relating this cruel scene to his brethren in England, 'it pleased the Lord to come in, and to fill my heart and tongue as a vessel full, and with an audible voice I broke forth praying to the Lord not to lay this sin to their charge, and telling the people that now I found God did not fail me, therefore I should trust him forever. For, in truth, as the strokes fell upon me, I had such a spiritual manifestation of God's presence as I never had before; and the outward pain was so removed from me, that I could well bear it; yea, and in a manner felt it not; although it was grievous, as the spectators said, the man striking with all his strength, spitting in his hands three times, with a three-corded whip, giving me therewith thirty strokes.'

"A few days later, and that meek sufferer, bruised and wounded so that for weeks he could only rest on his hands and knees, might have been seen stealthily threading his way through the forest wilderness between Boston and Providence, to escape the constable, who, with a second warrant, was hunting again for his prey; and as he drew near to the

Rhode Island asylum of freedom,* the voice of thanksgiving and songs of praise might have been heard 'for miles in the woods,' where pioneers of soul-liberty had gone to meet their suffering brother, to thank God for his deliverance, and to pour oil into his wounds.

"'It may serve as an index to the prevailing opinions, even in New England, two centuries ago, to mention that when this act of cruel persecution was severely rebuked in a letter from Sir Richard Saltonstall, in England, the Rev. John Cotton, author of the reply to Williams, entitled 'The Bloody Servant washed and made white in the Blood of the Lamb,' boldly justified and defended the whipping of Holmes, and the right of the magistrate to persecute, by the flimsy sophism that 'if the worship be lawful in itself, the magistrate compelling a man to it compelleth him to sin, but the sin is in the man's will that needs to be compelled;' and at that time *not a minister in New England could be found, with the exception of the Baptists of Rhode Island, to dissent from the views of Mr. Cotton, or to speak a word in favor of freedom to worship God!*"

PERSECUTION OF A BAPTIST CHURCH IN BOSTON.

"On the 28th of May, 1665, Thomas Gould, a member of a Pedobaptist church in Charlestown, Richard Goodall, a member of a Baptist church in London, and seven other humble disciples, after

* The Baptist Settlement of Roger Williams.

wading through a sea of persecution, formed themselves into the First Baptist Church of Boston. Fifteen years later, on the 8th of March, 1680, the doors of their humble sanctuary were nailed up by the marshal, and a notice posted thereon, warning 'all persons' against holding any meetings or opening the doors, 'as they will answer the contrary at their peril.' And the little despised band were compelled to meet to worship God under a temporary covering in the yard of their meeting-house.

"But soon a brighter day begins to dawn. Every experiment has only proved the utter folly of attempting to control the conscience by coercive means. The sun of soul-liberty, shining so brightly over the neighboring colony of Rhode Island, sends its rays beyond the limits of the noble little State; and at length light bursts into the minds of the ministers of Boston, and they begin to look with a more favorable eye upon the little company of Baptists in their midst, who have so long and so nobly struggled for 'freedom to worship God.' The march of freedom is onward, still onward, and the doctrine of Roger Williams (the Baptist apostle of 'soul-liberty,' or 'liberty of conscience,') is at last triumphant."

I might just add to the above, that a Baptist minister is now preaching regularly in the city of Boston, whose pulpit is on the very spot of ground where his brethren, for preaching the same doctrines he is now preaching, were so shamefully scourged at the whipping post!

The Baptists have continued as the firm, unflinching, undeviating advocates for perfect liberty of conscience to all the family of man. Thank God! we live to see this glorious principle triumphant in America. May our children live to see it triumphant throughout the world!

I will give yet one more quotation:

THE SUFFERINGS OF BAPTISTS IN VIRGINIA—DEFENCE OF THREE BAPTIST MINISTERS BY PATRICK HENRY.

"Numerous instances of persecution for conscience's sake occurred in different parts of the United States, from the time of Williams' sufferings onward to the Declaration of Independence, July 4th, 1776. In Virginia, as late as 1768–75, Baptists suffered from Episcopal persecutions. Preaching contrary to law was construed into a breach of the peace, and devoted ministers were incarcerated in common with the vilest men. June 4th, 1768, three men were arraigned as disturbers of the peace; and the prosecuting attorney brought this charge against them: 'May it please your worship, these men are great disturbers of the peace; they cannot meet a man on the road, but they must ram a text of Scripture down his throat.'"

The following instance of persecution seems to have been one of the last struggles of the demon, just before the Declaration of Independence. The facts were published by John M. Peck, in the *Baptist Memorial*, in 1845:

"Go back to the period just prior to the Declaration of Independence. Imagine yourself in the old court-house at Fredericksburg, Spottsylvania county,

Virginia. The king's judges are upon the bench, in great dignity, and the king's attorney is present to aid in dealing justice to all offenders. Numerous are the spectators on the present occasion, for three ministers are to be tried for no other offence than—'*preaching the gospel of the Son of God,*' contrary to the statute in that case provided, and consequently disturbers of the peace. The thunders which soon reverberated in the revolution had begun their mutterings, and many were the brave hearts in that audience indignant at what was transpiring, and at the impending fate of those inoffensive men, which apparently nothing could avert. But whilst the portentous preparations are going on within the court-house, a plain man dismounts his horse at the door. This was Patrick Henry, beginning to be known as a talented, patriotic lawyer. He had heard of this approaching trial, and, true to his noble principles, unsolicited he had ridden fifty or sixty miles from his residence in Hanover county, to volunteer his services in defence of these prisoners. No one can tell the feelings which agitated his noble heart at that time. What might seem to the common observer of little consequence, the punishment of three unimportant men, to him was freighted with moment, as embracing the principles of the revolution.

"As Henry entered the court-room, unknown to most present, and attracting no attention, the clerk was reading the indictment, in a slow, formal manner, in harmony with the august court assembled. He pronounced the crime with emphasis—'*for preaching the gospel of the Son of God.*' The reading of the indictment finished, the prosecuting attorney submitted a few words, all he thought necessary to convict the prisoners, and all which would have been necessary under ordinary circumstances. The judges were about to pronounce the ordinary verdict of condemnation, when Henry, who had entered the bar among the lawyers, arose, stretched out his hand, and received the paper. The first sentence of the indictment, which was being read as he entered, and had fallen upon his ear, was—'*for preaching the gospel of the Son of God!*' This was his key note. He commenced:

"'May it please your worships: I think I heard read as I entered this house, the paper I now hold in my hand. If I have rightly understood, the king's attorney of this county has framed an indictment for the purpose of arraigning and punishing by imprisonment three inoffensive persons, before the bar of this court, for a crime of great magnitude, as disturbers of the peace. May it please the court, what did I hear read? Did I hear it distinctly, or was it a mistake of my own? Did I hear an expression, as if a crime, that these men, whom your worships are about to try for a misdemeanor, are charged with—what?' and continuing in a low, solemn, heavy tone, '*for preaching the gospel of the Son of God!* Pausing amid the most profound silence and breathless astonishment of his hearers, he slowly waved the paper three times around his head, then lifting up his hands and eyes to heaven, with extraordinary and impressive energy he exclaimed, 'Great God!' The exclamation—the action—the burst of feeling from the audience, were all overpowering. Mr. Henry resumed:

"'May it please your worships: In a day like this, when Truth is about to burst her fetters—when mankind are about to be raised to claim their natural and inalienable rights—when the yoke of oppression which has reached the wilderness of America, and the unnatural alliance of ecclesiastical and civil power is about to be dissevered—at such a period, when liberty, liberty of conscience, is about to awake from her slumberings, and inquire into the reason of such charges as I find exhibited here to-day in this indictment! * * '

"Another fearful pause; while the speaker alternately cast his sharp, piercing eyes upon the court and the prisoners, and resumed:

"'If I am not deceived, according to the contents of the paper which I hold in my hand, these men are accused of '*preaching the gospel of the Son of God!' Great God!'*

"Another long pause, during which he waved the indictment around his head, while a deeper impression was made on the auditory. Resuming his speech—'May it please your worships: There are periods in the history of man when corruption and depravity have so long debased the human character, that man sinks under the weight of the oppressor's hand, and becomes his servile, his abject slave; he licks the hand that smites him; he bows in passive obedience to the mandates of the despot, and in this state of servility he receives his fetters of perpetual bondage. But, may it please your worships, such a

"If I am not deceived, according to the contents of the Paper which I hold in my hand, these men are accused of 'Preaching the Gospel of the Son of God.' Great God!"

day has passed away! From the period when our fathers left the land of their nativity for settlement in these American wilds, for liberty—for civil and religious liberty—for liberty of conscience to worship their Creator according to their conceptions of Heaven's revealed will; from the moment they placed their feet on the American continent, and in the deeply imbedded forests sought an asylum from persecution and tyranny—from that moment despotism was crushed; her fetters of darkness were broken, and Heaven decreed that man should be free—free to worship God according to the Bible. Were it not for this, in vain have been the efforts and sacrifices of the colonists; in vain were all their sufferings and bloodshed to subjugate this new world, if we, their offspring, must still be oppressed and persecuted. But, may it please your worships, let me inquire once more, for what are these men about to be tried? This paper says, 'for preaching the gospel of the Son of God!' Great God! for preaching the Saviour to Adam's fallen race!'

"After another pause, in tones of thunder he inquired, 'What law have they violated?' Then, for the third time, in a slow, dignified manner, he lifted his eyes to heaven and waved the indictment around his head. The court and the audience were now wrought up to the most intense pitch of excitement. The face of the prosecuting attorney was pale and ghastly, and he appeared unconscious that his whole frame was agitated with alarm; and the judge, with a tremulous voice, put an end to the scene, now be-

12

coming extremely painful, by the authoritative command—'*Sheriff, discharge those men!*'"

These quotations are but a little out of the mass of such as might be brought forward to show the character of the early Baptists of America, and the persecutions they suffered in the cause of Christ and soul-liberty, but I have not space for more, and will point the reader who may wish farther reference on the subjects to such books as "The Convert's Guide," "Baptist Denomination," "Baptist Martyrs," "History of the Welsh Baptist," and "Benedict's History of the Baptists," etc.

It may be easily seen that from the abundance of such matter, upon which I could lay my hands, and from the stirring character of the subject itself, I could readily present such thoughts, facts, arguments and reflections, as would not only relieve the name of our denomination from odium, but exalt it in the eyes of the people, and show where the real bigotry and persecution was, and where it always had been. I made free use of historical quotations, and piled on the applications, doing all in my power to make them stand up before the people like a mountain of glory. Whether I succeeded in this or not, one thing is certain, we breathed more freely afterwards, and by many were regarded with more respect.

While laboring in the Gate City an unpleasant experience occurred with the same Pedo-Baptist minister who was concerned with me in a debate at C * * *. I preached a sermon in defence of Baptist doctrine, and, as it had been previously announced, this minister, who was then in the city, and who did not want our doctrines defended, sent a reporter to take notes of my discourse, with the view of making a reply to them. When he gave his discourse in reply he declared, among other things, that he did not believe that immersion was baptism at all, and that no such thing was anywhere warranted in the Scriptures.

Immediately after this an article came out in the city paper which in substance was about as follows:

"PERSONAL.

"The Rev. Mr. * * *, who has lately been discussing the subject of baptism in this city, said, not long since, near the town of C * * *, in the hearing of many witnesses, while discussing the same subject there: 'I wish to have it distinctly understood that I believe in immersion as valid baptism, and I believe it just as strongly as any Baptist brother there is present; but I am going to show you that there are other Scriptural modes of baptism.'

"He now tells us in his last discussion: 'I do not believe that immersion is baptism at all; no such thing is anywhere warranted in the Scriptures.'

"Will this divine now be so kind as to tell the public which one of these two opposite statements expresses his real sentiment?"

What his real sentiment was I never learned.

CHAPTER XXIV.

BAPTISM OF A NUN, AND TROUBLE WITH THE CATHOLICS—IMMENSE CROWD AT THE WATER—THOUGHTS ON NUNNERIES—CONVERSION OF AN INFIDEL—HOW IT HAPPENED—HIS EXPERIENCE—AN INFIDEL CLUB BURNING THEIR BIBLES—THE CONVERTED INFIDEL CALLED TO THE MINISTRY—HIS DEATH—THE SHARPERS OF THE LOWER RAPIDS, AND HOW THEY MANAGED—WARNINGS TO YOUNG MEN—A THOUGHT ON PREACHING—A WEDDING IN CHURCH—CONVERSION OF MOST OF THE WEDDING PARTY—BAPTISM OF A LANDLADY, AND THREATS OF HER HUSBAND—HOW IT ENDED—THE FINANCIAL CRASH OF 1857–8—HARD TIMES—PROVIDENTIAL SUPPLY—REFLECTIONS.

WHILE I was preaching in Keokuk, there was an intelligent young Catholic lady, who was providentially employed in a Protestant family, through whose influence she was induced to attend our meetings. She had been well educated in a Catholic convent, and had already taken the white veil in a nunnery; but as she listened to the preaching of the gospel, the Lord opened her heart to attend to the things spoken. She repented of her sins in deep sorrow, and after receiving suitable instruction in the way of salvation, much concern being felt for her, she professed to have found peace in believing, and requested baptism.

This was soon known to the Catholics. The fact of her having taken the white veil, and the expectation that she would soon take the black one, made her case doubly aggravating to them. They looked upon it as an awful affair, and raised a tremendous excitement about the matter, declaring that if they ever could get their hands upon her they would give her such a baptism that she would never want another. They made so many threats of violence that she was in fear for her life, and by her own request we kept her secreted among us, to preserve her from outrage.

On the other hand, her case found deep sympathy with the Protestants, for they felt that in being saved from taking the black veil she was rescued from a fate worse than death itself. On the day when she was to be baptized we had a number of other candidates, and in view of the threats of the Catholics, we found it necessary, in order to allay fears and provide for general safety, to procure a police-guard, as an escort, to march with us from the place of worship to the river.

The First Baptist Church having a number of candidates to baptize at the same hour, its congregation met us at the water; and as a general excitement had been produced in the city about the threats of the Catholics, there was a grand rush to the river to see the ordinance administered, or witness the row, if there should be one. The numbers in the crowd of spectators that gathered along the wharf were variously estimated at from six to ten thousand people. It was a motley throng—merchants, clerks, shop-keepers, mechanics, day-laborers, hotel-boarders, strangers, doctors, lawyers, and preachers, Protestants and Catholics, saints and sinners, gentlemen, rowdies, wags, ruffians, women and children—all were there. In fact, it seemed that the inhabitants of the whole city, with all the strangers in it, had been stirred together in one vessel and poured out upon the river's side. It was a stirring time; and as it afforded an extra opportunity to make an appeal to the people, it was improved to the best advantage. The Catholics were present in pretty strong force, but they were so overawed by the masses and the presence of the city police, that they were obliged to hear the appeal, witness the immersion of the nun, and content themselves as best they could with grating their teeth, muttering their curses, and leaving us unharmed.

The young lady was again kept out of sight for a while, until the excitement seemed to have died away, when she shifted her quarters, and I lost sight of her, to see her, I suppose, no more; for, some time after I left Keokuk, I learned that by continued perseverance and repeated promises the Catholics had finally succeeded, through the aid of her relatives, in getting her among them again, and placing her in a nunnery at Dubuque.

Truly, there cannot be a much greater folly, not to say wickedness, in anything, than there is in those abominable institutions called nunneries. To think of a young lady, who is just in the prime of life's beauty and in the full glow of healthful spirits, designed by her Creator for happiness and usefulness in the world, thus coaxed, teased, and befooled into a nunnery—to take the black veil, live in imprisonment, in gloomy and solitary seclusion, under vows of perpetual chastity, all of which is contrary to nature, to say nothing of what may be her experience behind the veil—is, with me, calculated to stir my pity, and move my soul to feelings of abhorrence! Rather than see a daughter or relative of mine take such a step, I would see her in her grave! And I pray God that he may thoroughly purge our land, by the saving power of his gospel, from all such hot-beds of iniquity.

While I was preaching very loud in our chapel-room one night, a young man, who was a stranger in the city, was carelessly walking the street without any particular object in view, and overheard me. Supposing that something unusual was going on within, motives of curiosity led him to turn his course, and enter the sanctuary of God. While listening to the discourse he was suitably impressed, and then next night he came again.

While I was preaching the Lord applied the Word with mighty power to his heart, and such was his agony that he fell headlong upon the floor. When I invited the seekers forward for prayers, his physical prostration was such that he was unable to go forward with the others, and I had to assist him to the anxious-seat. When he was taken there, he wept and cried aloud for me to pray for him. Being very weary from vocal effort just at the time, I said to him, "Compose yourself as much as possible, my friend, and tell us who you are, what brought you here, and let us know something more about you, that we may be able to pray for you more intelligently."

He then related what in substance was as follows:

"I came from Ohio. I have a pious mother, who used often to warn me against wickedness; and when I left home, some two or three years ago, to try my fortune alone, she gave me a Bible, with the request that I would keep it carefully and read it often, and I promised her that I would do so. I was soon employed in running on the river, and ever since then steamboating has been my business. This kind of a life has thrown me into the company of rowdies, gamblers, drinkers, swearers, and nearly every class of wicked persons, and I became a vile sinner, wholly disregarding the counsels of my mother, and entirely neglecting my Bible.

"Our boat lies up for winter at any town where it happens to freeze in. Last winter it froze in at Quincy. While there I fell in with a lot of young men who had formed an infidel club, and I joined it. This club met occasionally and held meetings. Its exercises consisted chiefly in speeches and songs, which were sung in derision of religion. At length a meeting was appointed, at which each one of the club was to burn his Bible, and in the mean time a song was to be gotten up by one of the company, to be sung on the occasion, while the Bibles were burning. Each one was to burn his *own* Bible. When the meeting occurred the stove was heated very hot, in mock representation of the fiery furnace which was prepared for the burning of the Hebrew children. We formed a circle by joining hands, and promenaded around the stove, singing the song, while the Bibles were burning. Only one Bible was burned at a time, and when that one was consumed, the circle would halt until another one of the club would throw in his Bible, when the singing and promenading would be renewed.

"When I saw the first one thrown into the flames, it made me shudder! I thought of my Bible, which had been presented to me as the affectionate gift of a kind mother—of my promise to keep it carefully and to read it—of her pious counsels, and of my broken vows, until my feelings were distressed. The circle of infidels seemed to me like a company of damned spirits reveling in the orgies of hell. My heart panted as I thought my turn would soon come, and I feared I could not muster hardihood enough to burn my Bible. I would have given anything to have been away from the place, but there seemed to me no chance for backing out; I was ashamed to do that. I tried to encourage myself with the thought that some of my comrades were, perhaps, burning a mother's gift, and that it would be no worse for me to do so; but I found little comfort in that.

"My turn came, and I threw the sacred gift into the fire! As I saw its holy pages curl and squirm as things of life amid the devouring flames, my feelings were horrible, and I turned my eyes away

"The Circle of Infidels seemed to me like a Company of Damned Spirits reveling in the Orgies of Hell."

from the hellish sight! My thoughts and feelings were not known to the others, however, and the song and circle moved on until all the Bibles were burned, and the remainder of the evening was spent in ridicule, solemn mockery, and other kinds of sinful mirth.

"I resolved, when I left the club-room that night, that I would never enter it again; but as long as I remained in Quincy, I could not rid myself of the company and influence of those young men, and on that account I was glad when the river opened and let us away.

"This winter our boat is frozen in at Keokuk, and I am spending the winter here; but somehow I can't keep out of bad company, even here. I have been gambling considerable, and have spent my evenings chiefly at the saloons and card-tables. I was loitering about the streets last night, and as I passed this way, I heard a man speaking very loud, and turned in here to see what was the matter. I went home and told my wife that I had been to meeting, and was much interested, and she was surprised, supposing I had been to the saloons as usual. I told her I was going to the same meeting to-night, and persuaded her to come along;" and pointing to a woman who sat among the anxious, and was weeping bitterly, he burst into tears and said, "Here she is, a poor sinner like myself," and burying his face in his hands, he sat down exclaiming, "Oh, do pray for her and for me!"

By this time God's people were all on fire with interest, and we bowed together and had such a long and earnest season of prayer as seldom occurs. I then dismissed the assembly, that we might go to our homes; but such was the interest that the people would not leave, and we had another season of prayer. I then dismissed the second time, but they would not leave yet; and such was the prayerful interest, that we did not disperse until near two o'clock in the morning, when I finally dismissed for the third time. It was a praying, struggling time, indeed; the souls of the praying people were unusually humbled at the altar in behalf of all the seekers present, for there were several others, but more particularly in behalf of this young man, for we felt that he had walked to the very verge of the pit; but even then we were obliged to leave him sad and unsatisfied. Before the next night, however, he came into liberty and great joy. Blessed be God! It made rejoicing in heaven and on earth.

His wife and he afterward joined the church. He was ever after a devout Christian, was much beloved by the brethren, and finally began to study for the ministry. He was a man of marked intellect, and of great promise; but before he entered upon his proposed mission of love, the Lord took him, and he was not. He took the consumption, sank to his grave, and went home to die no more! His wife still remains to weep upon these mortal shores, but lives as a sincere Christian, in expectation of a happy reunion, to enjoy which may God finally bring us all. Amen, and Amen!

Gamblers and counterfeiters used to swarm about Keokuk, Montrose, and Nauvoo, in unusual numbers. Keokuk was one of the chief emporiums of the West, and travelers to and from all points of the compass halted there, and boats unloaded their freight there. In some seasons of the year, when the water was low, all the steamboat passengers were obliged to land at Keokuk or Montrose, and pass around the "lower rapids" by land. Those scamps swindled and gambled their living from the traveling public, and were always watching like so many sharks for a chance to gull somebody. They would draw a stranger on unsuspectingly, by forming his acquaintance, getting him into a saloon, under the pretext of taking only a social glass, then at the billiard or card table to while away a little time, or lead him on by other artful devices until he would become intoxicated with liquor or excitement, when his capital would be wrecked, his character and prospects ruined, and he would be ready to curse God and die! These fellows frequently shifted their quarters up and down the river from Montrose to Quincy, and sometimes when these places got too hot for them, they would retire from travel awhile, and hive up among the New Jerusalem saints at Nauvoo.

Many are the unwritten histories of the remorse and ruin of men, which had their origin and progress in the crafty doings of those deceitful rascals. Several such wrecks of humanity were saved from the jaws of death by our meetings. Many are the young men of promise who have forsaken the sober and pious counsels of their fathers and mothers, contemned their Bible, and have been caught in the webs and wiles of those wicked men; and I would to God that the experience related by the young man in our meeting would prove a timely and solemn warning to all young men who may read it. Young man! beware, lest you fall into the same evil net.

Notwithstanding our wholesome laws, such characters haunt our principal towns and cities even yet, and it is an easy matter to fall into their company. They may be seen hanging about those mouths of hell, called saloons and groceries; and I beseech you, young man, for the sake of your friends, and for the sake of your own soul and body, to shun them as you would a cave of venomous reptiles; shun the cup they drink, and the foul dens they inhabit, if you have any care for your own welfare, for time or for eternity. Their very steps take hold upon death, and you cannot get nearer to the pit of hell upon this earth than by entering those groceries and saloons.

The experience which has been related is suggestive of another subject—the true style of preaching. If this young man had not overheard my preaching from the street, and had not supposed that something was the matter, he would not have come into the meeting; but as it was, he did come, and he found out that something was the matter sure enough, and the Spirit showed him that the matter was at his own heart, the very last place he would have thought of looking in order to find it. I will not be so presumptuous as to attempt giving a full discourse on homiletics; but a practical thought or two may not be amiss. The delivery should ordinarily be in a voice so strong and full, and with a pronunciation so clear and distinct that the hearers may understand all you say, without the effort of straining their ears to hear. If such an effort is necessary, the passive hearers, who compose a large part of every audience, will receive no benefit. I suppose I must have been preaching quite loud when the young man heard me from the street; so that, in this case at least, it may be truly said that loud preaching was a means of great mercy.

On one occasion, when a house of God was thronged, and so many were standing around the windows outside that those who were the most distant from the pulpit were unable to hear the low voice of the preacher, sufficiently to distinguish one word from another, he at length lifted up his voice, and emphasized the single word "LOST!" There was one wicked man, who, with others, clearly heard the word pronounced; and though it was the only one which he understood during the whole sermon, it slew him as a sinner. The Spirit applied that word to his soul — "LOST!" The word seemed to echo in his ears. He tried to feel indifferent, but he could think of nothing but the word "LOST!" It suggested to him the future woes of the damned, and sounded through his soul as if it were a death-knell from eternity to his immortal spirit, to summon him to the regions of endless death. He tried to sleep, but that terrible word "LOST!" was ever before his mind as plainly as though it were written in flaming letters of fire upon the skies. He became miserable, nor did he find rest until as an humble penitent he sought for mercy at the feet of Christ.

"So then faith cometh by hearing, and hearing by the Word of God;" *and says God to Isaiah, "Cry aloud, spare not, lift up thy voice like a trumpet, and show my people their transgressions, and the house of Jacob their sins."† The word "*lost*" was the only word in that sermon which could have possibly done that sinner any good, for it was the only one he heard. It is true that God might convict a sinner by so faint a sound as the hum of a bee; but this is not His plan, for it has pleased Him, "by the foolishness of preaching to save them that believe."‡ Let us see to it, then, that as ministers we preach it truly; that we be not downy-mouthed and time-serving; that we do not cushion the face of God's gospel hammer with finery, to prevent its blows from hurting, or that we do not deal with sinners with gloves on our hands—we are too near eternity for trifling thus; but let us present the bare-handed, sin-killing and sin-provoking truth, in that plain, pungent, earnest style that will search the sinner's heart, show him his sins, awake his conscience, and alarm his soul; "not with enticing words of man's wisdom, but in demonstration of the Spirit and of power." §

One evening during my pastoral term at Keokuk, just as I had closed a sermon to my congregation, ten gentlemen and ladies who were fashionably

* 1 Rom. x : 17. † Isa. lviii : 1.
‡ 1 Cor. i : 21. § 1 Cor. ii : 4

dressed entered the congregation, walked up the aisle, and pressed toward the pulpit. As they were entire strangers to me, I was utterly astonished at their maneuvers, especially at their coming into church at such a time of night, when the meeting was nearly out. One of the party stepped up and reached me an unsealed envelope. As I opened it the mystery was solved. It contained a marriage license, in which was inclosed five dollars. After telling the audience what was to occur, I invited the bride and groom to step forth, which they did, each with an attendant, when I repeated a marriage ceremony, and pronounced them one until death should separate them. After the closing ceremonies I exchanged greetings and well-wishes with the newly-married pair, and said to them, that as they had now been, as I hoped, happily united with each other, I prayed that they might also both be wedded to Christ. Said I, "We are now holding meetings here every night, and I offer you my warmest invitation to come out and attend them; their object is to do the people good, and I hope they may prove a great benefit to you." I was then introduced to each one of the company, and invited them all to attend our meetings. One of the females, who was a fine-looking, portly, fashionable lady, was, I was told, the landlady of a hotel in the city.

After this the company attended meetings for many nights in succession; the Lord gave repentance, and one after another sought the Saviour until nearly all of them came out in religion. It was in the winter time, and when the landlady was soon after received for baptism, to be baptized the following Sabbath in the Mississippi, her husband, the landlord, sent me a word of warning, to the effect that if I baptized his wife in that way, he would surely shoot me. I did not know the landlord, and on getting this word I talked to the brethren about the matter. They said he was a resolute and desperate man, and that they scarcely knew what to advise me. All the brethren and sisters who were knowing to the message felt uneasy; my wife, in particular, felt quite dubious, and very much questioned whether or not it was my duty, under the circumstances, to attempt to baptize the lady; but on deliberation I concluded that it was my duty to baptize her, as well as all others who believed in Jesus and asked it at my hands, because it was the command of God; and feeling satisfied that while acting in obedience to Him, He would preserve me, I resolved to administer the ordinance and leave the result with Him.

When the congregation finally adjourned to the river, circumstances seemed to have combined to set forth the attempt in the most unfavorable light. It was raining in torrents; and a strong east wind, which was driving the rain in our faces, had also drifted the mush ice upon the shore so thick that we had not a little perplexity and delay in opening a baptistry through it; but we finally succeeded, and the landlady and several others were baptized, without our being molested by any shooting.

The wife of one of the deacons afterward went with her in an omnibus to assist her home, and to their surprise, when they arrived the husband waited upon them at the door, received them very kindly, and said nothing about shooting, nor did he ever afterward. But the Lord soon shot him. He came out to the meeting, was soundly converted to God, and the very next Sabbath he himself was baptised!

Thus through the medium of a wedding in church were a number of souls brought to Christ. I am glad to see that the custom of having weddings in church is becoming more common, and I wish that it might everywhere prevail.

The financial crash of 1857–8, and the hard times which followed during my stay at Keokuk, made my thousand-dollar salary come up minus. My brethren and friends would have gladly paid it, but they were nearly all either entirely bankrupt or almost hopelessly embarrassed, as were other people generally, and during my stay I shared embarrassments with them. Living in the city was expensive, and we were often taxed to our utmost to keep up a decent appearance, and hold out in the struggle to keep our heads above the waves. In such seasons the believer realizes more than commonly that "God is our refuge and strength, a very present help in trouble." *

I recollect that about this time, when our larder had run almost as low as that of the good widow of Sarepta once did,† and while I was sitting on my porch one day, wondering how I should provide for the wants of the morrow, a man drove up and in-

* Psalm xl:1. † 2 Kings iv:2.

quired, "Is this where the Rev. Samuel Pickard lives?"

Said I, "Yes, sir."

Said he, "I was ordered to leave you some flour and other things. Where shall I unload them?"

I told him that he must have got the wrong name and come to the wrong place, as I had ordered no such things from any one; but he said that he had no doubt about the matter whatever, and that he knew that the things were for me; so he unloaded them and went his way.

I never could learn who sent the things; but it was a good and timely store of substantials, which fed us many days, and we ate it with gratitude to the unknown donor, in remembrance of Him who fed Elijah by the ravens,* and in realization of the divine counsel and promise, "Trust in the Lord, and do good; so shalt thou dwell in the land, and verily thou shalt be fed." †

Had I space, I would further illustrate these and their kindred Scriptures by many incidents which I could give; but I have not, and I refer the reader to "Muller's Life of Trust."

* 1 Kings xvii : 6. † Isa. xxxvii : 3.

CHAPTER XXV.

UNDER APPOINTMENT OF THE HOME MISSION—VISITING ASSOCIATIONS—FINDS A VERY MISERABLE LODGING—CHICKEN AND POTATOES, ETC.—LIBERALITY OF WESTERN BRETHREN.

In the spring of 1859, I took an appointment from the Home Mission Board of New York, to labor as a traveling missionary or evangelist in south-eastern Iowa, and was succeeded in the pastorate at Keokuk by a Brother B * * *, of Missouri. He had helped us to a considerable extent in revival efforts while I was pastor, and we supposed him a suitable man; but the subsequent history of the Second Church was unfortunate. The settlement turned out unhappily for both pastor and church; but as this is no part of my narrative, I will not dwell upon it.

My principal field embraced Lee, Jefferson, Henry, and Van Buren counties; though I was at liberty to visit any section in the south-eastern part of the State. My business was to hold meetings with feeble churches, preach in destitute places, and organize new churches.

My salary was to be $600 a year, a part of which I was to raise on the field, and the remainder to be paid by the Board at New York.

I now felt that I was in my chosen element. I

moved from point to point, holding protracted meetings, and though I worked hard I enjoyed it greatly. During the year I traveled a great many miles, held many meetings, organized several new churches, and baptized a great many persons.

The statistics of my labors for this year I cannot now remember. I sent in a report of my labors to the Home Mission Board, and afterwards saw it published in an Eastern religious journal, but can not now lay my hands upon it.

During the fall of this year I visited seven Baptist associations in the western and more sparsely populated part of the State. On getting pretty well back, the roads were few, and the accommodations for travelers were miserable.

While making one of those tours westward to attend the meeting of the E * * * Association, having sent appointments ahead along the route for preaching, with the view of improving the time, I preached at a town called Chariton, in the evening, where my traveling companions were increased until our company was eight in number, including our beloved father W * * *, who was an aged minister, and his wife.

The next morning at sunrise we all set out together to go to the place of the association, which was yet about forty miles distant. We had two preaching appointments on the route during the day, and as the roads were bad, and the weather warm, we had to travel slowly, but had to keep moving in order to meet them, so that we could not possibly find time to stop for feed or dinner. At 4 o'clock, in the place of our last appointment, we found only about twenty or twenty-five persons present. We were all nearly worn out with traveling, and were weak from hunger, but it fell to my lot to preach, which I did the best I could under the circumstances. After we had attended to a few items of business with the church, relative to the association, I announced to the brethren that we had all traveled hard since sunrise without feed or dinner, and that as both ourselves and our horses were faint and weary, we wished that they would provide us with refreshments as soon as possible.

At this a large, brawny, overgrown, double-fisted brother, with an oval face and long snarly hair, arose and said, "I want you all to go home with me; I have a plenty for you, and of that that's good."

"But," said I, "here are eight of us with our horses, can you accommodate us all?"

"Yes," said he, "I can accommodate you all, and more, too, for I have a plenty, and of that that's good."

Said I, "that is all that we can ask for."

After dismission I inquired of him, "In what direction is your house?"

"It's right on in the road to the 'sociation," said he; and putting a sheepskin on the back of his Rosinante, he mounted it and said, "Now jest foller me, and I'll show you through;" and away we went.

We did not like the slovenly appearance of our guide, but he had talked so encouragingly about having an abundance, "and of that that's good," and seemed so hospitable, that we thought that, perhaps, after all every thing would be well when we got to his house.

We had not thought it worth while to inquire how far it was to his place, but supposed, of course, that it was but a short distance, and as we expected to alight at his door in a few minutes we were cheered, as with our aching bones and hungry stomachs we thought of a comfortable resting-place among his plenteous stores, where there was "a plenty, and of that that was good;" but to our surprise and disappointment he kept going on, and still on, mile after mile, until our poor tired and hungry horses were almost ready to drop from exhaustion. Night set in. We finally asked him how much farther it was. Said he, "It's only a little ways ahead now; we'll be there dreckly;" and we urged our jaded beasts onward. It grew quite dark, and yet no signs of a friendly light or cheerful hearth appeared. We were ready to despair.

"Aint we nearly there?" shouted one of the company.

"Yes," said the guide, "it's only a leetle ways further."

We kept on, but the "leetle ways" got very long, and the darkness and the bad roads made it seem longer still.

I was beginning to fancy that possibly some will-o'-the-wisp, or other apparition, was leading us away, to be lost and starved in the wilderness, when at last we saw a light! Our spirits raised at the sight; but on getting to it, what was our disappointment when we found that instead of taking us to his house, he had taken us to a place which was crowded with people who were expecting to hear us preach!

Said I, "Brother, where is your house?"

"Oh," said he, "it's further on."

"How far off is it?" I inquired.

"Oh, it's only a couple of miles," said he, "and as soon as this here meeting's out we'll go and have supper as quick as possible."

There was no help for us: the people who were there were eager to hear a city preacher, and we thought it might be hurtful to disappoint them, so we all went in to the meeting.

It fell to my lot to preach. I was so weak and faint that I did not see how I could do it, but there was no chance for retreat: I was pressed into the service, and was soon discussing the things of the gospel. As I advanced in the discourse, the people listened with such marked interest that it so inspired me to unusual effort, that my soul soon forgot the body and reveled among the delicious things of the Scriptures; nor did I think of our mortal wants for upward of an hour.

We then dismissed, and again followed our guide. Oh, what a long two miles it was to our guide's house! The night had grown darker and more cloudy, the roads got worse, and to add to our discomfort, we kept getting lost from the guide, who would persist in keeping too far ahead, so that we kept continually getting lost from the track, which obliged us sometimes to get out and feel about on the ground to find it, and to keep hallooing back and forth to know where we were.

At last we pulled up by a miserable cabin which seemed to stand in the edge of a field. It was wonderfully open at the top and had a repulsive appearance, but—"Drive in the yard, brethren," said the host, who had just let down the rail fence.

"Just onhitch there, brethren."

"Where shall we put the horses?" asked one.

"Why you'll have to hitch 'em to the fence! I'm sorry to say, I haint got any barn or stable."

"Well, we must water them," said one, "for they are almost famished. Where is your water, brother?"

"Well, I haint got any just right here, but down the holler a piece there's good water, and we will take the horses down there."

"How far is it," I inquired.

"It's only about a half a mile," said he.

"Well,' said I, "I think that is a good distance, if you have to carry it so far for family use."

"Yes," said he, "but there's plenty of it when you get there."

We felt that the horses must have some water, and, he leading the way, we led them behind us, and after groping our way down a dark hollow for what I thought a very long half mile, we found plenty of water, "and of that that was good."

When we returned, there were as yet no signs of life about the cabin; the family seemed to be asleep, and we found Sister W * * *, the aged lady who was with us, still sitting quietly and alone in her husband's vehicle.

"I'm sorry I haint got any corn for your horses, brethren, but I've got a stack of prairie hay there, so jest help yourselves," said our host.

"Have you no grain of any kind?" I asked.

"No," said he, "I haint got a bit; but that's mighty good hay, and there's plenty of it, and you can jest take all you want."

This was, to me, the worst misfortune yet. I had a noble horse, and he had been in the shafts since sunrise, traveling on heavy roads, without a bite to eat, and such was the case with all the horses; but it had to be endured, for we knew of no place within our reach where we could better it, and we tried to content ourselves as best we could in feeding them on dry hay.

We were then invited into the cabin by our host, who, for the want of chairs, set us out some benches made of split puncheons.

The next want was a light, that we might see each other's faces; but there was neither lamp nor candle, and our friend went out leaving us all in the dark. As he was absent some time I began to wonder at such a strange and apparently impolite movement; but at length the mystery was solved. He had been to the wood and gathered a back-load of dry brush, which he threw into the large fire-place, where it was soon roaring and crackling with a tremendous blaze and giving light in abundance.

We now began to take a survey of our quarters. The house was built of logs, and had but one room and one door, which was made of clapboards and swung on large wooden hinges. There was but one small window, to accommodate which one or two logs had been chopped out from one of the walls. For further ventilation, however, the roof, which was only partially covered with clapboards, was so open as to admit a handsome view of the sky and beautiful stars. The floor was made of broad puncheons, one of which I noticed was broken, leaving a hole large enough for a man to fall through. It looked dangerous; I wondered that some of us had not stepped into it when we first came in.

The north end of the house was mostly cut out to make room for the chimney, which was a huge pile, built of logs, sticks, stones and mud. A vacancy by the chimney, on the outside, had been thoughtfully improved into a chicken roost.

But our survey was soon disturbed in a way which was unlooked for. The burning brush waked up a host of flies, and bugs, and other vermin from all quarters of the cabin. I verily believe there must have been a bushel. They lighted on our hands and faces, and tried to creep into our nostrils and ears, and furnished us with unceasing employment and annoyance.

The house had but two beds, if such they might be called, and to one of these our host went and waked up his wife. She gave a yawn or two, and then crawled out.

She evidently had not taken off her clothes when she went to bed, for she put none on when she got up. She had dirty flaxen hair, which hung in strings and snarls about her head, and looked as though it had not felt a comb for a year; her feet and ankles were about the color of prairie mud. Her dress-sleeves were but five or six inches long, and those short patterns were torn into many slits and strings, each of which was so stiff with grease and dirt that it would have stood alone with very little help. When she was fairly upon her feet and had begun to move, I estimated her neat weight at something over two hundred pounds; and when she walked across the floor, it explained the circumstance of the broken puncheon.

As we thus became introduced to her, our prospects of getting "a plenty and of that that was good," were forbidding. She made a fire in a stove, in one corner, and got it very hot, and then threw more brush into the fire-place, to revive the light. The two fires now combined, as the weather was very warm and the room small, made the heat most oppressive to all, except the bugs and flies, which were more active and lively than ever. She then went to the bed and waked up the oldest daughter, whose name was Kate. When she arose she proved to be a chip from the old block. Her height, dress, and general appearance much resembled those of the mother, though she was not quite so fat.

Our attention was now arrested by a terrible fracas among our chimney neighbors, the chickens, who began to flutter and squall for dear life. We prophesied as to the cause of the disturbance, and our prophecy was fulfilled when the brother threw a large Shanghai rooster on the floor before us, with its head off. I thought it a pity to have killed him, for he seemed to be a real old stand-by. Kate was sent to the potatoe-patch for further supplies; and a pot of water was set on to scald the rooster. When the water was hot, the cook set the pot on the floor, plunged the chicken into it, and after due examination to see that it was well scalded, she stripped the feathers off with a vengeance, and threw them into the fire, and as she was not over particular, she was soon ready to dissect it.

She then got down to it on her knees, and cutting it enough to admit her hand, she reached in, and with one mighty surge she jerked the whole inside from the carcass, and threw them into the fire also. The smell of the burning offals now became very offensive, and some of the company stepped out for fresh air, but I was too deeply concerned about the destiny of the chicken to borrow trouble about such trifles, and I was determined to stay by it until the last.

The cook then put the chicken into the pot, without washing or singeing, and poured a good quantity of water in with it, with the view of making soup. She then inquired of her husband if Kate had not got back; and as he said "no," she put the pot aside and sat down. I wondered why she did not set on the chicken and have it cooking, but it appeared that all culinary operations had to be suspended until Kate returned. After a while she began to get restless, and inquired again for Kate; but she had not come. I inquired how far it was to the potatoe-patch, and learned that it was on the far-end of the farm, at the distance of about half a mile. I suggested that, as it was so far and so dark, she might have got lost, or that something else might have happened her, and that probably some one ought to go and hunt for her; but her father thought she was in no danger, because she was so well acquainted with the neighborhood.

It was now after midnight. I felt sorry for Sister W* * *, the aged lady who was with us, as she seemed scarcely able to hold up her head; but there was no chance but to wait, and to pass the time in the most pleasant manner possible, I fell to relating anecdotes and stories.

Suddenly the cook took a new impulse. Getting a large, old-fashioned buckeye tray, she filled it with meal and water, and setting it on the floor, she kneeled down beside it and with her hands mixed it into a tremendous batch of corn-dough; then getting a large dripping pan, which was about four inches in depth and capacious enough to hold a peck, she piled the dough into it as long as she could make it lie on, and set it in the stove. She then inquired again for Kate, but no Kate came yet. We knew well enough that it would take until near daylight for such a huge mass of corn-dough to bake, but we tried to feel resigned.

Finally, Kate made her appearance with a basket of fine large potatoes; it was a welcome sight to us, for we thought that if we could eat nothing else we could eat some of them. But the mother and daughter peeled them and sliced them without any washing, and, alas! threw them into the pot with the rooster!

After the large coffee-boiler was put on it was about two o'clock, but everything was now fairly under way; the rooster was boiling, the "dodger" was baking, the table was being set, and matters generally looked encouraging.

Supper was finally set — sooner than we expected. There was a scarcity of dishes, but we easily managed that by accommodating each other in the way of exchanges. The coffee was poured, but it tasted and smelled so badly that one sip was enough. We tried the chicken and potatoes, but the whole mess was so slimed over with pin-feathers, and looked and smelled so dirty and disgusting, that none of us could eat a bit of it. Our last chance was the corn-bread. This the woman cut and passed around, but we found that only a slight crust of about an eighth or quarter of an inch in thickness had been baked, while the remainder was nothing but dough. We thought that we must try to eat something, as we had told them we were very hungry, and for manners' sake we tried to nibble on the crust, but it was a sickly nibble. Seeing me shove back my coffee, the cook said that if I did not like coffee she could give me some buttermilk. I told her I was very fond of buttermilk, and would thank her very much for a bowl of it. She then took a vessel, and going to the churn, which was standing open, she brought me about a quart. When I attempted to take a sip, I noticed some flies in it, and as I set down the bowl and took a knife to lift them out, I happened to stir it a little, and found that from top to bottom the whole mess was a perfect mixture of flies, bugs, and buttermilk! I had for some time been trying to coax my stomach to be quiet, but this was too much; I hurried out of doors, feeling most deathly sick, and had a hard spell of vomiting. The rest of the brethren minced away at the table for a few moments longer, but could eat scarcely anything.

When all had left the table, the mother went to the beds and awakened the children; and they tumbled out one after another until we saw quite a squad of dirty, half-naked urchins about the room. When they first saw us they looked all over amazement and stupefaction, but in a few minutes they were all around the table, and seemed to have forgotten us entirely in the luxuries of the extra meal that was before them. The repast was a sweet one for them, and in a very little time nothing was left of the old Shanghai but the naked hulk. The corn-dough was all eaten, and the soup and potatoes, and every thing on the table, were licked up as clean as a kitten would lick a saucer.

The table being set aside, beds were spread upon the floor, and soon all were trying to sleep, but the bedding smelled so sickening that I had not lain long before I was obliged to hurry out of doors and endure another hard spell of vomiting. I sought for some place where I might lie down about the premises, but I could find none except where I would be exposed to the night air, which I dared not be. I went in again to try my bed, but it was no use; I could not endure the stench. Oh, what a long night it was!

Fortunately necessity was the mother of invention. I laid my valise about two feet from the bed, as a support to my head and shoulders, and poking my feet and legs under the cover, I put my handkerchief over my nose, and thus managed to bunk down under tolerably sweet circumstances. However, I could not get a wink of sleep, nor did my companions, generally; and as soon as daylight appeared we excused ourselves from staying to breakfast, and pushed on to the town of L * * *, a distance of fourteen miles, where we fed our horses bountifully, got our breakfast, and took a sound sleep.

It seemed strange that notwithstanding the way in which the brother lived who tried to entertain us, he had a large and excellent farm, and was in tolerable circumstances; but so uncultivated were his ideas of comfort that I suppose he really thought, as he had told us when he first invited us, that he had "a plenty, and of that that's good."

I will not say that what I have just related is a characteristic incident of the traveling minister's experience in the West, but I may safely say that he is often obliged to accept very rough and uncomfortable fare, and that he commonly sees twenty times as much of cold, coarse reality, as he does of romance.

The objects I had in view in visiting so many associations this fall were, first, to aid in raising money to liquidate a debt of several thousand dollars on the Baptist State Convention of Iowa; and secondly, to solicit patronage and circulate documents for the

Baptist College at Burlington. These things made my travels quite extensive on the frontiers of the State. The advantages and comforts we enjoy in the older settled parts, it seems to me, can scarcely be appreciated without a visit back among the border settlers. It was no uncommon thing to see people out there, both men and women, attend meeting barefooted; nor was it any less common to see ministers preaching without coats on, and sometimes they preached with their shirt-collars open and their sleeves rolled up.

At one of those western associations I could not but be pleased at the liberality of the brethren in behalf of the State Convention. The times were hard, and money was very scarce—in fact so scarce that very little calculation could be made on it, for there were but very few in the country who could command any; hence, when the wants of the Convention were presented, the prospects of getting anything seemed almost hopeless; but after the cause had been held forth, one brother said, "I have no money, but I want to aid the State Mission work, and if it will be of any help I will give a three-year old colt, worth seventy-five dollars. We gladly accepted this generous offer, and it was soon followed by others of a similar character. Some of them gave calves; some, home-made jeans; others, socks and stocking-yarn, and various other things; so that when the associational meeting closed we had quite a variety store. The three-year old colt and most of the things given we turned over to the missionaries, who were thankful to receive them, and the remainder we afterwards put up at auction and sold for cash, to apply on the debt; so that altogether it made a handsome sum. By such generous conduct among the brethren the cause of God has moved forward in Iowa, and it has taught us that where there is a will there is a way.

In such labors and travels, and in various revival efforts, I spent most of the year.

CHAPTER XXVI.

HOLDING GROVE MEETINGS—NATURE'S MEETING-HOUSES—A WISE INVESTMENT OF TWENTY-FIVE CENTS—THOUGHTS ON GIVING—MEETING AT P. G * * *—BAD USAGE—WHAT BECAME OF THE HOG AND FLOUR—LABORS IN AND ABOUT FORT MADISON—THOUGHTS ON CHURCH EXTENSION—BRIEF HISTORY OF THE FORT MADISON CHURCH—CONVERSATION ON COMMUNION—JOY OF AN OLD LADY ON LEARNING THAT THE BAPTISTS WERE ALL IN HEAVEN—EFFECTS OF POUNDING THE BAPTISTS.

In the spring of 1860 my appointment was renewed by the Board of the Home Mission Society of New York, and I spent the year following in traveling and holding meetings. During this time I witnessed under my labors the accession of about two hundred members to the churches in the various places where my meetings were held.

It was often the case that we could not get suitable houses in which to hold protracted meetings, and we would hold them in some grove. The first grove meetings in which I was engaged this year lasted about three weeks, in which time about thirty souls were added to the church as the result; and as God honored the plan I held a number of such meetings during the year with happy success. The novelty of the plan brought out a great many who, of course, came for the novelty only; but yet, without doubt, the meetings did a great amount of good. People would gather in by hundreds, some of them coming as far as ten and twelve miles, being enticed by the novel and entertaining character of the meeting. I remember, in one instance, talking to a man who was present, who said he had come a distance of twelve miles on foot, and he afterward walked home the same night, and said that he was well paid.

In the fall of the year, when the weather is favorable, a grove-meeting will draw out more people than a meeting will under ordinary circumstances; and to the scattered brethren living West, I will here say that you ought not to despair in the thought that you have no meeting houses, for in the various groves that are around you, the Lord has provided a great many large meeting houses. He has made for them arched ceilings of the canopy of heaven; he has frescoed them with the clouds, and hung about their walls and windows, with great artistic skill, scenes of pleasant and delightful landscapes, and over all the rich festoons and clinging vines from nature's smiling garden. But this is not all: he warms these audience-rooms with sunshine and lights them up with the golden lamp of day, so that you have no sexton to pay and no sexton-work to do. These houses of worship are each large enough to hold many hundreds of people, without being cramped for room, or smothered for want of pure air. They are all finished from floor to ceiling, except the small item of putting in a pulpit and seats, which can be done with a very little expense and trouble. Now these sanctuaries are waiting for use during several months of the year, and you ought to raise courage enough to move forward and occupy them.

While I was laboring in one of those grove-meetings, I was called away to attend an Association, and went in company with Brother G. J., who kindly took me in his carriage. I happened at the time to have but twenty-five cents by me, and as I wanted, if possible, to throw something into the hat at each collection, the best chance I could think of was to get my quarter changed into five cent pieces, and make it go the rounds as long as it would last. As toll was demanded on our way at a bridge on Skunk River, where it was proper for me, for manners' sake to pay it, I thought the quarter would have to leave me; but on telling Brother J * * * that it was all I had, and that I wanted to save it to throw in at the collections of the meeting, he insisted on paying the toll, and I got through to the Association with my quarter all safe in my pocket. Here, by throwing five cents into the hat at each collection, it was soon all deposited in the Lord's Treasury, and I was penniless. It was not long after the last five cents was gone, however, when a man who was a stranger to me, stepped up and greeted me in a very cordial manner, remarking that he had seen me before and that he had heard me preach, and with little ceremony he left $5 in my hands and went his way. Here, reader, is Scripture illustrated again by Providence. I have noticed the incident to enforce a good sentiment.

It is this: However, scanty our purse may be, we shall not be unwise if we intrust it all, or at least a part of it, to the Lord, for He whose word cannot fail has said: "Give, and it shall be given unto you, good measure, pressed down, and shaken together, and running over, shall men give into your bosom." * Be assured, reader, that you will not suffer for your generosity; I did not, in this instance, but had it returned in a signal manner, and increased twenty-fold; and if I were with you I could relate many similar instances of my own experience illustrating the soundness of the same sentiment. I know to my own satisfaction that I have always prospered best and felt the happiest when I was the most liberal with my purse, in God's cause. It is possible, of course, for a person to go beyond the bounds of sanity in such matters, but it is not probable. There is not nearly so much danger of ruin from that cause as there is from being struck by lightning.

I am now well advanced in years, and have known a great many liberal brethren, but I never knew a single one who had been ruined by his generosity, and hence I do not think that any caution of danger in that direction is necessary; but I do believe that there are many who are keeping themselves in poverty by murmuring about the Sabbath collections, and singing with their eyes shut when the hat is

* Luke 6: 38.

passed around. Such do not give except it be a little for shame's sake, and even that little is given grudgingly; consequently they do not receive the "good measure," which the Lord has promised on other conditions. If they were better stewards of what little they have received, it might be said unto them, "Well done, thou good and faithful steward, thou has been faithful over a few things, I will make thee ruler over many things." *

The next day after this occurrence we started back for our grove-meeting, at the distance of thirty miles, where we arrived at four o'clock, at which hour I preached a sermon, which was followed by other religious exercises, and just as the sun was setting we baptized seven happy converts. When I went to bed that night I felt that truly "the Lord" was "my refuge and strength."

During all these missionary labors I had still kept my family in Keokuk. It was an expensive place for poor people to live, and especially so with us, as our family had become large; but what little we had was there, and as it was the only place we could call home, we thought it best to remain there. I was expected by the Missionary Board to raise a part of my salary among those for whose benefit I labored; but the undisciplined and uninformed, whom I often fell among, would have it that as I was a missionary, I was getting a fine fat salary, of perhaps not less than a thousand dollars a year, which was paid by some of the rich folks East, who

* Matt. 25: 21.

had such a large amount of surplus money that they did not feel it, and as I was making money so fast that my family could live in the city, perhaps in fashionable life, they thought that such considerations afforded them a happy excuse for paying me nothing. The result was that I was often embarrassed in living; the four hundred dollars a year which I received from the Board being a good part of the time my whole dependence.

In one instance, having gone to spend a few days with my family and look a little after its wants, a deacon from the P. G * * * church, distant about thirty-two miles, called at my house, wishing me to hold a meeting with his church, and he wanted me to go immediately. I did not see how I could leave my family just at that time, as its wants were numerous, but he urged so hard and promised so encouragingly, and was so determined withal to take no refusal, that I finally consented, and went. I held a meeting with his people, in which I labored about two weeks with all my energy and strength, and the result was that about twenty souls were added to the church.

Before I left, a brother who was a licentiate went around among the people to get something for my remuneration; but he could not get a single cent from any one. He finally plead with the deacon who had urged me so hard to hold the meeting to pay me fifty cents, but he even refused to do that, though he had a considerable amount of money by him. At last he found one brother of moderate circumstances, who, though he said he had no money and could give nothing at that time, would, after he butchered his hogs, give me a hog and a sack of flour, and that he would deliver them for me at Keokuk. With this promise they all took an affectionate leave of me, and let me go home without a single dollar.

But I must tell how it turned out with the promised hog and flour. My family never got them. The following winter, however, the brother who had promised them came to the city with a load of produce, and after selling it out, in order to save paying a tavern bill, he hunted up our house and wished to get accommodations for himself and team over night. We kept him in the best manner we could.

His excuse for not bringing the hog and flour was that his plans for the season had not succeeded as he expected. The substance of it was that he had made the mistake of selling off his produce too closely, and consequently he did not have enough left to spare either the hog or the flour: thus the matter ended. The deacon who came after me lived only two miles and a half from the church at W. P * * *, but it was then struggling very hard to build a house of worship, and he kept his membership for the time at the P. G * * * church, which was six miles from him. Of course he could then do little or nothing to help the heavily burdened church at W. P * * *, because, as he would say, "I have to help the church over at P. G * * *, where I belong. After a while, however, it turned out that when the church at W. P * * * was built, the church at P. G * * * attempted to build a house of worship also, but he then concluded that as he lived so near the W. P * * * church it was his duty to unite with that. His ability was such that he might have been a good help to both churches, but he thus managed to get along with doing very little for either; and he still bids fair to get to heaven, if he ever does get there, as cheap as a man can.

Now, reader, if you are seeking to live religion on a cheap plan, the one just mentioned may afford you some valuable hints. This man was a Kentuckian.

Soon after this I held a meeting at another place, where I was invited to stop with an old Virginian, and though he was quite a wealthy man he gave me such miserable lodgings that I was compelled to go to a tavern for the safety of my health. There I got kept well.

During my stay I witnessed a number of conversions and organized a church in the place, but did not receive a cent. I expected a tavern bill to pay, but the proprietor of the house kindly refused to accept it. It is due to say of this wealthy brother, however, that he afterward went around among the neighbors and collected in my behalf about five dollars' worth of meat, flour, and garden sauce.

In the labors of the year I held several meetings in connexion with the Baptist church and pastor of Fort Madison. These meetings were held in and around the city at different points, and they were highly blessed to the strengthening of the church in the city and the salvation of souls. My experiences among those brethren and sisters were exceedingly pleasant. I have received many kindnesses among the churches from my kindred in Christ, but never was treated more nobly than by the members and friends of that church. This was a new organization: its history is one which is interesting, and one from which something may be learned. Though so large a place, up to about the year 1857 or 1858 there was no Baptist church in Fort Madison. There were some ten or twelve Baptist people, but there was no church organization of our order. Other denominations, however, occupied the ground with more or less success.

In the fall of 1857–8 the pastor of the Presbyterian church took a vacation, and went East on a visit, with the intention of being absent a number of weeks; and as the Presbyterian house of worship was unoccupied, some of our scattered brethren obtained permission to use it for holding some Baptist meetings. They then sent for the Rev. Morgan Edwards, now of Denmark, Iowa, who came to their aid and made a protracted effort of two or three weeks' duration, which resulted in the conversion of seventy or eighty souls. As the congregation was made up largely of the Presbyterian element, most of the converts being members or friends of Presbyterian families, they joined the Presbyterian church, which very much increased the strength of that body and proved to be of much benefit to it.

In addition to this, however, as the result of the meeting, a Baptist church of seventeen members was organized in the court house. Brother Edwards was then requested to act as pastor of the little church for the time, and he continued his revival efforts in the court house. At the end of the first three months, when Brother Edwards closed his labors with the church, it numbered about thirty-five or forty members, a part of whom had been brought to the Lord from among the best unconverted families in the place.

Rev. G. J. Johnson, formerly of Burlington, who was at the time acting temporarily as pastor at St. Louis, was then called to the pastorate. The church and pastor were happily united, and both were in an eminent degree sacrificing, enterprising, and persevering, and, as might be expected, they moved onward, increasing in numbers, grace and strength.

After Brother J * * * had labored efficiently for some time, he invited me to his assistance, and we held meetings together in the court house in the city, which were very successful. We then went out and stretched a chain of protracted meetings, from school-house to school-house, all around the city. Beginning near the river at the north, we moved around from point to point at a distance of from three to six miles of the place, until we closed up the siege near the river below. At these places men and women came out in religion, and all were received as members of the church in the city.

Thus the pastor continued, with great perseverance and activity, to besiege the city without and storm the castle within, and in less than two years from the time the church was organized, it numbered over two hundred members, and had begun to build a splendid house of worship.

The building of their house was a large undertaking, and cost them much time and struggling; but they finally succeeded in erecting an edifice which is an honor to the cause, and is one of the finest in the State.

A Campbellite church once flourished there, but as the Baptist church went up, the Campbellite church went down; and at the present writing its house of worship is desolate, being occupied in the basement by the hogs, and in the audience-room by the bats and swallows; while the Baptist church is still living in prosperity and moving forward.

I might give, with much profit, the history of other churches in Iowa and Illinois, which have had a rapid and successful growth upon much the same plan of operation; but this will suffice to show the most successful plan by which to operate in order to build up a church and save sinners. It also shows the elements necessary for a church and pastor to have in order to succeed. I believe that, as a general rule, where a pastor settles with a church, and ties himself in all his labors of visiting and preaching to the one little space immediately in the one congregation, while unoccupied fields, laden with abundant harvests, are all around him and within his reach, he is making a great mistake. If such ministers and churches wish to see themselves strengthened and enlarged, let them take courage, be more enterprising, enlarge the field of their operations, and thus increase their chances for usefulness and success. If this plan were more commonly followed in the West, I believe that twice as many people would be benefited by the labors of our pastors. A pastor might preach to one congregation for five years and never have a convert, when, at the same time, he might step out and preach a few evenings to another congregation, only five miles away, and gather a score of souls into the church.

There are brethren who have proved this by their own experience. It must be remembered, too, that the church and pastor must be active, and full of the spirit of pious enterprise; they must be engaged and ready both to pray and to do, otherwise Zion will continually languish. They should attempt great things for God, and expect great things from God.

God could convert the world with drones and mopers if he wished to, but it is not his plan; he loves to reward those who are the most pious and enterprising in his cause. Such he will surely prosper, and they shall see Zion enlarged. Then, brethren, arise and be doing, and may the Lord prosper you.

While I was laboring in Fort Madison, a certain Pedo-Baptist lady, upon whom I called, expressed a strong antipathy to our practice of restricted communion. She was determined to talk about it to her satisfaction, and give the Baptists a good raking.

She opened the battle very shrewdly. She would run on for a moment to tell how well she liked the Baptists, how much she admired the most of their doctrines and principles, how much she liked their style of preaching and the character of their worship, and thus praise them up to the mountain top; and then, when they were up high, she would try to hurl them all down suddenly with a mighty crash, by saying that their disgusting practice of close communion spoiled it all!

I quietly allowed her to continue this crashing process for some time, without making any reply, and after she had bounced the Baptists up and down to her heart's content, and emptied her mind upon the subject, she seemed quite relieved. I then introduced the following conversation:

"Now Sister * * *, will you tell me what are your greatest objections to our church communion?"

"Why," said she, "your close communion deprives me of a great religious privilege, and it's uncharitable."

"How long have you been connected with the church of which you are a member?" I asked.

"About ten years," she said.

"How often does your church have communion?" I asked.

"Every month," she said.

"And your people can have the privilege of having it as often as they choose, can they not?"

"Yes, sir, I suppose they can," said she.

"Well, as your church is so close by you, I suppose, then, you commune with it every month, do you not?"

"No, sir; not every month."

"Do you as often as every three months?"

"Well, I can't say that I do. In fact, I can't tell how long it has been since I was at our communion; the truth is, there are some in the church that I don't want to commune with, and I haven't been at the table for a long time."

"That is a pity," said I; "but here is an open communion church close by your house. You have been living by it a number of years, have you not?"

"Yes, sir, we have lived here a good while."

"I suppose," said I, "that they have communion as often as every month, do they not?"

"Yes sir, I think they do."

"Well, how often do you commune with them?"

"I don't know as —— I can't say that I am prepared to answer just now."

"Well," said I, "did you ever commune at this church at all?"

"Well," said she, "Mr. Pickard, really, to be honest with you, I believe I never did in my life!"

"Why, Sister * * *," said I, "can it be possible! And though you have lived here many years, and have been a member of a church close by you, which has communion every month, and another church at your door where you are invited as often, and have still other churches within your reach, and though you never commune with any of them, because you have no wish to, yet you say that the communion of the Baptist church is disgusting, and that it *deprives you of a great religious privilege!* You say also that our practice is uncharitable, while at the same time you have never asked our charity, and your own testimony declares that you have never needed it, as you say that your own people can have the communion *as often as they wish it!*"

"Well, really, Elder," said she, "I must confess I never saw it in that light before."

Thus the matter ended.

I have frequently found people who were anxious to make our communion appear as a great scarecrow, and such do sometimes succeed in creating a prejudice against us, where our doctrine is not understood, yet where we have a chance to present it coolly and candidly before the people, in the light of the New Testament, all the arguments against it are flimsy things, and the world may be assured that so long as the Bible is revered the doctrine must last.

Alluding to this subject reminds me of rather an amusing incident that lately occurred while I was holding a meeting over in Illinois.

While we were in the midst of a revival interest in which quite a number were seeking religion, a Methodist preacher came along, who instead of falling into the work of laboring and praying with us for the comfort of the mourners and the conversion of sinners, as he should have done, showed more of a disposition to raise a dispute, and immediately stuck up a challenge for me to a public debate with him.

As I thought he had more boldness than talent, I took no notice of it; nor would I under any circumstances have stopped the work of the revival, already in progress, to debate with any one. Before the man left the place, however, he seemed determined to try his little hatchet on the Baptists, and gave a discourse against our views. One of his main points was the telling of an old story, which has been worn thread-bare, of a dream, which some man was said to have told, to joke Elder Knapp.

There was an old Baptist sister who went to hear him, who though a well meaning woman, was said to be somewhat afflicted with lunacy. She took a seat near the preacher, and showed much concern of mind about the discourse, more especially the part pertaining to the dream. As he went on to tell how the dreamer dreamed that he died and went to heaven, and tried to find whether there were any Baptist people there or not, and how he looked all around, in one direction and in another direction, and couldn't find a single one, the old lady's feelings were wrought up to the most anxious interest, for she thought the search was about to be given up under the gloomy prospect that there was not a Baptist to be found in all heaven. At length the speaker said, however, of this remarkable dreamer, that he thought he asked the Saviour if there were no Baptist in heaven; when the Saviour took him to a place where he opened a trap-door, and told him they were all there, holding close communion.

"THANK GOD!" shouted the old lady with delight; "*then they are all there!*" said she.

Though I was not present, it was said that the effect of her sudden burst of feeling turned the point of the joke against the preacher, set the congregation into a glee, and turned the tide in our favor; at least it helped to enlist the public sympathy more largely in our behalf, and our meeting afterward went on with good interest and closed with success.

I have frequently observed, and many times heard it remarked, that our doctrinal opponents are more instrumental in making proselytes to the Baptist cause when they attempt public arguments against us, than Baptists are themselves; and I believe it to be a fact that the more we are pounded the better we prosper. A very clear illustration of this occurred while I was a merchant.

One of the little churches of which I was pastor at that time was close by the town of C * * *, and was surrounded by a strong Methodist community, which had a flourishing church near by. The Presiding Elder in going his rounds of love, appeared to take it into his head that our little church had better be out of the way, to make room for one that knew the way of God more perfectly. He then squared himself to the work, opened his batteries against it, and said enough, one would have supposed, to have blown it into fragments. Among other things, he said that the Baptist church was a mere upstart, of late origin, and of a mean origin at that, for the first Baptists were polygamists, they kept a number of wives, etc.

Being at some distance from the place, the brethren, who were much disturbed, sent word to me of the work of destruction that was going on, and thinking that I might be needed to gather up the pieces and bury the dead out of the way, I went up and a debate took place between us.

After the Elder left, his brethren, who did not seem

satisfied, sent for another man, who they thought was a larger light, to give the Baptist another heat. He in turn was met by Brother B * * *, a Baptist minister from Missouri, and after considerable discussion between them the debates ended; and the final result was that the Baptist church went up, and the other went down. The Methodist church having built a good house of worship in the town adjacent, so diminished in strength, and in the sympathy of the people, that they were unable to clear it from a mortgage which was resting upon it, and were compelled to sell it to the Baptists to pay the debt. We then moved our congregation into it, where it has worshiped ever since.

The Baptist interest is still prospering there, while Methodism has died out entirely, and they have not had a class, nor even a preaching station, there for some years. I felt sorry that they had been so imprudent, for I always regret to see any religious society decline; but so far as we were concerned in the unhappy event, we only aimed to act on the defensive, and that we were compelled to do to protect our church from abuse.

The lessons of history, however, ought to teach us the fact that the interests of religion can not be advanced by harsh measures; and we may be sure that where the spirit of persecution gets into a church there is death in the pot.

I wish that I might impress this fact upon all my brethren. It is better for us to bear patiently all the reproaches and hard titles that are heaped upon us and our churches, than for us to be the aggressors.

Forbearance is a Christian virtue. It is better to suffer wrong than to do wrong. It is safer to stand a siege than to storm a castle. The way to build a church is to labor for the conversion of sinners.

CHAPTER XXVII.

ENTERS THE ARMY—TENNESSEE RIVER—PITTSBURG LANDING—LAID IN THE HOSPITAL AT HAMBURG—PROSPECTS OF DEATH—RECOVERY—APPOINTED HOSPITAL CHAPLAIN—DESCRIPTION OF THE HOSPITAL—CONVERSION OF A YOUNG MAN—DREADFUL CRIES OF A WOUNDED MAN WHO WAS DYING—PRAYING FOR A WOUNDED CAPTAIN—SOLEMN WARNINGS—MOURNFUL INCIDENT OF TRANSPORTING A DEAD HUSBAND—REFLECTIONS—RETURN FROM THE WAR.

WHEN the Rebellion broke out I was aroused with the common feeling for the preservation of our country, and made speeches in various places to set the momentous issues of the day before the people in a proper light, and to call them to arms. I felt that matters of overwhelming interest were at stake, and in the month of February, 1862, I assisted in raising a regiment for the war, and volunteered myself. I was promoted to the office of first lieutenant, in a company which went out under Captain Archer, of Keokuk, a man whom I dearly loved, and whom I claimed as one of my sons in the gospel.

I did not allow my spiritual interest to die while I was recruiting, but held night meetings during a good part of the time. I felt that I was in a work which God would approve, and I went forward in it with all the zest which a full consciousness of right and duty could give.

When we began to raise our regiment it was after the capture of Forts Donelson and Henry, and the war spirit had in a measure subsided. This circumstance made it more difficult to raise the regiment; but we established our rendezvous at Keokuk, from which we went out in all directions into the country and kept at work, sending in recruits by squads and parcels, as we could enlist them, until our regiment was full.

My friend and brother, Captain Archer, was finally promoted to the well-merited position of colonel, which he afterward filled with high esteem from those of his command. He acted the true nobleman and the Christian throughout the service, and my prayer is that he may long live to honor his country and his church.

When spring opened we were ordered to move for the theater of war, and embarked upon the noble steamer "Warsaw." We stopped at Jefferson Barracks long enough to receive our arms, wagons, ambulances, and general equipments, and thence went aboard the steamer "Continental," and were soon on our way to Dixie's Land.

When the steamer first turned her bow from the wharf at Keokuk toward the fields of blood and strife, and we were permitted to take a farewell look of our weeping friends and relatives upon the shore, we were well-nigh overcome with the sense of our situation. As we looked forward to the dangers and uncertainties before us, and then looked back

14*

to the loved ones who were weeping for us upon the shore, and whom we feared we might never see again in the flesh, the fountains of our tears were unsealed, and many of us wept with the tenderness of children; but we were confident of the righteousness of our cause, and the mercy and justice of that God who doeth all things well, and felt comforted in the thought that "even the very hairs of our heads" were "all numbered."* and that we were "of more value than many sparrows."†

But oh, how many, many tears, have been shed over the partings and meetings consequent upon the "Great Rebellion," and how many have been the sorrows and disappointments!

After a prosperous voyage we landed at Hamburg, Tennessee, near the northwest corner of Alabama. I was delighted with the natural scenery on the Tennessee River. It is not a wide stream, but is very deep, and is navigable all the year round, for it is said that it never freezes over. Natural stone walls, of a peculiar whiteness, are seen in many places, standing up from the river's edge in a perpendicular form, which have smooth faces, and are crowned with a bold, natural cornice, at the top, that is often rendered most beautiful by a fringe of evergreen growing upon it. In other places the walls look as though they were yet unfinished, and the mason had merely stopped to go to dinner. Yet, strange to say, notwithstanding the enchanting beauty and great natural utility of this river, it is a

* Luke xii: 7. † Luke xii [illegible]

fact, that from Paducah, at its mouth, to Muscle Shoals, there is not a town upon it which is of any consequence whatever. Of all the little, dirty landing places that are upon it there is scarcely one that deserves the name of a town. This shows the blighting influence of the accursed institution of slavery. If that river had run through one of the free States of the North, its banks would have been lined with lively and enterprising towns and cities, and its waters would have been alive with the travel of commerce.

While we were quartered at Hamburg I visited the famous battle-ground of Pittsburg Landing, six miles below. As you step from the boat to the bank you see a small table land which runs back a few rods from the river, and beyond that is a hill running parallel to the river. To avoid this hill the road which starts back from the Landing turns a short distance to the left, and runs up a ravine which comes down through the hill to the river.

This ravine is the place through which the rebels attempted to pass down in order to get around to the river, and flank our army; but as their movements were anticipated by our men, they were met in the gap by the Union artillery, and suffered the most dreadful slaughter. They were thus caught in their own deadly trap, and were mowed down by hundreds. A rebel prisoner with whom I conversed, and who said that he was in the engagement in the ravine, acknowledged that out of an artillery company to which he belonged, which numbered one hundred and fifty members, only six were left alive.

In fact, it seemed marvelous to me that any man who stood anywhere upon that field in the time of action, could ever have got off alive; the underbrush all through the field was literally mowed down, and the forest torn in pieces by balls and shells. It seemed to me that there was not a square foot of ground upon the whole field where balls had not passed over!

The Shiloh meeting house, which was built of hewed logs, had been torn down and mostly carried away by visitors, as relics of the battle. Even the flooring had been split up in pieces for making walking canes; and I suppose that pieces of that house have been distributed into nearly every part of the civilized world. The number of spectators who have visited the place has doubtless been immense.

The sights that met our eyes about the various places where the thousands had been buried, were too hideous to describe; but the field, taken altogether, was certainly an awful monument of the horrors of sin and war.

When we landed at Hamburg, the left wing of the Union army was quartered there; it was its base of operations, and the place where the hospital was kept. We had not been there long when I took the typhoid fever, and had to be taken to the hospital—the very place which, above all others, I dreaded. Colonel Rankins, who was then in command of our regiment, showed much kindness in looking after my welfare, and was particular in charging the surgeon to take the best of care of me.

Shiloh Church.

for which I still believe I have reason to be grateful; but in spite of all that was done I took the chronic diarrhea, which grew upon me for some time, until I despaired of life. I suffered so much for several weeks that life became a burden. I expected to die, and tried to set my house in order, that I might be fully ready for an exchange of worlds; but as I thought of my dear wife and children whom I must leave behind, and the wants of the feeble churches and the perishing sinners back in Iowa, it seemed to me that there was so much for me yet to do and to live for, that the Lord would certainly spare me a while longer. One day, while I was lying in the hospital, and feeling that I was very near to the grave, there came up to my mind thoughts of the many and speedy answers to prayer which I had experienced in my past history, and I was suddenly possessed with the idea that a prayer of faith would save my life. With this my desire to live was quickened, and I fell to praying for my recovery. Never did I urge a plea before the Lord in greater faith. It pleased him that from that time I should begin to mend.

It had been written to my family that I was already dead, and they mourned for me as none but a wife and children could; but when they learned to the contrary, that I was alive and getting well, it was to them as news from one who had returned from the other world.

When I began to stir about again, I was appointed by the post surgeon temporarily as post chaplain in the hospital, with the understanding that I should look after the spiritual wants of the sick only so far as seemed proper for my health, for I was yet quite feeble. This hospital was, I suppose, one of the greatest infirmaries the world ever saw. It contained some six or eight thousand sick and wounded men, in the various stages of disease and suffering, and to a novice it was perfectly shocking to see the number of dead bodies that would be carried from it in one day. I was kept very busy in praying with and giving spiritual counsel to the sick; there seemed to be so much of this kind of labor for me to do that I was often induced to go beyond my strength.

While in this work it was my sad privilege to witness a great many deaths, and it is a fact worthy of the notice of all impenitent persons, that among them all I never saw one, howsoever wicked he may have been, who showed any signs of contempt for religion when he expected to die; on the contrary, all seemed to believe in sound orthodoxy, and such as were not Christians looked upon the fact as the cause of their most bitter regret. Never have I seen one, in a single instance, who, upon his dying couch, found any consolation in the doctrines of Universalism or infidelity. They were, then, generally ready to take the Christian's robe, and willing to give all they possessed for the Christian's hope; but, alas! with many it was too late. I have reason to believe, however, that my efforts for the good of souls in the hospital were not in vain.

There were those who, by their disease or wounds, were sobered and brought to view more seriously their spiritual state. Such sometimes received the offers of the gospel and recovered, and, I trust, will ever look back upon their experience in the hospital as one of the best portions of their lives.

I remember one young man, a very intelligent person, who was brought into the hospital one night, and as the surgeon examined him he said that he could not live until morning. He was very penitent in view of his past life, and told me his history in such a pathetic manner that it moved my feelings very much. I spent a considerable time with him in reading such Scriptures as I thought most suitable to his case, and praying for his salvation. He knew that his time was precious, and cared for little else than religion. He appeared to see the way of life, and joined most heartily in my prayers for his soul. After a while, to my great encouragement, he professed to have great joy in believing, and thanked me most heartily for the interest I had taken in his welfare. Soon after this he passed into the spirit-land.

One night there was a large, strong man brought in, who had been wounded. He had been told that he could live but a short time, and he was terribly frightened over his prospects for the other world. He would cry aloud to God for mercy for a few moments, then stopping his pleadings in fits of despair, he would utter his cries and lamentations, and tell his feelings of remorse with the full strength of his voice; and as his voice was very strong, he was heard by hundreds of patients who were about him. It is remarkable that those patients who were fearing death themselves had no complaints to make about his noise—they evidently felt that he had good reason to be terrified; but those who were convalescent, and felt that they were out of present danger, raised a hubbub of complaints. Some wanted him out of the place, some would call upon the attendants to go and stop his mouth. Some told him he was crazy and others cursed him most insultingly for being, as they said, such a great fool. But he gave no attention to any thing they said, and continued his cries for mercy or his wailings of despair. He seemed to have been a very wicked man. I prayed for him, and tried to instruct him and point him to Christ, the only way of hope; but he declared that it was all of no avail, for he was damned and was going to hell, and that nothing could save him; and he continued his loud and pitiful cries until his voice was hushed in death!

One peculiar case occurred, of a captain who from some disappointment became desperate and stabbed himself in a dreadful manner. He was conveyed to his tent in an ambulance, but as they attempted to take him in, he declared that he would never go in, or move another step, until Pickard would be brought to him to pray for him. One of his attendants came after me for that purpose, and I sent him word that I was too feeble to go at the time, but would call upon him after a while; but it was not long before the messenger returned, and told me that they could do nothing with the captain, unless by force, which they dare not attempt lest it would hasten his death. He said that he was yet outside the tent, still declaring that he would not enter it until Pickard was brought, and he urged me to go with him to the captain, if it was possible for me to get there. When I found him, he was in a very penitent condition of mind, and personally besought me to pray for him, with all my heart. After I had given him suitable instruction and prayed with him, he seemed to be satisfied for the present, and allowed himself to be taken quietly into the tent. Soon after this he began to recover, and finally he got well; but strange as it may seem, he never asked for any more prayer, and I suppose that up to the present time, if he is yet alive, he is trying to live without it! So far as could be tested, I found this to be most commonly the case with those who deferred repentance until the moment when the prospect of a speedy death was before them. Their repentance was not that of a real godly sorrow for their sins, but arose wholly from the fear of the consequences of sin, and they were simply terrified about death and hell. It is easy to see that where such thoughts only form the basis of repentance, it amounts to nothing; for, when they afterward recover from danger, this whole basis is gone; all those fears leave them for the present, and then their repentance is gone also. Such is the kind of repentance to which Paul alludes, as one that needs to be repented of. *

Let the careless sinner beware that he defers it not until the hour when life is in peril!

* 2 Cor. viii : 10.

"Of human ills the last extreme beware;
Beware, Lorenzo! a sudden death:
How dreadful that deliberate surprise!
Be wise to-day; 'tis madness to defer:
Next day the fatal precedent will plead;
Thus on, till wisdom is pushed out of life.
Procrastination is the thief of time;
Year after year it steals, till all are fled,
And to the mercies of a moment leaves,
The vast concerns of an eternal scene.
If not so frequent, would not this be strange?
That 'tis so frequent, this is stranger still.
Of man's miraculous mistakes this bears
The palm. 'That all men are about to live,'
Forever on the brink of being born." *

Some of the most affecting things I saw while at Hamburg, were in connection with the numerous visits of friends, who came for the bodies of their deceased relatives. In some instances, delicate women would come to attempt the task of conveying home the dead bodies of those they loved.

One day two women, the wife and mother of a soldier, called at my quarters for sympathy and help. The wife, who was burdened with a little child in her arms, said that they had heard that her husband was in the hospital somewhere in that part of the army, and that he was very sick, and they wished me to assist them in finding him. We very quickly ascertained, however, that he had been taken to another place, some miles distant, and the women left to extend their search. One or two days afterward they returned in a teamster's wagon,

* Young's Night Thoughts.

bringing a dead body with them. They looked as though they had been weeping bitterly, and when they recognized me they said, that before they found the husband he was dead and buried, and that they had taken up his body at a place about sixteen miles distant, with the view of getting it home. As I looked, I saw the body lying in the bottom of the wagon-box, at their feet, with only such a slight extra covering upon it, as they had been able to extemporize from their traveling apparel. In that condition the poor wife, with a child in her arms, and the mother, had ridden with the corpse that day the distance of sixteen miles, in the coarse lumber wagon, much of the time on a corduroy road, and all the way through a broiling sun; and to increase their trials, the body had become putrid and was every hour getting more offensive. They asked me to aid them in preparing the body so that they might take it with them to Kentucky. I had aided in such cases before, and knew how to dread such a duty, but their condition was so pitiful and helpless, that I could not refuse them. The only thing we could do to preserve the body at that time was to put it in alcohol.

After considerable trouble and heavy expense part of a barrel was procured, when we unheaded it, crammed the body into it, then headed the barrel again as tightly as possible, and the poor women, who were very thankful for my assistance, were soon embarked with their freight and journeying homeward.

Oh, how strong is the affection of a faithful wife or mother! How little do they merit abuse, and how much do they deserve our kindness, when they are thus ready to risk life and limb, and health and comfort, for our sakes!

Here was an attachment that was more than friendship—it was love. How sad is the thought of the thousands upon thousands whose hearts have been broken, whose hopes have been blighted, and whose spirits have been crushed in the slaveholders' awful rebellion, to satisfy the vindictive demon of war! May God hasten the time when wars shall be no more; when perpetual peace shall abound, and when "the kingdoms of this world shall become the kingdoms of our Lord and of his Christ."*

In the fall, after I joined the army, I was still so feeble in health that I felt compelled to resign. It was very trying for me to resign my post, and leave my friends and comrades behind, especially as so many opportunities were afforded for usefulness among them; but I was so reduced, and of so little use to the government, and had such a poor chance to recover my health, that it seemed unreasonable for me to remain.

On my return from the army my family received me with great joy, and for a time we enjoyed such gratitude and happiness over my safe return as, perhaps, none have ever realized who have not been off to the war. Here the joys and comforts of home were so reviving to my spirits that my health rapidly improved, and in a few weeks I was again ready for active service in the cause of the divine Master.

* Rev. xi: 15.

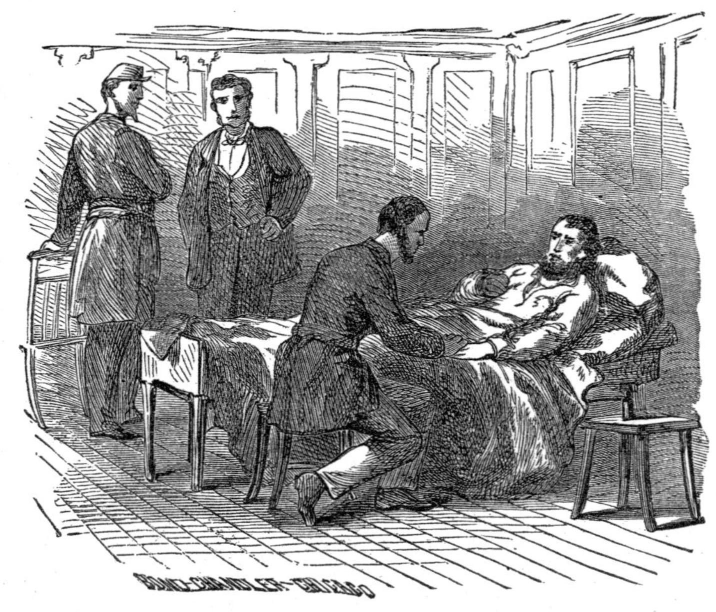

The Wounded Chaplain.

CHAPTER XXVIII.

REAPPOINTED A MISSIONARY—A REVIVAL IN V * * *—GIVING UP THE MEETING HOUSE TO TWO MINISTERS—THE RESULT—REFLECTIONS—MEETING NEAR DEACON C * * *'S—A DREADFUL FRIGHT—WANT OF MEETING HOUSES IN THE WEST—REVIVAL AT D * * *—MEETING AT S * * *—HAPPY RESULTS—REVIVAL AT Y * * * A * * *—TRIALS AND TRIUMPHS—LABOR FOR BURLINGTON COLLEGE—LIBERALITY OF THE CHURCHES—THE CHURCH AT A * * *—THE THIRTY-FIVE CENT COLLECTION—WHAT A CHURCH MAY COME TO—REFLECTIONS—HOSPITALITY OF A LITTLE PEDLER.

LATE in the fall of 1862 I received a new appointment from the Home Mission Board of New York, and again commenced laboring upon my old field, and spent the time until the close of the following winter, as usual, in revivals.

On going to the town of V * * *, for the purpose of holding a meeting, where there was no Baptist interest, I endeavored to find some place in which to preach, but there was no school house or building of any kind which could be had that was really suitable. There was, however, an old shaky meeting house in the place, which had been built in an early day by the Methodists, but for some time it had been entirely deserted. There was no religious interest that I could discover of any kind in the town, or in the surrounding community, nearer than the distance of two miles and a half, where there was a Baptist church.

There appeared to be a general disregard among the citizens in respect to religion, and I thought that rather than leave them without making some effort for their salvation, I would try to fix up the old meeting house in some shape to make it answer the purpose and preach in that. With this intention I inquired about the place, to ascertain where I should apply in order to get the privilege of using it. There were a very few individuals in the town who had formerly been connected with the church, but it had become so disorganized and forgotten that no one claimed to have any authority in regard to the meeting house whatever; yet every one said that if I wished to use it I might do so, of course, for it was standing idle and useless, and there would be no objection, for there was no one who cared about it in any way.

I then went forward with my plan, and getting the aid of some of the Baptist brethren who lived back in the country, we cleaned out and patched up the old barracks, arranged for heating it, and managed to make it answer the purpose tolerably well. In the mean while notices were circulated that a meeting would begin in the old house. The meeting finally began, and I soon had a good crowd; but there appeared to be an unusual hardness and indifference, and the truth was so slow in taking effect, that I preached every night for over a week with my utmost energy before I made any test of the feelings of the congregation. When I did make the test, however, a number arose for prayers, and designated themselves as seekers of religion. From this the reformation went on with great encouragement, and at the end of the second week fifteen persons had been hopefully converted. Besides this, the religious interest had spread from heart to heart, and there were many under deep conviction. The old house was thoroughly crammed each night; the people were giving the most solemn attention, and every omen was favorable to an extensive reformation throughout the community. But just at this point a most unfortunate move was made by a presiding elder and a circuit rider, who, having heard of the religious interest that was in progress, came to the place together and said that they had decided to hold a meeting there immediately, and would be compelled to use the house. They demanded, therefore, that I should give place to them. The movement gave me great disappointment, but it was a Methodist house—they had built it. I had no claim upon it except one of squatter sovereignty, and without any complaints I gave up the house to them, gathered up my converts, baptized them, and took them into the Baptist church, which was two miles and a half out of town.

As it was, however, our meeting was productive of great good. It greatly strengthened and encouraged the Baptist church in the country, and gave an impetus to the cause of religion and the Baptist interest, which is felt there to this day. But the outcome of the effort which was made by the Methodist elder and his colleague was somewhat singular. They commenced immediately with my congregation, while it was yet in a high state of religious interest, and though they preached, prayed, exhorted, stamped, and hallooed with all their might for two weeks, in endeavoring to appropriate that interest to the up-building of the Methodist church, they failed to get a single convert! The people knew how long the meeting house had been standing idle, and they felt that when the ministers came and took the meeting out of my hands, they were moved to do it by sectarian feeling, and it unfortunately excited their disgust. So unhappy was their fortune, that when they were about to leave the place it was with difficulty that the more orderly class of people prevented the boys from egging them.

Let it not be supposed that because I have related this unfortunate circumstance I do it to make a thrust at the Methodists, for I wish to turn it to better account. I wish to use this as a caution against bigotry. We are all liable to mistakes, and it is possible for us to have more concern for the up building of our own particular church and creed, than for the salvation of souls; and when Christians, in their efforts to do good, run into this mistake, they will surely fail in both those objects.

During the winter two brethren came after me to hold a meeting in the town of B * * *, in Jefferson county, and I went with them; but when we arrived we could not hold the meeting on account of the small-pox, which was then in the place, and we went out into the country in the neighborhood of Deacon C * * * 's, and commenced a meeting in a school house. As the school room, however, was so very much smaller than the crowd that would come out to the meeting, I thought it necessary, after preaching three or four nights, to close the effort.

During the meeting a young man came to my lodging under great excitement. His countenance and actions betokened so much alarm as to surprise me. I wondered what on earth could be the matter, but he was not long in telling. Said he—

"Mr. Pickard, I have been awfully scared, and I have come to you about it, for I don't know what to do."

Said I, "Why, my dear sir, what is the matter?"

"Why, sir, as I was going to meeting I met the devil on the road, right before me; and oh! but he was a most terrible sight! and he acted as though he was going to catch me. I tried to get away, and when I would run to one side of the road he would run to the same side, too, and stand right ahead of me. I was so scared that I didn't know what in the world to do. I just thought I was gone, sure. Why, sir, I couldn't tell you how dreadful he did look. He was as big as an elephant!"

"Why, how did you escape?" I asked.

"Why," said he, "I thought he was going to destroy me on the spot, and I prayed, but that didn't do any good; and then I ran, first to one side of the road and then to the other, and then I prayed again, but it didn't do any good yet; and finally I ran and hid behind a sapling, and after I had staid there a while he went off out of sight. But, sir, I am a great sinner, and I don't know what to do. I want you to pray for me with all your might, for I've been very wicked, and I am afraid he will destroy me yet!"

I kneeled down and prayed with him, and he seemed afterward to feel more at ease, but he soon went away, and I left the place. What was the final result of the matter I am unable to say.

There were very encouraging prospects for a reformation in the neighborhood, and I much regretted to leave, but it was midwinter, the ground was covered with snow, and there seemed no earthly chance to provide anything temporary in the way of a meeting house in which the people's health would be safe, and I felt compelled to give up the effort.

I will just say here, that the want of suitable houses in which to hold meetings has ever been, through the principal part of each year, an embarrassment to my labors; and the same is true of the labors of many of our brethren throughout the West. There are many churches, especially through the State of Iowa, which are making little or no advancement for the want of meeting houses. It is true that in many such cases it cannot be helped, but I believe that in a large proportion of them it can be, if the brethren in such places would only rally with more spirit and enterprise, and bring together their tithes and offerings. Every farmer, whether he be a saint or a sinner, ought to be impressed with the fact that a meeting house in his neighborhood will enhance the value of his property. Every one who can be persuaded of this, whether he be a good or a bad man, will feel an interest in such an enterprise and help to build. There are many strings to pull and many arguments to encourage such efforts, which may be drawn from interests both temporal and eternal; and a church of comparatively little strength can build a house of God, if they only have the spirit of pious enterprise. Where a church contains half a dozen brethren who are able to own tolerable farms, and clear of debt, that church can build, with the aid of the community, a good house of worship, and be no poorer in the end, and I heartily wish that all such would arise and be doing.

During the winter I held a meeting in the town of D * * *, where there was a feeble Baptist church with no pastor, though it had a small meeting house. The town in which the meeting house stood, as also the surrounding country, was settled by an excellent class of citizens, and they possessed more than an ordinary degree of intelligence. It was a most inviting field, and I remained and preached there four weeks, during which time about one hundred souls were converted, most of whom united with the Baptist church. There was a certain class who were very active in getting up lectures and parties, as is very commonly the case when a revival begins, but the Lord's cause triumphed over all opposition.

The church was made strong, secured a good pastor, and has continued to prosper to the present time. I have since been permitted to visit it on different occasions, and rejoice with many warm friends.

The fall preceding this I went into the neighborhood of S * * *, to hold a meeting. There was but one Baptist in the community, and she was a widow. She had moved in from the East, and was very anxious to have me make some attempt for the reformation of those around her.

I had a notice circulated that I would preach the next night in their school house, which was a good and large one, and the people came out well, and gave very good attention. At the close of the service I told the audience that I was willing to remain and preach to them a few nights, but that, as I was an entire stranger to them, I did not know that it would be very much desired, and that if I should remain, I should like to do so by their encouragement. I then took a rising vote to ascertain their wish in the matter, and was gratified in seeing nearly all who were in the room at the time arise to their feet. I then went on with the meeting, which continued ten days, and, according to the best of my recollection, every unconverted one who voted for the meeting was converted before it closed. The congregation was greatly increased after the first night, and there were scores who did not embrace religion, but of those who did, a good church was organized, which is flourishing and sustaining regular preaching to this day.

Somewhere near this period I paid a visit, by in

vitation, to Illinois, and held a meeting in the town of Y* * * A * * *. A feeble little band of brethren had struggled nobly to build a house of worship in the place, and after getting it up, and making hard trials to clear it from debt and complete it, they were at last about to have it sold from them to cancel a mortgage which was resting upon it. The brethren were about despairing, but concluded to make one more effort for the salvation of sinners before the meeting house went out of their hands.

As soon as we began the work, it seemed that nothing was left undone which could be done by the devil, to prevent the salvation of souls. In the first place, he sent off and got a Universalist preacher to hold forth, in order to keep the people from our meetings, but in this the man could not succeed—the people would come to the Baptist meeting. A dancing master was then sent for, to get up a dancing school to draw away the young people; but prayer was made unto the Lord, and the work of grace went on, while the dancing-master got sick, and every other scheme of opposition failed. Though the meeting was not of long continuance, some fifty or sixty persons united with the church, the debt was finally rolled off from the meeting house, the church took a new start, and, I believe, has enjoyed a fair degree of prosperity ever since. To God be all the glory.

In the spring of 1864 my appointment as missionary was renewed, but soon after my attention was called to the wants of our Baptist college at Burlington. That institution was originated and built chiefly under the zealous labors of Elder G. J. Johnson, and a very few generous friends and brethren who co-operated with him. They justly felt that the wants of the denomination in the West for such an institution of learning, in particular with reference to fitting young men for the ministry, were great.

Actuated by motives the most generous and noble, they had begun the enterprise and forced it through, so far as they had gone, in the face of many difficulties, and had succeeded, by the blessing of God, in doing a vast amount of good. Many of the sons and daughters of our families had there received mental elevation—it had helped to enlarge the educational interests of our people—and above all, it had sought out young men of ministerial gifts, aided them in preparing for the ministry, and sent them forth until its representatives were preaching in Iowa, Indiana, Illinois, Missouri, California, and Oregon. In addition to these things, the enterprise had accumulated a property in grounds and buildings, and various apparatus, from its different donations, to the value of $25,000. Under the paralyzing effects of the war, however, the institution had become burdened with a debt of $6,000, and under the circumstances it was so discouraging as to threaten the life of the school. The brethren thought that my extensive acquaintance with the churches would insure me success, as an agent, in soliciting contributions to aid in canceling the debt, and fully persuaded me that it was my solemn duty to give my assistance. Though a work like this is

Burlington Collegiate Institute,

(*Corporation, Burlington University,*)

BURLINGTON, IOWA.

not such as any one can have an appetite for, I suppose, I felt that it was one which was important to the cause of our churches, and started forth, and after a somewhat lengthy effort, which was assisted by two or three other brethren, we closed with success. In this tour I visited and preached to many churches, renewed many old acquaintances, both in Illinois and Iowa, and, I trust, enlarged my circle of friends. I was especially thankful in finding that in most of the places where I visited the spirit of Christian benevolence had been greatly enlarged among our people, and that in about the same proportion God had blessed them in temporal prosperity. With but very rare exceptions, indeed, I saw no turning of the cold shoulder because I was an agent to collect money for the Master's cause, but on the contrary, both myself and the claims I presented were generally received in the true spirit of Christian generosity.

Among those churches which responded to my appeals to aid the college, I am happy to make most favorable notice of Independence, Bonaparte, Des Moines, Winterset, Oskaloosa, Denmark, Fort Madison, Jefferson, Oquaka, Fall Creek, Sugar Grove, Edgington, Monmouth, and Young America. Of all the churches, however, that have aided in this college enterprise, the First Baptist Church of Burlington has borne the heaviest burdens. It has been a strong tower upon the walls of Zion, and its leading brethren have been characteristic cross-bearing and self-denying men.

In one place which I visited, however, of which I

may make profitable notice, the brethren have never burst their shell; and I wish the Lord's sledge-hammer would fall upon it and break it in pieces, and let them out into the sun, so they can look upon the light of gospel day. The case in question was that of a church in the village of A * * *. It contained about one hundred members, many of whom were among the most able farmers in that part of the country. Their temporal ability is such, that if they could be brought into sympathy with the self-denying labors of their brethren who are straining and giving to advance the interests of religion in the West, they might do a great amount of good.

Knowing of their ability, and hearing that they were seldom called upon to give anything to the cause of religion, I made a journey of thirty-two miles, going nearly half the way on foot, in order to visit them in behalf of the college. The first place at which I stopped among them was at the house of a brother who preached occasionally, who owned a large farm, and was worth at least $10,000. I told him all about the institution, and all about the good it had done by educating ministers and sending them forth to bless the world, and how much help it had been, and still would be, to the cause of religion, if we could keep it moving, and then appealed to him for aid.

After he had quietly heard me through, said he, "My observation and experience proves that for preachers to have too much learning ain't good;" and after trying some time to show to me, by arguments the most contemptible, that what he had said was true, he refused to bestow a single dollar. I plead hard for the small sum of one dollar, that he might have a little interest in the matter, but it was no use, he stubbornly refused. I then made a number of calls upon the brethren, but found them all like the first, and could not get a single cent. Feeling disappointed that I had lost all my time and travel in getting there and going about among them, I resolved to push ahead, and get away as fast as possible to more generous climes; but the brother with whom I had dined, and who was also a preacher, urged very hard for me to remain over the Sabbath and preach. I told him that as I could not get anything from them, I could not afford to give them my time in that way, for it was too precious — the college was suffering, and I must go at once and visit such churches as would aid it; but after urging me some time in vain, he finally said that they would give me a good collection on the Sabbath if I would remain and preach, and with considerable encouragement in that direction I consented. He also promised that after dinner he would go around with me among the brethren, and try to stir them up on the subject a little.

While we were waiting for dinner I thought I would read the news. Said I, "Have you the *Christian Times?*"

"What, me!" said he, in apparent surprise. "No, thank God; I never had it in my house. They say it's an abolitionist paper."

"Have you any religious paper?" I asked.

"No," said he, "nor I don't want any of them. They say it's them papers that's brought on this war."

I found that there were four such preachers in the church, all of whom I visited. One we found in the field threshing, with whom I made an earnest effort to get something, but it was of no use whatever. While I was with him, however, a peddler came along, of whom he bought something, causing him to display the contents of his pocket-book, which could not have had less than $500 in it at the time.

The last preacher whom we visited did not believe in colleges, or educated ministers either, and would give nothing; and though he was well off in point of property, all the library which I could see in his house was a Bible and an old greasy hymn book. Aside from these, according to the best of my discoveries, the place was as destitute of any books or other sources of information as any Indian hut. As I had arrived there on Friday, and had agreed to preach three times, the people had become pretty well stirred up, so that when Sabbath came we had a good turn-out at the meeting.

When I was in the midst of my sermon the people's hearts seemed to be moved very much; one brother, especially, became so extremely happy that he lifted up his voice while I was preaching. I began to think that matters looked very encouraging for a good collection, and closed the sermon while all were in a high state of feeling. Thinking that that would be the best time for me to get them to do their duty to the college, in as prudent a manner as I could I changed the subject to an appeal for them to give. The hat was then passed round and returned to the desk, and on counting the contents, lo! it was but *thirty-five cents!* With a look of amazement I then held the precious little bunch up before the congregation, between my thumb and fore-finger, and made quite a speech about it, reminding them of their promise to give a good collection, and of the time I had spent among them, and of the preaching I had done for them, and would frequently shake the little bunch before them and tell them to look at the result! Finally, I told them that I did not wish to keep the money, for if I did keep it, it would go into the published report of our collections as the contribution of their church, and hence it would be laid before the world that they had given only *thirty-five cents*, and it would be a disgrace which I did not want to see published against them. I then begged of them that, for the honor of the cause, they would come and take their money back; but no one would come to take the money, and the whole amount was left in my hands.

At night I preached again, but the taking of the collection had so destroyed their religious feelings that all was very cold and dull. At the close of the last sermon I begged to know if some one of the brethren or friends would not help me forward, in the morning, by taking me a few hours' drive on my journey to another point; but not one would offer, and so little was their sympathy for my mission, that when the meeting was dismissed not one of them even invited me to a lodging, but all dispersed and left me standing alone with the *thirty-five cents.*

Now, reader, you may see what a church will come to where its members do not believe in taking religious newspapers, building colleges, giving to religious enterprises, helping to educate ministers, nor sustaining salaried pastors; but, above all things, do believe in hating a contribution box. The thirty-five cents was, as near as I could find, the first public collection which had been taken in that congregation for many a day—the people discouraged it.

Their house of worship looked as if it had been built for a barn, and afterward changed into a meeting house. I believe that there was not a particle of paint on any of the inside work; every thing about it looked dreary and uninviting.

I will just here state what I believe—what *I positively know.* I will not make the statement upon theory, but facts—upon the result of long and varied experience, and extensive observation. *Let a church banish the contribution box, and discourage public collections, and it will surely decline in spirituality, and in a few years die of dry rot, and become a stench in the nostrils of the Almighty!*

It is easy to see that such a result is natural. When we suppose we are excused from bringing our offerings to the Lord, and presenting them upon his altar, it accommodates *self,* which will then get the upper hand, and when it fills our hearts, the spirit of pious enterprise is gone, because there is no room for it. This will encourage all those ruinous ideas of which I have spoken, such as opposition to religious newspapers, opposition to building colleges and educating ministers, opposition to sustaining salaried pastors, and in fact opposition to every religious enterprise, at home or abroad, where it will cost any sacrifice to carry it through. I heartily wish we might all learn to follow more closely the apostolic injunction, "Upon the first day of the week, let every one of you lay by him in store as God hath prospered him." * "Take heed," O ye churches, "and beware of covetousness; for a man's life consisteth not in the abundance of the things which he possesseth."

While I was yet standing near the church, deliberating as to what I should do, a little man, who was a peddler, and who it appears had heard of my situation, came along with a pistol in his belt, and appeared to be in high dudgeon. I heard him, as he was coming, inquire of somebody in a very blustering style, "Where's that preacher that nobody wants to keep over night?" Directly he came up and invited me home with him, where he treated me the best he knew how, and the next morning took me aboard of his peddler wagon, and hauled me about sixteen miles.

* 1 Cor. xvi : 2.

CHAPTER XXIX.

A RIDE WITH A PEDDLER—CONVERSATION WITH A REBEL AND HIS ARREST—SUCCESS OF THE COLLEGE ENTERPRISE—LABORS AGAIN AS A MISSIONARY—REPORT OF ONE HUNDRED AND TWO DAYS' LABOR—ATTACKED BY TWO UNIVERSALIST MINISTERS—THE RESULT—SOME POETRY FOR UNIVERSALISTS—THE GREAT HARVEST—CALL FOR LABORERS—FAREWELL ADDRESS.

THE blustering little peddler who had become my traveling companion, was a very small man, but terrible ferocious, and seemed to be in for the "Union," soul and body. The chief topic of his conversation was about the Rebels and Copperheads, against whom he had an awful spite. As our route was not far from the State line of Missouri, we were passing through a country which had been much threatened by guerrillas, and which was being flooded with refugees from Missouri, who were mostly rebels at heart. The peddler was armed equal to a pirate, and was ready for any emergency. In fact, from what we could learn, the traveling looked rather squally, and I wondered that the little man would dare to risk himself and his goods alone in such a country; but he declared that he was not afraid, and that nothing would please him better than to have a chance to shoot some of Uncle Sam's straggling enemies. While on our journey we overtook a man who we thought looked rather suspicious, and about the following conversation ensued.

Peddler. "How do you do, stranger?"

Stranger. "Very well, I thank you. How do you do?"

Peddler. "All right, sir. Where are you from, stranger?"

Stranger. "I am from Ohio. I am a minister of the gospel, sir."

Peddler. "Ah! to be sure. Have you been preaching any around these parts?"

Stranger. "Well, not exactly in this neighborhood. I have been up more in the northern part of the State, and have just come in here. I am now trying to find a man by the name of D * * *, with whom I have some business, and I was told that he lived in or near the town of C * * *. Can you tell me, sir, whether I am on the right road to C * * *?"

We both happened to know that the man whom he inquired for was suspected of being a traitor, and that complaints had already been laid against him for harboring rebels; but the peddler said,

"Yes, sir; this is the road to C * * *."

"Where did you spend the Sabbath?" I asked.

Stranger. "In the village of A * * *, sir."

"Ah!" said I, "I preached there last Sabbath."

Stranger. "Is it possible, sir! Then you are a preacher, too, are you?"

"Yes, sir," said I.

Stranger. "Well, I am glad to see you, then. What kind of preacher are you?"

"I am a Baptist preacher, sir," said I.

Stranger. "Well, indeed, that is just what I am."

"Ah! indeed, sir."

Stranger. "Yes, sir; and I am trying to find some church that wants a minister, and perhaps you can tell me where I can find such a place."

"I expect I could, sir, for people need preaching in many places; but if you are a Baptist minister I am surprised that you would spend the Sabbath so near the church where I preached yesterday, and not come to meeting once."

Stranger. "I was not very well, sir."

"Well, you seem to look pretty stout again to-day," said I. But the peddler was getting impatient.

Peddler. "Where did you stop yesterday and last night—whose house was it at?"

Stranger. "At Mr. G * * * 's."

The peddler knew it was a falsehood, and quick as thought he bounced from the wagon, with his pistol in his hand, saying, "Surrender, sir, or you are a dead man!" and his pistol was held close to the stranger's face, all ready to fire, so that he durst not move a hand. His hands were then bound behind him securely, and we set him on the top of the peddler's box, and moved on.

"Now," said the peddler, "set there, you infernal rebel, you. You've lied enough for one day."

The man begged hard for his freedom, but his jailor ordered him to be quiet, and we rolled ahead.

This was after the battle at Athens, which was on the Iowa line; and as it was believed that Anderson's guerillas were near the border at the time, we suspected that this man was a spy who was sent ahead for information. At any rate, the peddler took him to the town of C * * *, where he was lodged in jail, and was afterward proved, I was informed, to be one of the worst of rebels. He was kept in jail a considerable time, but what finally became of him I never knew.

When the college was found to be clear of debt, a brother in Quincy, according to previous promise, gave five thousand dollars more toward its endowment, which, with another claim of twenty thousand dollars, held by the institution, will, when all is settled as it is hoped, leave it worth about fifty-five thousand dollars, clear of all embarrassments. My prayer is that it may be well sustained from this time henceforth, and do a vast amount of good.

At the close of my labors for the institution, I attended the K * * * Association, which was held at the town of D * * *, in Iowa, and saw so many tokens of the growing spirit of enterprise as did my soul good. All the leading objects of Christian benevolence were presented, such as the Home Mission, Foreign Mission, Bible Society, Education Society, Church Building Fund, etc., and every appeal was responded to most liberally; especially in view of the fact that the Association had been in existence but two years, and covered but a small territory.

During the fall and winter I was again continually engaged in revival efforts, under the employment of the Home Mission Board. That the reader may form some better idea of the hard labors of a traveling missionary than any I have yet given him, I will here give an account of the labors of one hundred and two days, performed by me in the winter of 1864, and sent in my report to the Mission Board.

Number	of miles traveled - - - - - - -	700
"	of sermons preached - - - - -	118
"	of visits made - - - - - - - -	310
"	of prayer meetings conducted - -	87
"	of conversions - - - - - - - -	180
"	baptized and added to churches -	107

I much regret that this is the only report upon which I can now lay my hands; but short as it is, however, it will serve to show that the life of a missionary is a stirring one.

I shall mention but one meeting which I held during the winter. It was one which, though none were converted, proved a happy success.

I was sent for by a few brethren to go back into the State of Iowa about fifty miles, to hold a meeting in a destitute place where there was no church, though it was in a considerable village. We obtained the use of the school house, however, and commenced the meeting. It was not long when some unconverted men became very angry at my plain way of telling them their sins, and in order to spite me they made up a purse of fifteen dollars, and dispatched a couple of men, who were known to be drunkards, after two Universalist ministers, to set up an opposition meeting.

The ministers came on. In the first place, they wished me to let them occupy the school house. They said that as I had now occupied it for several evenings, it would be no more than fair for me to step aside for a time and give them an equal chance; but I could not see the point. Not succeeding in this, they went across the street into an old frame house within a few rods of my meeting, and commenced preaching there. Notices were posted up about town, and the biggest gun was set up to preach, in order to draw the people away from my meeting; but when they had done their best they could only succeed in getting the most wicked class of the community to hear them. They, however, hammered away against us as long as the meeting lasted, and succeeded in raising the spirit of controversy, and preventing the salvation of souls for the time; but the result of the controversy was, that the better class of the people felt disgusted at their uncalled-for attack upon the Baptist cause, and their sympathies were all aroused and enlisted in our favor. We then seized the opportunity which was presented in the general sympathy, to get pledges and subscriptions from the citizens for building a house of worship, and such was the interest taken in our enterprise, that within three or four days a sufficient amount was raised to erect a good building, and before I left the materials were on the ground.

This is another illustration of what I have already said, that the more the Baptists are pounded, the better they prosper; and we ought not to murmur at such experiences, for the reason that they make us fruitful.

I have not space to deal with the doctrines of Universalism at any length in this book, but will here present a simple piece of poetry, which I never saw a Universalist who was able to manage.

"Thus Pharaoh and his mighty host,
Had God-like honors given;
A pleasant breeze brought them with ease,
And took them safe to heaven.

"So all the filthy Sodomites,
When God bade Lot retire,
Went in a trice to paradise
On rapid wings of fire.

"Likewise the guilty Canaanites
To Joshua's sword were given:
The sun stood still that he might kill,
And packed them off to heaven.

"God saw those villains were too bad
To own that fruitful land;
He therefore took the rascals up,
To dwell at his right hand.

"The men who lived before the flood
Were made to feel the rod;
They missed the ark, and, like the lark,
Were washed right up to God.

"But Noah, he, because, you see,
Much grace to him was given,
He had to toil and till the soil,
And work his way to heaven.

"The wicked Jews who did refuse
The Lord's commands to do,
Were hurried straight to heaven's gate,
By Titus and his crew.

"How happy is the sinner's state
When he from earth is driven;
He knows it is his certain fate,
To go straight up to heaven.

"There's Judas, too, another Jew,
Whom some suppose accursed;
Yet with a cord he beat his Lord,
And got to heaven first."

I have not yet returned to the place of my contest with the Universalist ministers, but now that the Baptist meeting house is built, I intend to at an early day, God willing, when I hope to reap a harvest of souls.

Though the Lord has done wonders for us as a people, in raising up churches throughout the West, there are yet many large fields for missionary enterprise. Though our people are now numbered in the State of Iowa by thousands, I trust that they are yet to be *multiplied*, and that the work of our denomination has but fairly begun.

The great harvest is ripening fast, and rapidly increasing in abundance, and to all such as feel that they are called of God to enter the field I will here say, Come over into Macedonia and help us, for "the harvest is plenteous and the laborers are few."

With all the trials and crosses that are incident to a missionary's life, he has his joys and comforts. No class of men can be blessed with a larger number of warm personal friends, and this in itself is a fortune. Though, so far as worldly wealth is concerned, he may expect poverty, if he is entirely devoted to his work, yet he will be fed and clothed, and may constantly look forward with joy to the time when evening shall come, and when the Lord of the vineyard shall say unto his Steward, "Call the laborers and give them their hire."

To young men who are trembling and halting under the pressure of the Spirit, let me say, Wait no longer, but equip yourself for the work without delay. Hasten to a School of the Prophets, at Alton, Burlington, Pella, Chicago, or some other one within your reach, and there prepare yourselves with every qualification of grace and learning which Providence will allow, that you may become "workmen that need not to be ashamed, rightly dividing the word of truth." Fear not, you are in the morning of your days; and with the long life that seems open before you, you may truly accomplish, with active piety, a glorious work; for the Master has said, "Lo, I am with you alway.'

To older men who may be called to enter the work at the eleventh hour, let me say that you will likewise receive your penny. One brother of my acquaintance, who had formerly been a deacon, entered the ministry about five or six years ago, when he was upward of sixty years of age, and has been an active, useful pastor, approved of God and the brethren, ever since. If you feel that you would be but small stones in the temple, remember that we have many small niches which you will fit, where large stones will not answer.

I must here, however, offer a word of caution to any brethren who are already in the ministry, and contemplate coming to Iowa to settle. There is but little in the State to invite you, if you require everything made ready to your hand; but if you can and will labor, and are willing to endure hardness as good ministers of Jesus Christ, and strive to *make a place for yourselves*, there are opportunities rare and inviting. On this point I will insert part of an article clipped from the *Christian Times*.

"TO THOSE SEEKING PASTORATES.

"If any Baptist minister who reads this is wishing to come to Iowa, and who has got grit, patience, zeal and benevolence of heart which have made him beloved where he has lived and labored, let him write to our worthy General Agent of the Iowa Baptist State Convention, Rev. S. H. Mitchell, at Oskaloosa, and he will tell him of fields of labor where these qualities will not only be appreciated, but be productive of glorious fruits. For such as only aspire to metropolitan parishes, those of Iowa are too large and too important, with few exceptions! There is work here to be done, and truly blessed is he who knows how and will do it. Such will find a welcome that will warm their hearts.

"IOWA."

Let such, then, as are called for in the above article come forward, of both old men and young men, that we may sow, and reap, and finally rejoice together, bringing our sheaves with us.

But, reader, I must close this rude and imperfect sketch. I am sorry for its deficiencies, as well as for all others of my life; and for all my mistakes, which I am confident are many, I humbly crave the forgiveness of both God and man. As I look over the wide field where God has so abundantly blessed the labors of myself and my brethren, I cannot but remember with deepest gratitude the hundreds of brothers, sisters, and friends, who have received me kindly and rewarded me generously, as a minister of the Lord Jesus. To such is this volume sent as a tribute to the memories of by-gone days, and as a token of my regard. Let me ask you that while I remain in this mortal tabernacle, which is now becoming weather-beaten, you will pray for me, that my remaining days may be useful.

Finally, let us not lay aside our armor in the church militant until we enter forever that rest which remaineth for the people of God. There I trust that we shall have a happy reunion,

> "Where, upon a green and flowery mount
> Our weary souls shall sit,
> And with heavenly joy recount
> The labors of our feet."

FAREWELL.

APPENDIX.

THE BARREN FIG-TREE.

(REPORTED BY REV. E. H. WARING.)

TEXT.—"Then said he unto the dresser of his vineyard, Behold, these three years I come seeking fruit on this fig-tree, and find none: cut it down; why cumbereth it the ground? Luke xiii: 7.

MY text is a part of the parable of the fig-tree. I am sorry there are so few persons present this evening; but I have no doubt there are those here who need to be instructed in the ways of eternal life, and I seldom ever meet a congregation in which there are none who are not Christians. You perceive already that my text is designed for those who are out of Christ; and you may think it strange that I would introduce such a subject upon this occasion, seeing there are so few here who are not professed Christians; but I presume there are those present to whom the subject ought to be preached. This parable is full of meaning; and as the Saviour often used the parable, or figures, or metaphors, for the purpose of illustrating some great truth, so in reference to the one in which stands our text.

I am aware at the same time, that a great many people claim that a parable is without meaning, and therefore want to set it aside, simply because it is a parable. But when you come to look into these parables, you will find them big with meaning, as everything else the Saviour has spoken; and he designed by this parable to teach a very important lesson.

The parable speaks of a vineyard, and it is stated that in this vineyard there was a tree that is repre-

16*

sented as barren; and here I want to depart a little from the language of the parable, that those who are not familiar with the idea of a vineyard may understand my meaning the more clearly. You may be more familiar with the term "orchard" than with that of the vineyard; and as I do not want to entertain you now with a description of the vineyard, with the wine-press, etc., we will, to bring it down to every one's capacity, call it an orchard, which will illustrate the same thing. There was, as we read in the parable, a husbandman, who issued the order to cut down this tree; and this husbandman represents God, the owner of the vineyard. But the vine-dresser plead for the life of the tree, and this vine-dresser represents Christ. The vineyard represents, as we claim, God's universe. So then you get the meaning of these expressions in the parable.

Coming, then, to the subject of the parable, there are two reasons why this tree is ordered to be removed. The first reason is its barrenness; for says the owner of the vineyard, "Behold, these three years I come seeking fruit on this fig-tree, and find none." The second reason for this order is because it is an encumbrance to the vineyard, and hence the question is asked, "Why cumbereth it the ground?" And I would have you understand, fellow-sinner, that you are, by your rebellion against God, not only bringing destruction upon yourself, but you are assisting very materially, by your influence, in the damnation of your fellow-men; for you see these two charges are brought against the tree—it brought forth no fruit, and it encumbered the ground. You, therefore, not only refuse obedience to God yourself, but by your unholy influence you encumber the souls of those around you. You are not only refusing to enter the kingdom yourself, but you are actually hindering those who otherwise would enter in. Now I wish to use this parable to illustrate the condition of those who refuse to enter upon God's service. There is a meaning to every thing in the parable, and it is important for us to try and understand it.

Now, here is the farmer, he goes to the nursery from which he gets his trees, and he selects the best piece of land he has for those trees, and he cultivates and improves that land, and he takes those scions from the nursery and carefully plants them in that orchard. Now, he knows that those trees are not capable of bearing fruit, or of yielding him any remuneration for the expense and labor he has bestowed upon them, or for the ground which they occupy. Yet he takes all the care possible of those trees, defends them from injury, cultivates and brings them on, and by the blessing of God—the sun, and the air, and the rain—they grow, and at length become large fruit-bearing trees. We want by these trees, thus planted and cared for, to represent the infant race. God does not demand of the infant the fruits of faith and obedience, until it has arrived at the years of accountability. It cannot labor in the kingdom of God for the promotion of his glory, and God does not demand of it fruit, any more than the husbandman requires fruit of the tree before it is capable of bearing fruit. And yet, after that tree has occupied the land until it has had sufficient growth and age to produce fruit, the husbandman looks for the necessary fruit from the tree. And he has a right to expect it, has he not? Certainly he has. Every man knows that this is reasonable. Now I want to know on what ground the husbandman would demand fruit of that tree? Why, it is his. It occupies his ground, and do you not admit that it is his prerogative, that he is its owner, and that he has a right to look for fruit from it?

Now, so it is with the family of man. Here the child is cared for and protected, and grows up to years of knowledge—to know good from evil. And God gives it the necessary instruction and means of doing good, and I want to know if he has not the right to claim fruit from that child when come to years of accountability? Is not this reasonable? And if so, then I want to know why every man should not respond to the claim of God, the owner of this great vineyard, whose land we are occupying, whose air we are breathing, and whose blessings we are enjoying all through our lives? Is the demand unreasonable? Now if the individual is here to-night, who is in his sins, who has reached the years of accountability, and feels that this is unreasonable and unjust that God should demand fruit of him, let him raise up his hand. But there is not one here—no hand comes up.

Now let me change it a little. We read—the husbandman came three years seeking fruit from this fig tree. Now it was not because this tree could not bring forth fruit—that it was barren. There it was in the vineyard, surrounded by other fig trees that did bring forth fruit; and if it could not have brought fruit the husbandman would not have made any such demand upon it. Now so it is with the sinner. It is not because he cannot bring forth fruit unto God—that he does not. If so, God would not make any such claim upon him. Then, when you come to look at the justice of the claims of the husbandman upon the tree, and to see his care of it, and how it grows and flourishes year after year, and brings forth no fruit—nothing but leaves—no fruit, that it is barren and unprofitable, you can see why the husbandman should be provoked with it, and want it cut down. It has not only disappointed his hopes, but provoked him to cut it down. Then why may it not be cut down? Ought it not to be cut down if it cannot be made to produce fruit? It certainly can bear fruit as well as any other tree in the orchard, and why should it not be cut down and the ground disencumbered, that something more profitable may take its place?

Then I come to you, and ask you if you have arrived at years of accountability, and have brought forth no fruit, why should not God issue his orders to the sheriff, Death, to cut you down, seeing you are hardening and callousing your heart in sin, and, by your influence, hindering others from entering into the kingdom of God, and laboring for its extension in the world? Why, do you not see it would be just for God to remove every such individual from his vineyard, when you have had every facility and means to do right; and God has done everything possible for him to do, to bring you into the kingdom of his dear Son? And still you rebel against him. Can you see any reason why such an order should not be issued against you, to take you out of the way? You know you have borne no fruit, and that God has come, by these various means, year after year, seeking fruit from you; but yet there has been nothing but rebellion on the part of incorrigible sinners. Now, why should not the tree be removed? Why should the vine-dresser cry, "Spare it yet another year?" "Lord, let it alone this year also, till I shall dig about it, and dung it: and if it bear fruit, well: and if not, then after that thou shalt cut it down."

Now here the vine-dresser speaks of the cultivation of the tree. You know the nature of the parched soil of the earth. Under the influence of the burning sun the ground becomes naturally very hard, and would very much impede the growth and fruitfulness of the tree; and, therefore, the husbandman says, "Let alone this year also." He does not say it cannot bear fruit, or that it has had no good opportunity—that it has been afflicted—that it has not been permitted the privilege of bearing fruit, or anything of that kind; he does not say that it ought not to be removed—that it has not been barren—that it does not cumber the ground; no, nothing of that sort; but he says it is a pity that such a tree, in such a situation, and that has had so much care, should not be spared. And now, he says, "I will cultivate it, and I will use means to strengthen and improve the soil, and I will see if I cannot get a crop from it; and then, if it brings forth fruit, all will be well; and if not, then thou mayest cut it down." Now, just so Jesus intercedes for sinners. We have seen that he is represented in this parable by the vine-dresser. See how the man pleads for the tree; and so, my dear friend, with reference to you, it is only through the intercessions of Christ, the great vine-dresser, that you are here to-night. It is not because you have rendered obedience to the commands of God; but because Jesus pleads for you that you are here. You are capable, if you will embrace the means within your reach, of bearing fruit; and it is a great pity that such a spirit as yours, made to be happy, should be cast down into hell—that that man with the towering intellect, for the simple reason that he refuses obedience to the government of God, that justice should require that he should be cut down; and yet it will be, unless the person can be induced to yield his stubborn heart to the mandates of heaven.

Thus, you see, the vine-dresser goes to work. Here you have a view of some of the implements that are used for the purpose. See the man with his pick, digging up the soil—the hard soil. So God's Word represents the heart of man as being hard as the flinty rock. Now it is our duty to go to work and dig with the pick of divine truth into the parched soil of the sinner's heart. God has represented the hard ground of the sinner's heart by this rocky soil: "Is not my word like a fire? saith the Lord; and like a hammer that breaketh the rock in pieces."

Now, as the vine-dresser has to use some implement to break up the hardened soil, so with the sinner's heart. And the prophet speaks of "breaking up the fallow ground." Here there is another implement. The hard soil needs the plow to turn it up, that it may be prepared for the seed. And we must have the plowshare of eternal truth, which must be driven right through the parched soil of that wicked heart to break it up and soften it, and prepare it to bring forth fruit. There is no other way of doing it; for without it you may cast the seed upon the sinner's heart—and it is compared to the stony ground—and you may continue to preach the gospel to that hardened sinner year after year, and the fowls of hell will follow the plow and gather the seed out of the heart. You know the seed that was cast on stony ground—the fowls of the air gathered it up and devoured it; and how can it be gathered out of the heart, unless it is in the same way by which it is put in? Hence we claim that it is the fowls of hell that gather up the seed that has been sown in the heart, and the person brings forth no fruit.

So I say we have to use the plowshare of divine truth to break up that heart. It must be done by the Holy Spirit, but the gospel is the means. Turning back to the prophet again, he speaks of other implements: "Is not my word like a hammer that breaketh the rock in pieces?" The sledge-hammer of the law must be brought down to break the flinty heart; and when it has been broken up, you have to enrich it by pouring into it gospel truth. The mind must be stirred with gospel truth to illuminate, and lead it to obedience to Christ.

But again, we notice that the Holy Spirit has come, and the heart has been moved again and again, for we read, "These three years I have come seeking fruit thereon." I would inquire of the sinner, "How often have you been impressed with the necessity of giving your heart to Christ? Perhaps, not once, nor twice, but many times you have been so influenced. He is the husbandman, the owner of all this great vineyard. And can you be astonished, this being true, if you should never be visited again—that you would never have another opportunity—that your soul would never be impressed again—that you would never have another invitation to repent? Would this astonish you, knowing that for so many years God has knocked at the door of your heart, in order to do you good and bring you into a saving relation with himself? Barren sinner, look here! God will not chide. How long has he stood at the door of your heart, and knocked? You read, "Behold, I stand at the door and knock: if any man hear my voice, and open the door, I will come in to him, and will sup with him, and he with me." Rev. iii: 20. The opening is your duty. God stands, in the person of his Son, and by his truth and through his Spirit he is knocking at thy heart, and he waits with patience for you to unbolt that door, with the promise that if you do, he will come in to renew your heart, and dwell in you, the hope of glory. But if you do not do it, He will issue the sentence to the sheriff of the skies, "Cut down that hardened sinner;—why cumbereth he the ground?"

Now God complains, again, that you are cumbering the ground. You are not only found to be barren in spirit, but you are in the way of others—you are cumbering the ground.

Now turn to the orchard again. There stands the tree; and frequently we are asked by the skeptic, "If religion is such a blessing, we want to know why there are so many poor professors among you? Why don't you own more wealth, and have better houses and larger plantations?" Do you see that barren tree? Perhaps it is the most flourishing of any in the orchard. And why? Because its substance has never been exhausted by supplying a return to its owner. It is absorbing all its substance to itself, and it is encumbering the ground; and the more it adds to its growth, the more it cumbers the ground. Any one of common observation can see it. Does it not absorb the rays of the sun from the whole circle of the ground it covers? Why you may go and sow the best seed under that tree, and wherever it interposes the seed will bring you no return. I have noticed some such trees that have destroyed the productiveness of the ground for a quarter of an acre. Nothing would grow there. Now, if the tree is unfruitful, why should the farmer spare it? If it was removed how much larger crop he would have! Then why should he spare the tree? Now I charge upon the sinner that he is necessarily in the way of others. I do not charge that he means to be in their way, but that he necessarily is in their way. You go and inquire of the tree. You see it has prevented the growth of the wheat, or oats, or corn, that has been planted beneath it, that has been cultured and cared for; but when harvest came there was no crop. Now interrogate the tree, and the tree says, "I did not intend to interfere with the growth of the crop!" But do you not know, in the nature of things, that tree could not have been there without interfering with the crop? Why, it is as clear as the noon-day sun.

Now how are you going to remedy the influence of the tree upon the ground which it occupies?

Only by removing the tree. It is utterly impossible for the tree to avoid having its influence upon the soil which it occupies. Now this illustrates the influence of the sinner. He cannot avoid exerting an influence, and the sinner should reflect on the number of souls he is encumbering by his refusal to serve God. It is true he may not design to do this, but it is impossible for him to occupy the position he does without affecting the interests of some immortal souls. Every man has an influence; and I will tell you that your influence is in exact proportion to your moral character and standing in the community. It cannot be otherwise.

There, for instance, is that husband and father. He may be a skeptic in religion, and he exerts an influence over every member of his family. Is it at all probable that any of his family can be affected by gospel truth, and brought to Jesus Christ, and be made fruitful Christians, until his encumbering influence is removed? Not at all. Why does not that wife and those children go to the house of God, and become Christians? Because of the controlling influence of that skeptical husband and father; and his influence forms a wall around them which is positively insurmountable. Is it not probable, then, that if it were not for that father's influence, they would be converted? Certainly. Now how are they to be reached? They are hardening in sin and imperiling their eternal interest every day they live. How are they to be reached? I ask if it would not be better, if that husband cannot be prevailed upon to become a Christian—if it would not be wisdom for the maker of that man to remove him out of the way, that the members of his family might be reached and saved?

"But why did the husbandman want to remove that tree?" you ask. "Had he not plenty of land besides?" Certainly, but what was the use of that land being occupied with that tree that never brings any fruit, and has he not a right to remove it? And so I ask if it is not God's prerogative to take such men out of the world, that those whom they encumber may be brought to repentance and salvation? I have labored in some places where there have been such hoary-headed sinners, who seemed to be in the way of their friends coming to Christ. In one case that I think of, I felt moved by the Spirit to pray that the person should be taken out of the way. He was the father of eight children, a hardened wretch, who was in the way of his wife and children being saved; and I felt moved to pray that if he could not be saved, he should be taken out of the way. And he was taken out of the way, I do not know how, and that wife and those children were all converted and brought into the Church of Christ.

Oh yes, "Cut it down, why cumbereth it the ground?" That is the important question propounded here. Why should it? You may take that young man who delights so much in amusing himself in the house of prayer. In several places where I have labored I have found such young persons banded together not to be influenced by the preacher, and not to seek salvation. In one case I felt impressed to pray for the young man who seemed to put himself forward as the leader of the rest, and the result was that he was converted.

And so you may take that young lady. She may exert her influence over other young ladies, and lead them to refuse to yield their hearts to Christ. I have met with such, high-headed, stiff-necked, proud-hearted young ladies. I know it is a wonderful pity to see a young woman put herself in opposition to Christ, to be too proud to bend to the Nazarene, and to use her influence to prevent others from coming to Christ. Why, some people seem to think that such a thing ought scarcely to be mentioned. I was asked in one case, by a young man, "Who gave you the authority to say that a young lady was in the way to hell?" Why, I tell you, God will damn the young lady just as quick as he will the beggar on the dunghill. There is no difference with Him. And if the young lady takes this position, I want to know why she should not go down to perdition as well as the male? I tell you the ax is laid at the root of every tree. It matters not whether they are male or female, high or low, black or white, if they are cumberers of the ground, and are standing in the way of anybody else, they are in danger of being cut down.

Now, barren sinner, you see if you did not cumber the ground, the barrenness of your soul would bring destruction upon you. But, when you combine with this the encumbering of others around you, are you not afraid the ax will be used to cut you down? So it is Christ would teach us these important lessons by this parable.

Without protracting these exercises further, I want to inquire of the congregation, who are impenitent, if it is not the prerogative of God to issue this order at any moment? Certainly it is. No one can dispute it. Then, we are ready to remark, there are none here to whose hearts He has not come seeking fruit, one, two, three, or many years. How long is it, friend, since you came to years of accountability? And now how old are you? Ascertain that, and you may find out how many years you are in debt to God, for sparing and taking care of you. And all this, with nothing to pay for one moment of misspent time! Poor miserable bankrupt, as thou art! And I want to say, it is nothing but the intercession of Christ that has spared you thus far. Oh, how you have insulted Him! and yet he pleads: "Spare, oh, spare the sinner another year! My servants shall pass round and deliver another gospel message. My spirit shall again strive with that mind. I will yet wait to be gracious, and if he will repent and bring forth the fruits of righteousness, all shall be well. If he has misspent much time, and neglected many opportunities, and squandered may gifts and talents, yet, after all, if he repent after another message has been delivered, it shall be well. I will accept him, though he has done despite to my Spirit, provoked me, done injury to my cause, and prevented others from enlisting under my banner. If he will now accept my Son, and reverence Him, all shall be forgiven. He shall be brought into my kingdom, receive my favor, and be an heir of everlasting salvation. And it shall be with him as if he had commenced to obey me at the beginning."

But if not, there will be the last time when Jesus will plead for the guilty soul. He will then say as he did of the tree, "Cut it down." It may be very soon—we cannot tell; but we are going to commend you to God, and to the word of his grace. Hazard not the interests of your soul any longer, but seek repentance and the remission of sins. Tarry not in all the plains of iniquity. "Seek ye the Lord while he may be found, call upon him while he is near." And may God forbid that you should ever again reject his Spirit when sent to bring you to himself; and may you finally be crowned with everlasting life in the kingdom of our dear Redeemer. Amen.

THE GENERAL JUDGMENT.

(REPORTED, PHONOGRAPHICALLY, BY REV. E. H. WARING.)

TEXT.—"And I saw the dead, small and great, stand before God: and the books were opened; and another book was opened, which is the book of life: and the dead were judged out of those things which were written in the books, according to their works." Rev. xx: 12.

The last verse of the chapter reads: "And whosoever was not found written in the book of life was cast into the lake of fire."

To say the least, my friends, there are three books mentioned, or included in the declaration in this text, "books." You perceive that this term is used in the plural; and the third book is the Lamb's "book of life," which I may call, to make it more plain, God's Family Record, in which are inscribed the names of all his saints.

Before I enter upon the investigation of this subject, I want to present one or two facts. The first is, that to the church of Jesus Christ there has been given no legislative power to enact new laws for the government of the subjects of Christ's kingdom. These books contain the will of God, as revealed in Jesus Christ—the only law that has been, or ever will be, given for the government of the kingdom of God on earth. It is also true that to this church there has been given no dispensing power to set aside, or revoke, any law that has been enacted in the council chamber of heaven for the government of the church on earth, as you will notice from one or two declarations in the context. One of them is this—"And if any man shall take away from the words of the book of this prophecy, God shall take away his part out of the book of life, and out of the holy city, and from the things which are written in this book."*

Then we are to understand, taking this view of the subject, that our salvation is based upon humble obedience to the revealed will of God, as contained in the New Testament Scriptures. And I will remark further, that while many claim that there is no punishment for sin in a future state of being, notwithstanding God has threatened to punish sin, according to the declarations contained in the Bible, I claim that God cannot avoid punishing those who fall in their sins beyond the grave. Not to do it would be to make him violate his own law; and we claim that while God is a covenant-keeping God, he is also a law-abiding God, and will stand by his own truth. No matter if infidels are angry, and if all the devils in the universe go frowning around and raise their objections to the Word of Life, it will stand firm as the pillars of heaven. God can not violate his own truth. I want to enforce this idea upon your minds. Let me illustrate it. Many have asked, "How can God be happy in heaven, when he knows that multitudes of his creatures are suffering under the penalty of his law forever?" Let me remark that if the sinner is damned, he damns himself. God's law and God's plan of salvation have been clearly revealed, and the sinner may become acquainted with them now, and need not wait until the judgment day to know what God requires of him for salvation. For instance, the thief knew before he committed the act of theft what the penalty was, just as well as he learned it afterward. Now the law is known, what is the duty of the judge? The man has stolen your horse, he has been arrested, brought into court, the evidence is had, the jury have taken the case and retired,

* Rev. xxii : 19.

in a little while they return and announce a verdict of "guilty." Now what is the duty of the judge? Would the criminal speak to him to enact a new code to exonerate him from the penalty of the law? Not a word of it. That judge is there to administer the law as it is, and to administer it faithfully. Now would it not be unjust for that thief to brand that judge with being a hard master for exacting the penalty of his crime? Could the judge do otherwise without being himself a violator of the law? Would he not be a perjured man if he did not administer the law according to his oath and the nature of the case? Is it not his duty to find out the penalty attached to the crime, and administer accordingly? Now, here is God's law. You may all know it. In it is revealed, "the wages of sin is death." We may all know this, and know it before as well as after we commit sin. The thief knew the penalty as well before as after he did the act of theft.

Many are troubled about this thing. One says, "I wish I knew how it will be with me in the judgment day!" "I wish I could assure my heart whether I will be happy then, or not!" You need not vex yourself about that. If you will go to God's book you may dismiss all these questionings. You may know your duty here, just as well as you will know it beyond the grave. God will make no new requirements there, but will judge every man according to his works.

But about these books. The books mentioned in the text are the Old and New Testament Scriptures. I might take up the book of nature, and the book of conscience, and other things, in relation to this subject; but I will speak only of the Old and New Testament Scriptures. The books are opened.

But you may ask why the Old Testament Scriptures are present in the day of reckoning? You may say, "Why, I supposed we were from under the Old Testament, and under the New Testament dispensation?" That may be true now; but in the general judgment God will have as much to do with the Old as with the New Testament. It would be unjust, for instance, to hold Adam accountable for obedience to New Testament requirements. Adam received but a very brief law, and will be held accountable only to it, and not to a law revealed many years after Adam had passed away from earth. That age of the world is compared by historians to the starlight. But as the world passed on, there was raised up one and another through whom God communicated his will to men; and as knowledge increased, men's responsibility increased also. Here comes Moses, through whom God revealed his will, and then one prophet after another, and thus the light increased; and so it is written, that "the word of the Lord was unto them, precept upon precept, precept upon precept, line upon line, line upon line; here a little and there a little."* And this prophetic dispensation is compared to the moonlight. You know how much larger the moon is than the star, and how much fuller the light. Thus man's responsibility continually increased; and thus we may pass through the Old Testament Scriptures, to show that they will be introduced in the day of general judgment. All that lived and died under the Old Testament dispensation will be judged by Old Testament law; and this will be just, for God is going "to judge the world in righteousness."

Now we come to the New Covenant. I know there is a controversy going on with reference to the exact time when the Old Covenant closed up and the new one was introduced. Well, one thing is certain, that we were never held by the Eternal amenable to both laws at the same time; that is,

* Isa. xxviii : 13

that God would not hold the people responsible to the Old and New Testaments at the same time. Therefore, just when the old covenant closes the new one commences; and it is remarked that, "The law and the prophets *were* until John: since that time the kingdom of God is preached, and every man presseth into it."* Therefore, since the old dispensation passed away, we are held answerable to New Testament requirements. The reading, studying, and searching of New Testament requirements, as God's will revealed to a ruined world, ought, therefore, to be interesting to every man. And why? Because we are responsible to God's revealed will as contained in the New Testament Scriptures. Now, mark you, there has been a change in the law. Here come up new ordinances and new duties, and this dispensation brings up all the claims of God upon us. They are all revealed—all made known—and here is a rule by which the Christian world will be governed. Here we have it—Heaven's great code. You may all have it. This is the rule by which the great court of the universe will be governed, so far as respects us, in the great day of reckoning.

Now the Eternal has prescribed that this code shall be preached to every creature—not to every nation, but to every creature. And then, again, that they might be made acquainted with the requirements of God—that they might know what they must do to secure salvation—they have only to learn the will of God as here revealed. And these men of God take this Word and go forth, publishing salvation, with all its consequences, to every nation and every creature. And Jesus tells us plainly that this gospel of the kingdom is to be preached in all the world, for a witness unto all

* Luke xvi: 16.

nations, and then shall the end come.* Do you know that when you are slighting this Word, you are slighting one of the witnesses that will appear, for or against you, in the last day? If you will have nothing to do with the Word of Life here, it will have much to do with you in that day. Is it nothing to you that you pass it by? How many do pass by this Word as though it was nothing to them! And yet it will be here, and it will be yonder. Men must have something to do with it; and if they will not here, they will yonder. This book will be there. I do not mean to say that this combustible, material book, will be there; but every principle, every truth, every promise, every threatening, will be there, and will be presented by the judge, and we must answer to it. And this Word will be the rule of judgment there. Jesus says, "He that rejecteth me, and receiveth not my words, hath one that judgeth him: the word that I have spoken, the same shall judge him in the last day."† And if this Word is to judge us, will it not be just for it to be there? Men will not be able to controvert it then. They may do it now, but they will not do it then; and when the great judge himself interprets it, there will be no excuse for not having obeyed it. It may be no plainer then than now. There will be no excuse then, and there is none now, when we consider how clear is the light in which it has been revealed—how it is adapted to us—how it elevates us—what a source of joy it has been to us; and we shall be surprised that we have ignored the book of God, by which we are to stand beyond the grave. And thus we see that God has provided for the publication of this Word to every nation, in every human ear, that there may be no excuse for sin in that day.

There is another thing connected with this: "the

* Matt. xxiv : 14. † John xii : 48.

things which were written in the books." Now, when you look at those things, do you think there can be any repeal of them, or any power granted by which they can be set aside? No, not a word of it; they are permanently fixed as the pillars of heaven. Now we are to be judged "according to the things which are written in the books, according to their works." Now let us see whether we have observed the things which are written in these books, and we may know in ten minutes whether we shall be condemned or acquitted there.

Now you know it is made our duty to *repent.* It is a very simple thing, and I want to bring it down to the capacity of every one of you. The doctrine of repentance is a doctrine of this book. It is *written* here, and the text says emphatically that the dead will be judged "out of those things *which were written* in the books." Now, have you repented of your sins? How many there are that have never been exercised with a godly sorrow that worketh repentance unto life! Now compare your conduct with the things written in these books; and if you have never repented, God could not refuse to damn you without violating his own law. Is not that clear? How can the judge pardon that criminal who has been convicted at his bar? He has not the pardoning power, for that the man must go to the Governor. Then you cannot be excused unless you repent of your sins. And yet you refuse to repent, and stand and wonder whether you will be saved or lost. Why God cannot have you without repentance, without violating his own laws. Now here the doctrine of repentance is revealed. Just what God asks you to do is made plain; and he gives the means to aid, assist, and lead the souls of men aright in the journey of life, if you will only yield obedience to his requirements.

Again, there is the duty of *faith.* We read in the

Scriptures that "with the heart, man believeth unto righteousness; and with the mouth, confession is made unto salvation."* Have you ever with the heart believed, and with the mouth made confession unto salvation? Have you ever? If not, believe me, dying sinner, you stand condemned by the law of heaven, by your own conscience, and by the long catalogue of crime which you have committed against the law of Christ.

He also requires every individual that thus repents and believes to be *baptized.* This is the very next thing that is written. I am not going to argue any mode of baptism this afternoon, but simply to enjoin it upon you as one of those things that you are to attend to. Have you done this? If you have never been baptized, you have never rendered obedience to the requirements of Christ.

And, brethren, after you have done these things, you are required to come out from the world and be separate. Indeed, I might spend much time in bringing out these things that are written in these books, but we must proceed.

I would look around again. You gather up a band of Christians. You see them happy. You see them laboring for you. What induces this brother (referring to the Sabbath-school superintendent) to come here and labor in the Sabbath school, from Sabbath to Sabbath? Do you line his pockets with greenbacks? Is that the motive that prompts him? No; but it is to advance the glory of God, and secure the salvation of souls. And so it is, doubtless, with the teachers, every one of them. Now, why do Christians toil? What is it all for? Why, they are going to be rewarded according to their works; and they labor to fit you for the service of the living Christ. If you ask them their

* Rom. x: 10.

motive, they will perhaps tell you that Christ has moved them by his Spirit; and that, exercising a godly sorrow which needeth not to be repented of, they believe in Christ, and they have received that influence which creates a man anew in Christ Jesus. They have turned unto God, who has had mercy on them, and have partaken of Christ by faith. Then you ask them, "Have you gone on doing what Christ has told you?" "Oh, yes." They tell you that they know they are of the truth, and can assure their hearts before him, and that truth works in them; and they labor to bring their fellow-men to Christ, feeling that their works shall be rewarded at the last day. And, my brethren, I know you call all to go along with this class of individuals, and be presented with them to the Father, and share in their reward; for God will reward every man that feareth him. "God is no respecter of persons; but in every nation, he that feareth him and worketh righteousness, is accepted of him."* Then men from every clime will be rewarded, and their reward will be glorious. You may know what that reward will be now, and need not wait to know it. I think God has told us what "the penny" will be. I think that of all people on the earth, Christians should be the most happy. You hear them talk about poverty sometimes. Yes, they are down in the depths of poverty; but yet they are the richest people upon whom the sun has ever shone. Christ was poor; but is it not written that "though he was rich, yet for your sakes he became poor, that ye through his poverty might be rich?"† And who, in view of what he has promised, would talk about poverty?

Now the Christian labors in every possible way to bring men to God, to glorify his Father which is

* Acts x : 34-35. † 2 Cor. ix : 9.

in heaven, and thus to do his appointed work, knowing that he will be rewarded in that day.

And now, with reference to the ungodly. You see men will be judged according to their works. You may flatter your wicked hearts that you will be saved, although you have never complied with the first principle of Christian obedience. Now you can tell for yourselves what your works have been. Just stop and think for a single moment, and then tell me, if you please, if your are willing for God to reward you according to *your* works—according to *your* past history and present standing in the sight of the Eternal? Are you willing? God has promised to do it, and you cannot say it is unjust for him to do it. And I want to know, then, if this afternoon should bring you to the final reckoning, and you should be rewarded according to your works, whether blame could attach to the judge? Certainly not. Could blame attach to the judge for having faithfully performed his duty in inflicting the penalty which the law has affixed to the crime, when the man has been duly tried and convicted, upon sufficient evidence, of the crime of which he was charged? Certainly not.

Now, here come the books, and among them is the book of conscience, which you have written with your own hands. Here is the law which God gave you through his Son, who died for you on the reeking cross. Here are the requirements of God, and every one of them is reasonable, and such as you must approve. Here is the written Word, and there is the book you have written. I want to know how God can save such a man. Here is the gospel which was preached unto you, and there are the people of God, entering in through the gates into the city, who were saved by that gospel! How can *you* be saved? You neglected the gospel. You rejected Christ, and counted the blood of the covenant, wherewith God sought to sanctify you, an unholy thing. How can *you* be saved? Yes, the books will be opened, and the time is coming when you shall see the justice of God in the damnation of the sinner. You will have to see it—you cannot escape. Your sins will sink you beneath the wrath of God for ever and ever, while the lightnings of Sinai will flash throughout your darkened soul through all eternity. And you have done it yourself! While God invited you, while the church wooed you, while the ministers of Christ besought you, you have gone on ignoring the blood of the covenant, and neglecting all the means which God has provided for your salvation; and thus, by your own conduct you have destroyed your own salvation, and made your bed in hell. Now, can any blame attach to the Eternal? No, never, never. But I must hasten. I might go on and enumerate crime after crime that you have committed; but I must not dwell upon it now.

Now, after this gospel is preached to all nations for a witness, then will the end come, and this Word will appear against you; and, to come to the third clause in the text, there must be a general resurection: and all this will occur immediately after the close of the gospel dispensation. When the gospel will cease to be preached, and the lips of the ministers will be sealed, then God will summon the world to judgment. Then shall the tenants of the tomb "come forth; they that have done good unto the resurrection of life; and they that have done evil unto the resurrection of damnation."*

And this shows, as I have already said, that we are to be judged according to our characters. As we have formed them here we shall appear in that day. And now, at the blowing of the trumpet by

* John v: 29.

the angel Gabriel, the dead will come forth, and every man will appear in his own order. And then this third book—the Book of Life—will be produced. Oh, with what interest the Church of God will look upon that book! It is God's family record. It contains the names of all God's people—every one of them. Here we may be imposed upon. We may enroll upon our church records unworthy men. There may be a baptized sinner—a Simon the sorcerer, numbered with the people of God—but there will be no mistake there. That record is kept above—kept in heaven—and it will be absolutely correct; and this record will be produced. With what interest, I say, will we look upon that record, when we come to appear in that day. I understand that the names of every Christian will be in that book, and all whose names are not in that book will be cast into the lake of fire. How anxiously we shall look to find out whether all the family are there! "Where is John? Where is Mary? Where is father—mother—husband—wife? They have fallen here and there, and some, perhaps, in distant lands. Oh, how interested we shall be to know whether all their names are there!

And now the judge proceeds to inquire, "Did you do my will? Did you keep these requirements that are written in these books?" Now let your works come up, not by way of merit, but as acts of obedience—works of righteousness; let them come up, and let us compare the one record with the other. Happy is that man who can then say, "I have kept the prophecy of this book." Is there not a blessing pronounced upon obedience to God's law? Oh yes. "Blessed *are* they that do his commandments, that they may have right to the tree of life, and may enter in through the gates into the city."* Now, who would not be of the truth!

* Rev. xxii: 14.

Who would not keep the commandments of God! Who would not so live as to assure their hearts before him in that day!

That book—that family record—is open; here are the family coming up—all gathered together, and there is to be a final separation. To illustrate it, suppose we were to divide this congregation, placing on one side all who keep the commandments of Christ, and on the other side all who disobey him. Would not families be divided? Here is the husband—a good husband and kind father, but without piety in his soul—he is on the left of the line. There is the wife, who enjoys Christ in her heart—she is on the other side. Oh, what a division this would make in your families even here! And there will be families divided forever, according to the revelation which God has made in the Bible. There are persons who have repented, believed in Christ and obeyed him, who shall be on the right hand of the judge; and others who have ignored the Bible, and have fallen in death with their sins upon them, who shall come forth to the resurrection of damnation. Oh, what a solemn day that will be when this book will be opened! Where do you stand, sinner? The record declares emphatically that Christ "shall separate them one from another, as a shepherd divideth *his* sheep from the goats. And he shall set the sheep on his right hand, but the goats on the left."* The family of man will be divided, the good from the bad, the saint from the sinner; and while the one class is received into the heavenly family, the other is cast off to wail in perdition for ever. They are severally rewarded according to their works. Now, you see clearly where you stand. That is the day of reward. You do not hear any more the inviting

* Matt. xxiv: 32–3.

voice of the gospel. You are not asked to come to the mercy-seat. The day of probation has gone, and the time of reward has come. "Oh, reach out your hand, poor sinner, and take the cup of wrath and drink it to its dregs; and when you have heard the sentence of the judge, then turn away, while the heavens are rolled away as a parchment scroll, and the elements melt with fervent heat, and bear your doom forever, down amid wailing and woe that shall never end! You are a lost spirit, and must be shut out forever. Your works have been evil continually continually, and you must be rewarded according to your works!"

And now, in leaving the subject with you, I want to say to you that the books have not yet been opened. You are still surrounded with mercy. Your day of probation has not passed. Will you still ignore salvation? Will you still turn your back upon the bleeding Lamb, and pass by, and say, "It is nothing to me?" Will you not stand where you now are, and say, "I will pray to God that he will lead me to repentance and salvation, that in that day I may be found on the right hand with the righteous, and with them wear the robe and bear the palm, and go up through the emerald gates into the city?"

Let me say that I believe our infant children will all be saved in the world to come—all whose names are written in that book—all, ALL will be saved, and garnered in everlasting glory. We sincerely trust that you will all be found on the right hand in that day. We want you to be saved. Every day you live in sin you are getting farther from God. Repent of your sins, and yield to be saved by grace. May God bless you. Amen.

AN EXAMINATION

OF THE COMPARATIVE STATISTICAL RESULTS OF THE LABORS OF ELDER JACOB KNAPP, IN THE STATE OF MASSACHUSETTS. BY A. WILBUR.

The following examination and calculations on the results of the labors of Elder Jacob Knapp, in the State of Massachusetts, were made in the autumn of 1846; at which time there seemed to prevail a general impression, at least in the Baptist denomination, that the effects of his labors with the churches were anything but salutary. The pulpit and the press proclaimed the "disastrous results,"—such as "spurious converts," "excommunications," "unsettling ministers," "dividing churches," and the like. The spirit so prevailed with the clergy, that it was rare to hear an occasional sermon or an address, or even a Sabbath-school essay, but it would contain some direct or indirect missile at the "revival," or its "measures." We conscientiously believe ministers and writers were not aware to what extent their minds were led by the spirit of the times.

While these things were thus passing, it occurred to us, "Is it so?" Are these statements and representations facts, or are they specters of the imagination? Instead, therefore, of following the multitude, and crying, "Away with such a fellow from the earth!" we quietly retired to our domicile and examined our documents carefully, "whether these things were so." And we are compelled to say, we were surprised at the results. We found our own mind had been borne away by the tide of public influence to an extent we could hardly have believed.

Our examinations then extended to four years inclusive, commencing with the associational year of the evangelist's labors in each church; including that, and the three successive years. The following was the result:

Mr. Knapp commenced his labors in Massachusetts with the Baptist church in New Bedford, in the Taunton Asssociation, in the summer of 1841. That church, during the four consecutive years, baptized 262, and excommunicated in the same time 28, or about 10½ per cent. on her baptisms. All the other churches in that association, taken together, in the same four years, baptized 488, and excommunicated 105, or nearly 22 per cent. on their baptisms.

At the end of the four years the church in New Bedford had gained in numerical strength 205, or 80⅓ per cent. on her former number. All the other churches in the association had gained in the same time 284, or 18½ per cent. on their former number.

The church in New Bedford separately, and the other churches collectively, have excluded *annually* about an equal proportion compared with their numbers, viz., averaging about 1½ per cent. on their whole number.

His next labors in the State were in the Boston Association. Here they were mostly confined to five churches in the city of Boston. Two of the city churches did not invite him into their pulpits. One of these, with its pastor, was decidedly unfriendly to the whole movement, from beginning to end.

Those five churches where Mr. Knapp labored, baptized, during the four years, 1,054 persons, and excommunicated 158, or 15 per cent. on their baptisms.

All the other churches in the Boston Association, taken together, baptized in the same time 1,775, and excluded 336, or nearly 19 per cent. on their baptisms.

The two churches in the city where Mr. Knapp did not labor, baptized 122, and excluded 36, or 29 per cent. on their baptisms.

The church that was unfavorable, and took no interest in the movement, baptized 22, and excluded 12, or 54½ per cent. on her baptisms. All these churches, thus separately classed, have excommunicated, on an average, *annually*, within a fraction of 1½ per cent. on their whole numbers.

The five churches where the evangelist labored, have gained in numerical strength in the four years, 904 members, or 51 per cent. All the others in the association, together, have gained 670, or a little over 13½ per cent.

The two churches in the city above named, taken separate, in the same time have lost in number 72, or 8¾ per cent. on their former numbers.

The next labors of this evangelist in the State were in the Salem Association. Here also they were mostly had with five churches, viz., three in Lowell, the Second Church in Salem, and the church in Marblehead; although his labors in Marblehead were small compared with those of the other four churches. These five churches, during four years, commencing with the year of his labors, baptized 817, excluded 143, or a little over 17 per cent. on their baptisms.

All the other churches in that association, in the same time baptized 669, and excommunicated 207, or 31 per cent. on their baptisms. These five churches also have excluded annually, on an average, about $1\frac{1}{2}$ per cent. on their whole numbers. The other churches a mere fraction over.

The five churches have gained in the four years, 508 members, or 26 per cent. The other churches gained in the same time 198, or a fraction less than 6 per cent.

These examinations, as before said, were made after the close of the four years; and they show to every candid mind, that the constantly reiterated complaints of "spurious converts," "numerous exclusions," etc., having reference to the evangelist's labors, were without a shadow of foundation. But, on the contrary, the churches where he did not labor excluded many more, in comparison with their receptions, than those with whom he did, and each class about an equal proportion to their whole numbers.

We stated these facts, at the time, to several brethren, who said the public ought to have them; and at one time we fully concluded to publish them, but were deterred for reasons that will be given hereafter.

A few months since, a friend, who learned we had some facts relating to Mr. Knapp's labors, asked the loan of them. Our attention being thus again called to the subject, we concluded to extend the comparison throughout the State; and although the examination absorbed more time than we knew how to spare, yet we pursued it, and arrived at the following results:

It will be remembered, Mr. Knapp labored with eleven churches in this State: one in the Taunton Association, five in the Boston, and five in the Salem Associations. The results of these labors were reported in three associational years, viz., 1841, 1842, and 1843. In making up the aggregate of baptisms, etc., of the other churches in the State, the intermediate year of 1842 is taken as the year of commencement.

The eleven churches, then, where he labored, commencing in these churches with the year of his labors—as will be seen above—baptized in four years 2,133, and excluded 329, or a little over 15 per cent. on their baptisms. All the other churches in the State, taken together, baptized in the same time 6,746, and excommunicated 1,578, or 23⅓ per cent. on their baptisms.

Having recently shown the above to a brother, he suggested the idea of extending the comparison still further. Wishing to make our examinations as satisfactory and conclusive as possible, we concluded to continue them for four years more, so as to include eight years; supposing any further calculations would be needless, as all influences for good or for evil would not extend beyond this.

In eight years there had been added to the associations in the State, 42 churches, containing 3,394 members. These are mostly new churches; some few are churches of some years' existence, but have recently united with the associations. These 42 churches are not included in the following calculations,—only the churches which existed at the commencement of 1842. The propriety of this will be seen when it is remembered that these new churches are made up from all the churches in the State, assisted in some instances by members from other States; and if their statistics were included, their whole influence would be on the side of the churches in the State in 1842. Leaving out the new churches, and deducting the eleven in which the evangelist labored, there remained in the State, at the commencement of 1842, 193 churches. Between these and the eleven the comparison is made.

We find, then, in eight years, inclusive, the eleven churches baptized 2,625, and excommunicated 613, or 23 per cent. on their baptisms. The 193 other churches in the State, in the same time baptized 8,673, and excommunicated 2,456, or 28⅓ per cent. on their baptisms. The original number in the eleven churches was 3,984. They had gained in the eight years 1,266, or nearly 31 per cent.

The original number in the 193 churches was 21,432. They had gained in eight years 254, or a little more than 1 per cent.

This discrepancy of gain being so great, it occurred to us, perhaps the 193 churches had been more largely drawn upon to form new churches. So again we betook ourselves to the task of examining the dismissions, and found the following result:

The eleven churches, in the eight years, have dismissed to other churches, and to form new ones 1,543 members, or nearly 33½ per cent. on their average numbers.

The other churches in the same time have dismissed 6,403, or nearly 30 per cent. on their average numbers.

So we found the eleven churches had done their full share, according to their numbers, in contributing in membership to build new churches.

We have given the facts; let them speak for themselves. They have been gathered from official documents, examined and compared with much care and labor, and, we think, may be relied on.

Any way one may look at the eleven churches, compared with the others, either of their associations or of the whole State, they show themselves on the advantage ground.

Now, suppose the result to have proved just the reverse—as has been represented, and is to this day supposed to be the fact by the community—we say, suppose these eleven churches had appeared comparatively to as great disadvantage as they do to advantage, what might, with propriety,—nay, what would be said? We offer no comments.

But it will be asked by some: Why bring these things out at this late period?—(and we shall look for censure from a certain class)—why were they not given to the public while the subject was before the people's mind? To this we answer, first, as before said, when the examination of the first four years was finished, we showed the results to several brethren, who strongly advised us to publish them. We concluded to do so, but took occasion to show them to two brethren who were unfriendly to the revival movement, and spared not to speak against it. We chose to see what effect it would have.

After carefully reading our document through, they handed it back, saying, "Well! what of all that—*it proves nothing.* If they [the converts] are not excluded, there are hundreds who ought to be."

It appeared to have no effect to suggest to their minds the possibility that they might be in an error. We were convinced that the public mind generally, at least in our denomination, was so fixed, that evidence on this subject, however conclusive, had lost its power.

Second, our attention has recently been called to the subject, as we said. It was again suggested that "these facts ought to be given to the public." We concluded also that the public mind, *generally*, (not in all cases) is now so unbiassed that men can look at facts impartially, and give them their due weight.

Another incentive to publish was, that probably these lines would fall into the hands of many desponding disciples, who for some years past have been exercised somewhat, as probably most of Christ's numerous disciples were, when the news spread over Palestine that "Jesus of Nazareth was crucified." Their meditations have been, "What did all this mean?" "We verily thought we were exercised by true religion." "If this is spurious, is not all religion spurious?" "If these converts are mostly spurious converts, am not I such? and are not all such?"—or "where is the evidence of the true?" and the like. We met with many such, and endeavored to comfort them by assuring them that the generally received reports concerning those revivals *were not true*, and that, so far as our knowledge extended, the converts of those revivals were, considering their numbers, as true and lasting as any converts of any revival we ever witnessed. We have sometimes thought, perhaps, for the sake of such disciples, it was a mistake not to have published before.

We will now propose a question to the reader of this pamphlet in Massachusetts.

Admitting that the revivals in 1841 and 1842 were as really the genuine operations of the Holy Spirit as have been any revivals since the Apostles' days, and let the same course be pursued as was pursued by the ministry, the press and the laity, towards the means, the measures and the converts, might we not reasonably suppose it would legitimately produce precisely the state of things in the churches as was found in 1844, 1845 and 1846?

There is something unaccountable in men, good men, pious men, with reference to evidence of the operations of the Holy Spirit. No matter how judicious, candid or pious, (or all of these combined) a man may be, and no matter how the Spirit may be operating, if from any cause his mind happens to take a turn against those operations, there seems to come over him a moral mist or darkness that wholly disables him to receive evidence in favor of the Spirit's power. Evidence, that would be abundant and conclusive in any other case, is no evidence in this; or it is sometimes perverted and becomes evidence against instead of in favor. We think we have observed this in many instances in the course of our pilgrimage, and in several have detected it in ourself. Never have we seen this indefinable,—what shall we call it?—delusive mysticism! no, that does not convey our idea; and we know no words in our circumscribed vocabulary that will. It is an indescribable something that comes over the mind and perverts the judgment on this particular subject, and effects no other. We say, we never saw it prevail in our denomination as it did in 1844, 1845 and 1846, in regard to the revivals of 1842. Inferences were drawn from false premises, and given forth to the public as true. Statements were made and sent out, directly contrary to facts. Reports, almost innumerable, were circulated, which had no shadow of foundation; and some of the above were from good, well-meaning men, who intended no misrepresentation, but verily thought they spake and wrote truth. Our charity for the Jewish Council which sat in Jerusalem in the year 29, with Caiaphas in the chair, was enlarged fifty per cent.; and never before did we so fully understand the spirit of that prayer, "Father, forgive them, they know not what they do." It would be endless and useless to revert to these statements and rumors, and then show their unreliableness: but for the sake of showing how easily a good man may slide into an error, and unintentionally misstate things, perhaps we may be permitted to name one fact.

In 1844, (it might have been in 1845) a pastor in this city wrote to a distant body, that the people of his charge "had so lost their confidence in him [Mr. Knapp], that not twenty of his church would hear him preach unless he was a reformed man." We heard that such had been written. It so happened, a short time after this, Mr. Knapp was to preach on a Sabbath evening in the Tremont Temple. We attended the lecture, and sat on the side of the hall, where we could see to recognize about half of the congregation; and seeing quite a number present from that church, we had the curiosity to count them, and we saw fifty-two from that church whom we knew. As the congregation was passing out, a prominent member of that church came by, whom we asked if there were not more than twenty members of his church present. "Yes," said he, "more than a hundred." And we verily believe he spoke the truth.

We have named this circumstance only to show facts. We well know that pastor, and will say no one holds a higher place in our Christian affection than he. Further, we are ready to bear testimony that he will not intentionally misrepresent; but such was the general impression, and he imbibed it so strongly, that he felt assured he stated the truth.

May we venture an opinion?—and whether correct or not, we are confident it would be supported by a large proportion of that church. Our opinion is, that there has not been a time since he labored in Boston, that any other man in the United States could call together a greater number of that church, to hear a sermon, than Mr. Knapp.

www.ingramcontent.com/pod-product-compliance
Lightning Source LLC
LaVergne TN
LVHW020108110826
845151LV00001B/95

* 9 7 8 1 4 2 5 5 4 3 5 5 6 *